Safe Zones

Safe Zones

Training Allies of LGBTQIA+ Young Adults

Edited by Kerry John Poynter

ROWMAN & LITTLEFIELD

Lanham • Boulder • New York • London

Published by Rowman & Littlefield
A wholly owned subsidiary of The Rowman & Littlefield Publishing Group, Inc.
4501 Forbes Boulevard, Suite 200, Lanham, Maryland 20706
www.rowman.com

Unit A, Whitacre Mews, 26-34 Stannary Street, London SE11 4AB

Copyright © 2017 by Kerry John Poynter

British Library Cataloguing in Publication Information Available

Library of Congress Cataloging-in-Publication Data Available

ISBN 978-1-4758-2526-8 (pbk : alk. paper)
ISBN 978-1-4758-2527-5 (electronic)

∞™ The paper used in this publication meets the minimum requirements of American National Standard for Information Sciences—Permanence of Paper for Printed Library Materials, ANSI/NISO Z39.48-1992.

Printed in the United States of America

This book is dedicated to the student leaders from the Lesbian, Bisexual, & Gay Student Association (LBGSA) at Ball State University from 1990 to 1995.

Contents

Editor's Note

Rowman & Littlefield has made 31 handouts—which supplement the curriculum and assessment pieces of this book—available as a single PDF formatted for easy and clear printing on 8.5" × 11" paper. These resources may be printed and reproduced in limited quantities for private use without obtaining written permission. To acquire a copy of the PDF version of these resources, please email resourcematerial@rowman.com with your request, providing both the title and editor of the book, *Safe Zones: Training Allies of LGBTQIA+ Young Adults* by Kerry John Poynter, along with proof of purchase (e.g., a scan of the receipt).

Due to copyright protection issues, any part of this book beyond this resource section may not be reproduced in any form without written permission from Rowman & Littlefield.

Safe Zones relies on the contributions of many scholars or workshop facilitators who have shared their work online or that have been disseminated at workshops or conferences over numerous years. (See the acknowledgments section and chapter 1 for details.)

The editor has made every effort to credit everyone where possible, but any omissions are completely accidental or were unknown. Please share your experiences using the activities, handouts, and curricula design or any questions by joining the online community at www.facebook.com/SafeZonesBook or www.twitter.com/safezonesbook. You can write me at safezonesbook@gmail.com.

Acknowledgments

THE CONTENT IN THIS BOOK OWES A GREAT DEBT TO EDUCATORS AS WELL AS WORKSHOP FACILITATORS THAT came long before its creation. Some of the ideas and concepts contained here are decades in the making. Many of us have shared resources and documents and presented ideas at national conferences, with the intent to help each other with little thought as to keeping track of the original authors. Perhaps we should have cared more about intellectual property, yet it was never about that. We just wanted to give back to our colleagues who were often like us, working in a new profession, a sub-profession, LGBTQIA+ student services in higher education. My thoughts are with all those people from the last couple decades. I particularly acknowledge the practitioner scholars and student services professionals from the Consortium of Higher Education LGBT Resource Professionals. Thank You.

I am also thankful to my former colleagues from Duke University, namely Dr. Karen Krahulik, and the Columbia University Office of Multicultural Affairs. They provided valuable resources that allowed me to tinker with new ideas. Essentially these campuses became a sort of experimental lab that allowed for trial and error. Much of that learning shaped what became the University of Illinois Springfield Safe Zone program and thus this book.

SPECIAL THANKS
Dr. Juanita Ortiz, former Safe Zone committee member and facilitator at the University of Illinois. She was instrumental in helping to design many parts of the Safe Dating as well as Multiple Identities sessions. It was volunteer faculty like her, a rare breed in my experience, that allowed a small staffed office to create something so unique. She is a treasure that is sorely missed on the campus.

Nancy Jean Tubbs has been my partner in crime, so to speak, all these years. The work she has shared, produced by her and the students at the University of California Riverside, continues to be adapted by many of us nationwide.

Michael Stephens, my former graduate assistant at the University of Illinois Springfield, who gladly researched just about anything I threw at him whether screen name acronyms or an unwieldy database.

Dr. Michael Murphy, associate professor in Women & Gender Studies at the University of Illinois Springfield, for lighting a fuse under me by deftly pushing to present all of this in a draft book proposal at his sexualities series on campus.

All of the people that provided feedback of book chapters including Phillip Bass, Dr. Jason Pierceson, Dr. D. A. Dirks, Dr. Michelle Miller, and Dr. Holly Kent. Finally, all the many co-authors and contributors that have shared their work so broadly in the past few years and have allowed this volume to be created.

CHAPTER 1

An Overview of Safe Zones

In 1992, a dedicated group of LGBTQIA+ students, with no resources, thanks to an intransigent Office of Student Life, dared to do what administrators should have: educate the campus, provide support services, and start the first ever Safe Zone program! It was a special time for student activism on this college campus long before public role models such as Ellen DeGeneres, before movements for marriage equality, before trans inclusion was a glimmer on the horizon, before organizing on the Internet. The queer admissions gods recruited a certain band of future leaders that created a proving ground of sorts for new educational interventions on campus. Work that this author still finds himself doing today.

As far as I know, a group of student leaders, my friends: David Speakman, Kenton Campbell, Brian Ernsberger, and Tim Goldman, originated the Safe Zone idea. Many others continued the efforts, such as Lisa Avery, Stephanie Mineart, Rose Young, Tracy Clark, Brian Craig, Toni Kelly, Jody Crabtree-Hoffman, myself, and the organization advisors, Sue Wanzer and Joe Goodwin. After hosting a string of regional student leader conferences, the program idea spread across the Midwest.

The program began with a simple sign in black and white on a yellow card that read "SAFE: Students, Administrators, & Faculty for Equality" with interlocking male/male and female/female symbols. Participants were required to attend a brief orientation session and post the sign on their office doors so to take allies "out of the closet"—a first ever visible support system. The bottom half of the sign advertised the "SAFEline" hotline phone service that these students ran as peer to peer counselors under the training and supervision of the Counseling Center on campus. The relationship built with the Counseling Center endured for years later as the professional staff, under the direction of Dr. Jay Zimmerman, continued to build the program as Safe Zone. "At Ball State, we're more than just educators—we're educational entrepreneurs" (from the Ball State University home page). No doubt.

How far we have come. Since the 1990s, North American educational institutions have implemented Safe Zone allies programs as a means to improve campus climate and thus retention of lesbian, gay, bisexual, and transgender, queer, and questioning (LGBTQIA+) students. Such programs have proliferated at hundreds of universities and high schools in response to student demands and unsupportive campus environments.

The core of Safe Zone programs is a series of educational and self-reflective workshops on various LGBTQIA+ themes and issues. Upon successful completion of the Safe Zone curriculum, participants become members of the campus Safe Zone program and are able to display a sign outside their office indicating they are allies to the campus LGBTQIA+ community. Public identification of allies encourages dialogue about LGBTQIA+ people (who may not be readily visible) and allows LGBTQIA+ students and others to identify supportive staff and faculty without fear of bullying, retribution, and harassment.

However, there has been no standardized curriculum or reference on the topic, and no centralized place to gather knowledge, resources, activities, and experiences of those who run or facilitate these Safe Zone ally developmental programs. University staff and administrators who oversee such programs are continually "reinventing the wheel" and dependent on hand-to-hand/word-of-mouth dissemination of curricula, workshops, and handouts—usually through professional consortia or associations.

Moreover, administrators are typically not afforded research and writing time in their job descriptions, and no standardized reference or training manual has previously been in print on this topic. As a result, Safe Zone programs have been in a loosely organized "cottage industry" phase in need of a centralized, consolidated resource.

OVERVIEW OF THE CONTENTS

This book offers a model Safe Zone curriculum and a step-by-step guide for prospective Safe Zone trainers. It contains all the tools needed to implement, coordinate, and train participants in a Safe Zone program. The real-world tested curriculum is based on the author's years of experience creating and facilitating Safe Zone programs at several major U.S. colleges and universities. It consists of two introductory chapters that explain Safe Zone programs and the learning style employed in the trainings followed by 6 chapters, each devoted to a specific Safe Zone workshop. The content draws on a number of academic disciplines: LGBTQ Studies, Women and Gender Studies, Sociology, Criminal Justice, History, Anthropology, and Psychology. A final chapter offers a comprehensive model of assessment. All handouts and activities used in this book are available as a download from Rowman & Littlefield.

Chapter 2 explains the history, justification, and coordination of these Safe Zone programs. It emphasizes a required training curricular model and provides a best practice general outline of an initial fundamental workshop session. Answers to frequently asked questions explain how to respond to political considerations.

Chapter 3 advocates for a constructivist pedagogy for Safe Zone programs, social justice work, that employs an experiential learning style. The author draws on years of social justice training to explain the facilitator role, quality questions, and how a parallel process should occur that mirrors the real world outside the session. "Tips for facilitators" and an annotated bibliography, reoccurring items in the curricula chapters, help new trainers/facilitators hone their skill sets for social justice training.

Chapters 4 through 9 detail the six workshop sessions. Each of these curricula chapters includes an introductory contextualization of the learning material taken directly from the workshop session, and an annotated bibliography of key readings for new facilitators to attain. Readings are to be used to supplement their knowledge in prep for facilitating the session. The curricula for each workshop contain a list of required materials; set-up directions and facilitation instructions; example process questions, statements, and points to use while facilitating; tips for leading successful workshops and avoiding/handling problems. The workshops, handouts, and activities are presented in such a way that they can be replicated or adapted for the needs of a specific school or audience. Handouts, activities, and Safe Zone logo artwork are available as a download from Rowman & Littlefield.

Chapter 4 covers fundamental learning outcomes such as terminology, the coming out process, LGBTQIA+ historical icons, and a student peer-led education activity and panel. This session begins with a guided imagery that asks participants to walk in the shoes of an LGBTQIA+ young adult. Many topics, such as sexuality over the lifespan, are introduced that are intended to whet the appetite for further learning in the advanced sessions (chapters 5–9).

Chapter 5 delves deeper into sexuality over the lifespan by reviewing terms such as bisexual and pansexual, then uses the experiences in the room in an anonymous activity to visibly make real the spectrum of sexuality. Myths of bisexuals are tackled with a matching game and a role play activity gives example as to how biphobia can manifest within interpersonal relationships.

Chapter 6 is brave. It addresses the intersection of faith or religious belief with LGBTQIA+ identities. The authors document a way to facilitate this topic without devolving into a debate on scripture(s) within an Abrahamic faith tradition. The point is to give light to how some LGBTQIA+ people have resolved conflict with their faith beliefs with a liberation theology view. Key challenges for LGBTQIA+ people are introduced, supportive resources are explained, and participants practice conversing with a hypothetical LGBTQIA+ young adult using the GRACE model.

Chapter 7 provides visibility to transgender topics. The curriculum begins at breaking the supposed binary of gender by introducing a continuum, reviews common terms, introduces the science of transgender as well as intersex, and common challenges in higher education. Activities are designed to have participants consider how they create and express their own gender as well as how their reinforcement of a binary in their everyday life polices the genders of others.

Chapter 8 provides an honest sex positive curricula with the intent of safe healthy dating, safe sex, and relationships for LGBTQIA+ young adults. Topics include hooking up online, dating scripts, debunking "gay sex," HIV/STI disclosure, and intimate partner violence. These are topics that are not usually part of the vernacular due to a variety of reasons. It is past time that these topics come out of the closet so LGBTQIA+ young adults develop healthy behaviors and healthy relationships.

Chapter 9 recognizes the multiple identities of the LGBTQIA+ community, including the intersections of race, culture, gender, and sexual orientation from a global perspective. Topics include terms that are non-Western European, understanding identity conflict and resolution for multiple oppressions, a tour of global gender and sexual minorities, and creating a personal action plan. This session attempts to bite off more than it can chew as the depth of potential cultures is beyond the time frame of discussion, yet it is an introductory framework to understand how multiple minority LGBTQIA+ people navigate communities that may or may not privilege aspects of their self.

Chapter 10 provides an example model assessment intended to help understand if the program is meeting previously stated goals and desired impact. The chapter advocates for assessment throughout the life of the program from inception, facilitation learning, learning outcomes for members, steps for policy change, and repetition when needed.

ACRONYM: LGBTQIA+

The use of the acronym "LGBTQIA+" (lesbian, gay, bisexual, transgender, queer, questioning, intersex, agender, asexual) in this book is intended to be inclusive of the vast diversity of genders and sexualities present in the human species. It is for the labeling, or even attempts at no labels, the typical aged sexual and gender minority college student is describing. An attempt to represent a spectrum of identities including pansexuals, genderqueers, and all others that are breaking the binary of a limiting description of sexual orientation and gender identity.

STATISTICS

The median age that young adults come out—confirm their identity as a sexual or gender minority—is 20 years old (Pew Research Center, 2013), the exact typical college age. This means many young adults are coming out at earlier ages and expecting that colleges and universities are places for them. Estimates of the number of LGBTQIA+ students at institutions of higher education are difficult to come by. Universities do not typically ask for sexual orientation on admissions applications, although many are now asking for gender identity inclusive of trans applicants. The often-cited 10 percent of the population statistic (Kinsey, 1998) could mean that as many as 2 million college students in the United States (Strayhorn, Johnson, Henderson, & Tillman-Kelley, 2015) identify as LGBTQIA+.

Other studies in recent years indicate that, depending on geographic location, anywhere from 2–10 percent of the population identifies as LGBTQIA+ (Williams Institute, 2013; Gates & Newport, 2013). However, much of this depends on identification with labels such as "lesbian" or "gay," which hold Western and White cultural significance for some people of color or international students. UCLA, for example, who regularly assessed their student population, found they received a more accurate representation of their non-heterosexual student participants when asking "attraction" over a limiting "LGB" demographic question, effectively doubling numbers from less than 4 percent to 8.3 percent (Eyermann & Sanlo, 2002).

At Brown University about 12 percent of students polled by the *The Brown Daily Herald* (2010) identified as "gay or bisexual." The *Yale News* (2010) student poll found 17.7 percent of men and 8.1 percent of women were exclusively attracted to their own gender while an additional 12.2 percent of women were attracted to both women and men (three times that of men).

While some people, including student services administrators, would cite small numbers as justification for not needing to address the systematic concerns of LGBTQIA+ people in higher education, clearly there is a significant population present at colleges and universities in the United States. Any attempts to minimize the need to provide resources or respond to this population, particularly transgender students, because of small numbers, should be met with skepticism. Exact numbers should not determine the need to educate and provide services, whether a school has 100 or 500 LGBTQIA+ identified students.

AUDIENCE

This book is intended for staff that are charged with providing student support services that are inclusive of LGBTQIA+ students. Although its contents are easily transferrable to the classroom, the explanatory style has administrators in mind who largely plan activities that occur outside of those classrooms. Students that are not exclusively online spend the vast majority of their time, of their learning, not in the classroom. Yet it is administrators that are tasked with teaching these students how to engage with each other with civility, with respect. That is not possible without finding ways to help understand the realities of our multicultural society—a society that increasingly realizes that lesbian, gay, bisexual, transgender, queer, questioning, intersex, agender, asexual (LGBTQIA+) students are an important facet of the student population. To not support and affirm this student population is to shoot your recruitment goals, your retention goals, your successful matriculation in the proverbial foot.

WHAT NEXT?

There are topics not addressed adequately in this book. There is room for future workshop session development on intersexuality and asexuality and possibly other topics. It is the hope of the author that a wellspring of educators will begin to create or share their ideas as a result of this publication. Interested educators can join this effort or just ask questions, receive feedback, and share their ideas on social media (Facebook.com/SafeZonesBook, Twitter.com/safezonesbook) and through email (safezonesbook@gmail.com), and meet at national conferences.

Kinsey (1998)mentioned that he found people in his studies in the 1940s that were outside the "X" of his scale of sexual orientation, but it was not until the advent of the Internet that asexuality found a voice. A reportedly small group of people with this sexual orientation has found community. There is much work to do to theorize the development of this true sexual identity that is increasingly found among sexual minority communities. Bogaert (2012) and Scherrer (2008) are early works of note.

Unlike the absence of asexuality, intersexuality is included with the transgender workshop session; however problematic that can be as the connection is tenuous at best. It is past time that those of us doing this work find space to develop the tools to work with these young adults and educate our colleagues. It is my hope that this book will help to illustrate how glaring this absence is in our work and encourage the development of educational interventions. Finally, an opportunity exists to test the learning outcomes of this curricula on a national basis, figure out what works best, and adapt the curricula.

REFERENCES

Bogaert, A. (2012). *Understanding asexuality*. Lanham, MD: Rowman & Littlefield Publishers.

Eyermann, T., & Sanlo, R. (2002). Documenting their existence: Lesbian, Gay, Bisexual, and Transgender students on campus. In R. Sanlo, S. Rankin, & R. Shoenberg (Eds.), *Our place on campus: Lesbian, gay, bisexual, transgender services and programs in higher education*. Westport, CT: Greenwood Press.

Gates, J., & Newport, F. (2013). *Gallup special report: New estimates of the LGBT population in the United States*. Accessed from the Williams Institute, August 23, 2013, at http://williamsinstitute.law.ucla.edu/research/census-lgbt-demographics-studies/gallup-lgbt-pop-feb-2013/.

Kinsey, A. (1998). *Sexual behavior in the human male*. Bloomington, IN: Indiana University Press.

Pew Research Center. (2013). *A survey of LGBT Americans: Attitudes, experiences and values in changing times*. Retrieved October 30, 2015, from http://www.pewsocialtrends.org/2013/06/13/a-survey-of-lgbt-americans.

Scherrer, K. S. (2008). Coming to an asexual identity: Negotiating identity, negotiating desire. *Sexualities, 11*(5), 621–41.

Serna, D. (2010). One in four, maybe six. *Yale News*. Retrieved October 30, 2015, from http://yaledailynews.com/blog/2010/02/10/one-in-four-maybe-six.

Strayhorn, T. L., Johnson, R. M., Henderson, T. S., & Tillman-Kelly, D. L. (2015). *Beyond coming out: New insights about GLBQ college students of color*. Columbus, OH: Center for Higher Education Enterprise, The Ohio State University.

Weiss, S. (2010). About 12 percent of students identify as gay or bisexual. *The Brown Daily Herald*. Retrieved October 30, 2015, from http://www.browndailyherald.com/2010/11/12/about-12-percent-of-students-identify-as-gay-or-bisexual.

What Is a Safe Zone Program?

Kerry John Poynter and Nancy Jean Tubbs

"My Ally sticker has already impacted my ability to connect with students. I've had a few ask about it, which gave me a chance to describe the Ally program. In addition, one student from the Winter term asked about the sticker, talked about his experiences with coming out, and then requested information and resources. It is a small sticker, but a powerful symbol. And it has helped me better serve my students. Thank you for that!"

—Community college assistant professor, California

"The Allies sticker in some ways gives people a reason to stop (learning to be a better ally). I would rather they go on."

—LGBT Resource Center Director, California

"I see the Allies program as a way to start conversations and open the door to educational trainings. We allow the contract to expire after three years, and we are considering an online 'refresher' course for staff & faculty."

—Multicultural Center coordinator, South Carolina

HETEROSEXUAL AND CISGENDER PEOPLE ARE OFTEN ASKED TO BE ADVOCATES FOR LESBIAN, GAY, BISEXUAL, transgender, queer, intersex, and asexual (LGBTQIA+) people on many campuses nationwide. Yet, these willing allies have few skills or resources available to them and no personal experiences to guide their own development in advocating for LGBTQIA+ student populations. Nonetheless, with adequate resources and training, staff, faculty, and students can have a significant effect on creating a positive culture on a college or university campus.

Washington and Evans (1991) define an ally as "a person who is a member of the dominant or majority group who works to end oppression in his or her personal and professional life through support of, and as an advocate with and for, the oppressed population" (p. 195). Allies of different groups of people are instrumental in effecting positive change in the dominant culture. It is important to note that LGBTQIA+ people can also be allies within their own community, but may choose not to be due to fear, discrimination, or harassment. Therefore, heterosexual and cisgender allies hold much power to affect change that contributes to a more accepting campus climate.

In the early to mid-1990s educational policy makers and program planners began to recognize the potential of Safe Zone allies programs (Alvarez & Schneider, 2008; Ballard, Bartle, Masequesmay, 2008; LBGSA, 1992; Poynter & Tubbs, 2007). Developing heterosexual allies could make the culture of a college or university campus more accepting toward LGBTQIA+ people (Bullard, 2004).

Additionally, individuals including students and young adults are likely to believe that their peers hold negative attitudes about LGBTQIA+ people resulting in adjustment of behavior to emulate this misperception (Bowen & Bourgeois, 2001; Worthington, Savoy, Dillon, & Vernaglia, 2002). Heterosexual males will feel the need to fit in and be accepted by others that hold negative attitudes about LGBTQIA+ people, thus emulating their peers (Franklin, 1998). The public identification of allies through an LGBTQIA+ Safe Space Ally program will help to alleviate previously held misperceptions, encourage affirming group identification, and encourage others to participate while creating a more accepting campus.

A number of colleges and universities have developed LGBTQIA+ Safe Space Ally programs (Evans, 2002; Henquinet, Phibbs, Skoglund, 2000; Hothem & Keen, 1998; Poynter & Schroer, 1999; Poynter & Wang, 2003; Poynter & Barnett, n.d.; Sanlo, Rankin & Schoenberg, 2002; Tubbs, 2003; Tubbs, Bliss, Cook, Poynter, & Viento, 2000; Ballard, Bartle, Masequesmay, 2008). Names for these programs include Safe Zone, Safe Space, Safe Harbor, SAFE on Campus, and Allies.

Goals of these programs include improving the campus climate, increasing awareness, increasing conversations around LGBTQIA+ issues, providing safe space, educating members and providing skills to members to confront homophobia, transphobia, biphobia or heterosexism. Although it is unclear where the "Safe" idea originated, the earliest reference found is the Ball State University program called SAFE On Campus (Lesbian, Bisexual and Gay Student Association, 1992).

The hallmark of these "Safe" programs is the public identification of allies by placing a "Safe" symbol, usually incorporating a pink triangle or rainbow or the word "ally" or a combination of all three, on office doors or within living spaces. Typical components of these programs consist of a resource manual and sticker or sign. Many programs also require an orientation or training session(s) of varying lengths. Other components may include a listserv, advisory board/committee, web page resources, assessment, periodic socials, and additional items to identify members such as key chains, buttons, and pens.

There is no "'Center for Safe Zone Training' a staff person can attend . . ." (Hothem and Keen, 1998, p. 367) and no comprehensive written resource in existence for campus coordinators. Until recently, minimal published information existed about these programs and what little is available is still scattered throughout the Internet (Evans, 2002). Essentially there has been a lack of comprehensive information to inform others about how to implement, coordinate, facilitate training, and assess these programs. As a result, these programs can still be based on little shared knowledge or experience. The exceptions have been the "Safe on Campus" DVD (Poynter & Wang, 2003), which is outdated and now unavailable, and the "I am Safe Zone" DVD (2012) by Jessica Pettitt which can be financially burdensome to programs with little access to funding.

JUSTIFICATION FOR SAFE ZONE PROGRAMS

Safe Zone programs have proven to be useful in affecting campus climate change (Evans, 2002), while the associated trainings create more accepting attitudes among Safe Zone members (Finkel, 2003; Worthen, 2011). According to the National College Climate Survey (Rankin, Weber, Blumenfeld, & Frazer, 2010) LGBTQIA+ students, staff, and faculty rate the overall climate at their school less positive than their heterosexual peers. "All (LGBTQIA+) students rated their campus environment less positively than did 'straight' students" (p. 2), and LGBTQIA+ "individuals (are) the least accepted group when compared to other under-served populations and, consequently, more likely to indicate deleterious experiences and less than welcoming campus climates" (p. 9). Other studies nationwide, have found that LGBTQIA+ students encounter a less than welcoming environment at the collegiate level (Noack, 2004; Rankin, 2003).

The public identification of Safe Zone members can help alleviate the real or perceived climate concerns for the LGBTQIA+ population. The Safe Zone program can also help students in the earlier stages of coming out, as well as students in the general university population, to understand their multiple identities (race, sexual orientation, etc.) in order to better process through the life issues they will encounter throughout their college experience (relationships, family, religion, etc.).

ALLY DEVELOPMENT

Evidence suggests that these programs do make a difference. Assessment results from various institutions support that their individual programs increased visibility, improved the environment, increased conversations, and increased the comfort levels of the participants in the program (Ballard, Bartle, Masequesmay, 2008; Evans, 2002; Poynter & Lewis, 2003).

Participants may report that they do not have many interactions with people on campus as a result of participating in the program (Evans, 2002; Poynter & Lewis, 2003). However, conversations do increase for some and as a result, awareness around LGBTQIA+ issues is fostered. A large public university in California found that 42 percent of the members reported that students had come to talk with them about LGBTQIA+ issues (Ballard, Bartle, & Masequesmay, 2008). Other tangible benefits also are apparent such as indirect interactions such as

LGBTQIA+ people feeling an increased comfort level and changing a perceived negative campus image (Evans, 2002).

Even if members do not report an increase in conversations, there may be an increase reported in their comfort level after attending workshop sessions (Poynter & Lewis, 2003). At worst, members may report that the program had not increased conversations or comfort due to already high comfort levels that existed prior to the program. More information about assessment of these programs can be found in chapter 10.

ALLY IDENTITY DEVELOPMENT

Program planners should become versed in the identity development process of becoming a heterosexual and cisgender ally. These programs need to meet potential members at their developmental level. Joining a Safe Zone or Allies program, completing a workshop session, and hanging an Allies/Safe Zone sign does not make one an ally. The personal journey is not complete (Lewis & Purcell, 2015). An ally has to understand that this is an ongoing learning process, one that means continued self-learning, learning to be an advocate by practicing action-oriented skills, making mistakes, listening to queer people criticize you and taking it to heart, adjusting your thinking, and moving forward with the process of becoming a better ally.

Program coordinators should have an understanding of heterosexual ally development (Broido, 2000; Evans & Broido, 2005) as they coordinate a comprehensive Safe Zone program. Coordinators need to continually engage members involved in the program. It is not enough to simply require members to participate in a training session and post a membership sign. It is impossible to prepare members to become the best of allies in a training session (Woodford, Kolb, Durocher-Radeka, & Javier, 2014). Putting up a Safe Zone or Allies sign is an action-oriented component but it cannot be the end of action! Program coordinators should plan carefully as to what content the institution needs with a balance of knowledge acquisition, personal development, skills practice, and steps to institutional inclusiveness.

Some curricula have had a sole emphasis on training members about identity development models. In fact, researchers (Ryan, Broad, Walsh, & Nutter, 2013) have found that an emphasis on identity development for heterosexual allies, as the sole focus of training, was not found to be reflected in the stories of their Safe Zone members. Members referred to their participation as professional duty as opposed to a personal developmental process. Designing a training solely on majority development can have the result of unintentionally leaving out important dialogues of learning on LGBTQIA+ topics.

"Providing equal treatment to all students" (Ryan, Broad, Walsh, & Nutter, 2013, p. 98) is a fine non-discriminatory ideal to uphold but it is not entirely possible if you do not understand the LGBTQIA+ community. A variable training program and coordination should meet potential members at their developmental level as opposed to solely teaching about the coming-out process. "Initially I think the way a lot of these trainings were developed was about what if somebody comes out to you? How do you prepare for that moment? Many of these trainings have moved on from that (concern). It's still a component . . . (but) our students have moved on from that (need)" (D. A. Dirks, personal communication).

Advanced topical sessions (such as transgender, faith, multiple identities, bisexuality/sexuality over the lifespan) are needed (Ballard, Bartle, & Masequesmay, 2008). The chapter authors also believe that if facilitators depend on sexual and gender identity development models, such as the coming-out process, as the sole focus of training then there is insufficient information and skills building provided to the potential members.

An assessment of a Safe Zone program at a large, public university in California found that "over three-fourths (78%) of the faculty/staff said they would like follow-up or additional training. Over half requested advanced training on effective ways to be an ally or advocate, relevant legal issues, and on topics of gender and sexism, and transgender issues. Nearly half requested training on the intersection between LGBTQIA+ issues and ethnicity, race/racism, and religion, as well as more role playing scenarios" (Ballard, Bartle, & Masequesmay, 2008).

Since membership in these programs should be voluntary, the self-selected participants in the trainings are likely to already have a basic level of knowledge and awareness. Ongoing "refresher sessions" (Draughn, Elkins, & Roy, 2002) or models with "incremental designs offering successive trainings on specific topics" should represent all the populations found in the diversity of the LGBTQIA+ community (Woodford, Kolb, Durocher-Radeka, & Javier, 2014, p. 320). The curriculum provided in this book is intended as a longer-term process of knowledge and skills development, organized into advanced sessions, that meets potential members at their developmental level.

This chapter condenses various items of published and non-published information into a comprehensive resource that, based on the experience of the authors, advocates for a model LGBTQIA+ Safe Zone program that includes a series of learning or skills-building sessions and assessment component.

ORGANIZING AN LGBTQIA+ SAFE SPACE ALLY PROGRAM

When creating an LGBTQIA+ Safe Zone program, many strategic questions must be considered. Who will organize and administer the program? How will the campus administration respond? How will the campus LGBTQIA+ community respond? What resources are available?

Programs at different institutions are either coordinated by a professionally staffed campus LGBTQIA+ services office (Sanlo, Rankin, & Schoenberg, 2002), staff and faculty, or by student organizations. Often an advisory board consisting of staff, faculty, and students may have responsibility for coordination, recruitment, and training. Regardless of who coordinates the program, colleges and universities should not rely solely on students to provide services and education to the campus community.

Strengths of staff and faculty coordination:

- Continuity of organizers who remain many years on campus
- Knowledge and expertise of student affairs staff or faculty
- Resources of campus offices (e.g., copy machines, desktop publishing, access to rooms and funds)
- Legitimacy when supported by administration

Strengths of student coordination:

- Energy of student organizers
- Student empowerment
- University-recognized student organizations may have access to more funding than departments

Including all potential stakeholders in the development of the program—students, staff, faculty, and administration—will help to provide legitimacy. Planners should invite influential campus leaders such as administration and student leaders to serve on an advisory board. Responsibilities of the advisory board should include assistance in identifying potential allies and providing a sounding board for ideas. Board members should be prepared to stand up for the program in public, and should agree to attend or facilitate trainings.

Meanwhile, many campus offices or academic departments may have an interest in helping to launch the program. Approach women's centers, cross-cultural centers, counseling centers, Greek advisors, residence life, health education, student activities or student unions, academic advisors, women's studies departments, sexualities/LGBTQIA+ studies departments, and supportive student groups for assistance.

Organizers must also be cognizant of possible challenges by campus administration. If challenges are expected then strategies for responding should be outlined before launching the program. There are several possible strategies that may be used. For example, turn to current literature on the needs of students "coming out." Use campus climate surveys to examine whether safe spaces are needed on campus. Look at student affairs mission statements and staff job duties to emphasize the right of every student to a safe learning environment.

Programs created by students or by staff/faculty outside of a particular office must consider whether to seek official university recognition. Independent programs may have more freedom from administrative pressure. However, resources must be paid with donations and fund-raisers, and meeting space may be difficult to find. The campus administration may also attempt to co-opt the program for political reasons, such as using its existence to defend against charges of a hostile campus climate. The pros and cons of how the program is recognized should be weighed depending on the environment of the particular campus.

CURRICULAR PROGRAM MODELS

Curricular components of most LGBTQIA+ Safe Zone programs are somewhat similar across campuses regardless of how they are named. Training sessions must be a required part of these programs. A fundamental training may consist of a number of elements including panels of LGBTQIA+ students, staff, and employees;

referral guidelines for counseling and harassment reporting; role plays; information about identity development; resources available on and off the campus; and general LGBTQIA+ information. Each school should design a training program specific to the goals of their program and the assessed needs of the campus. At the conclusion of training participants are then asked to sign a contract or values statement affirming their participation in the program.

There are variations in the types of trainings that institutions employ. Four variations were found by Woodford, Kolb, Durocher-Radeka, and Javier (2014) with each having different design characteristics. Some schools employed a combination of multiple variations. The various curricular models are: "(1) understanding LGBTQIA+ concepts and developing awareness of biases, (2) understanding LGBTQIA+ issues and recognizing discrimination and heterosexual privilege, (3) becoming support persons to LGBTQIA+ individuals, and (4) becoming advocates to create LGBTQIA+-affirming campuses" (p. 318). The curriculum explained in this book employs variations of each of these four. We recommend using campus climate assessments such as the Campus Pride Index (campusprideindex.org) to encourage allies to make inclusive policy change as well as working with faculty to design classroom-specific sessions.

Recruit facilitators from across campus that have backgrounds in the academic areas covered during your sessions. Plan for practice sessions to receive useful feedback before launching. Consider the presentation styles of each facilitator (Young & McKibban, 2013) and how their personal narratives will help to shape the sessions. See chapter 3 for an understanding of the learning style described in this volume.

The drawback to requiring training is that fewer people may participate in the program. However, since those in attendance have taken the extra step to attend it is more likely that all members are committed to the goals of the program. In addition, people will self-select whether or not participating as a member is right for them and thus you will likely not need to screen out those that cannot fulfill the goals of the program.

On rare occasions people interested in participating in a program will want to "save" or help LGBTQIA+ people through religious conversion therapy. Providing a required training ensures that you know that the participants have seriously and critically considered what it will be like to be affirmative toward LGBTQIA+ people. The chapter authors wish to convey our preference for a required training.

TRAINING JUSTIFICATION

A required training should be an integral part of a comprehensive LGBTQIA+ Safe Zone program. Automatically assuming that all interested participants will be able to function and communicate when in contact with LGBTQIA+ people does not take into consideration the impediments to this contact. Posting a "safe" sign or symbol is helpful in communicating nonverbal support but not all persons that post a sign or display a symbol are going to be able to communicate effectively when conversation occurs as a result of the sign. Training will help to alleviate barriers to this conversation.

An impediment to contact with LGBTQIA+ people and issues can be anticipated discomfort about future interactions with LGBTQIA+ people (Mohr & Sedlacek, 2000). The fear of unintentionally exhibiting homophobic or prejudiced behavior is also an impediment for future contact with LGBTQIA+ people (Devine, Evett, & Vasquez-Suson, 1996; Mohr & Sedlacek, 2000). Providing educational interventions, such as a required training in an LGBTQIA+ Safe Zone program, that create interpersonal contact with LGBTQIA+ people, demonstrate affirming conversation techniques, and provide skills-building activities can help reduce discomfort and fear before members post signs or stickers.

EXAMPLE INTRODUCTORY TRAINING OUTLINE

Each college or university will need to design a training based on the specific needs of their own campus. The comprehensive curriculum explained in this book advocates for completion of an initial Fundamentals session and two of five advanced sessions of any choice before signing a contract and receiving a Safe Zone sign. Members are encouraged to attend other sessions as time permits to continue their development. Potential members can test out of the initial Fundamentals session online and skip forward to advanced sessions of their choice.

The following outline contains the most fundamental elements of an introductory training session.

1. INTRODUCTIONS & GROUND RULES

   Use the introductions as not only a way to get to know the participants but as an avenue to learn. For example: Ask for name, affiliation (major/department), as well as a brief example or story that illustrates how and why they are affirming toward LGBTQIA+ people. Ground rules should set the stage for a safe space that includes confidentiality, respect for opinions, and an open, sharing dialogue. Ask for participants to share the pronouns people should use for them, if any. Including pronouns during introductions sets the stage for other demonstrations of trans-inclusion.

2. CAMPUS AND LOCAL RESOURCES

   A brief overview of resources available on campus and in the local community may include the campus counseling center, student groups, LGBTQIA+ Office, harassment reporting, and LGBTQ+-friendly coffee shops, restaurants, bookstores, and local organizations. This information should be condensed into a document for later perusal.

3. TERMINOLOGY

   Provide for a discussion on common terms such as heterosexism, homophobia, biphobia, transphobia, various labels, and LGBTQIA+ symbols. Ask for audience questions and provide a written vocabulary of definitions.

4. LGBTQIA+ & ALLY PANEL

   An interactive question-and-answer format with self-identified LGBTQIA+ and heterosexual or cisgender ally students, staff, and faculty who raise firsthand issues, concerns, and experiences on campus. Due to time constraints a moderator may need to limit the type of questions asked. Provide note cards for participants to write questions on and then choose a diverse set to use.

5. LGBTQIA+ DEVELOPMENTAL THEORY & ALLY/MAJORITY DEVELOPMENTAL THEORY

   Using sexual identity formation theory (Cass, 1979; McCarn & Fassinger, 1996) explain that LGBTQIA+ people may have different needs. Emphasize that people may be at different stages in different areas of their life (school v. job v. family v. friends). Allow participants to examine their own level of homophobia using the Riddle Homophobia Scale (Riddle, 1996) while using majority/ally identity theory (Broido, 1997; Broido, 2000; Evans & Broido, 2005; Gelberg & Chojnacki, 1995; Mohr, 2002; Pearlman, 1991; Sullivan, 1998; Worthington, Savoy, Dillon, & Vernaglia, 2002) to explain that heterosexual people have different needs as well. Use panelist stories to illustrate examples.

6. ACTIONS TO BE BETTER ALLIES TO BISEXUAL/PANSEXUAL PEOPLE, LGBTQIA+ PEOPLE OF COLOR, & TRANSGENDER PEOPLE

   Focus on direct actions participants can take to be better allies for marginalized members of the LGBTQ community. Resources such as "Ways to Be an Ally to Nonmonosexual/Bi People," "Tips for Supporting Queer Trans People of Color," and "Action Tips for Allies of Trans People" can be presented to spur dialogue and translate ideas to action. Further questions on these topics can be used to motivate participants to attend more advanced sessions. Provide a copy of the results of the Campus Pride Index to give new members advocacy ideas on policy, programmatic, and operating procedures to make the campus more inclusive.

7. OPTION: SIGN CONTRACT/VALUE STATEMENT; PROVIDE SIGN, STICKER, ETC.

CONTRACT

The contract is an agreement to provide a "safe zone" for anyone dealing with sexual orientation or gender identity issues. It emphasizes that an ally is meant for support and referral and is not a professional counselor (University of California Riverside Allies Contract, n.d.). Signing the contract is required before anyone can hang or use the sign or identifiable resources of the program. Once again, we recommend further advanced sessions beyond the basic fundamentals session before signing the contract, becoming a member, and hanging a Safe Zone sign. Signing a contract helps staff, faculty, and students consider whether they can meet the responsibilities of being a member.

One challenge some people of faith must consider is whether they can be affirming when they hold religious beliefs contrary to being supportive of LGBTQIA+ people. In these cases, the potential ally can be asked if they would be able to refrain from challenging someone based on their religious beliefs, and if they could refer visitors to another ally or to a campus resource that will be supportive in spiritual matters. Many potential allies recognize a duty to be supportive of others, especially if they are staff or faculty seeking to create a safe learning environment, regardless of their religious beliefs. Others cannot make this commitment and participate in the program. However, they have gained knowledge and resources, and sometimes they choose to join at a later time when they can sign the contract and make the commitment with sincerity.

POLITICAL CONSIDERATIONS: FREQUENTLY ASKED QUESTIONS

[Adapted from the Northern Illinois University Ally program. Used with permission.]

Campus members may resist posting a Safe Zone sign/sticker that is only for LGBTQIA+ support. The following are a few of the typical critical questions with example responses.

WHY DO WE NEED AN ALLIES SAFE ZONE PROGRAM WHEN OUR CAMPUS NON-DISCRIMINATION POLICY INCLUDES SEXUAL ORIENTATION? ISN'T THAT ENOUGH?

The reality is that not all people on campus are supportive, knowledgeable, and understanding of LGBTQIA+ people. Most of these people are not actively affirming either. This is the difference between posting a "safe" sign that conveys a strong message of support as opposed to posting a blanket statement of non-discrimination already included in campus policy.

All participants in these programs should agree to be supportive and affirming of all people regardless of sexual orientation or gender identity. Some schools, such as Indiana University, have avoided this issue altogether by designing a program that attempts to be inclusive of everyone on campus. Finally, the need to support transgender people through education and ally development is actually underlined by campus nondiscrimination statements that often include sexual orientation, but not gender identity or expression.

I DON'T KNOW ANY BIAS INCIDENTS OR INSTANCES OF HARASSMENT OR DISCRIMINATION AGAINST LGBTQ+ PEOPLE ON MY CAMPUS. WHY, THEN, DO WE NEED A SPECIAL PROGRAM FOR A PROBLEM THAT DOES NOT EXIST?

LGBTQ+ people may underreport incidents of bias, harassment, or discrimination for fear of being "outed," facing retaliation, or simply believing nothing will be done. If a campus does not publicly report bias incidents, harassment, or discrimination, then you may be unaware of the negative experiences for LGBTQ+ people on campus.

I SUPPORT DIVERSITY ISSUES IN GENERAL. WHY SHOULD WE FOCUS ONLY ON LGBTQIA+ PEOPLE, WHEN ALL SOCIAL IDENTITY GROUPS MAY REQUIRE MY SUPPORT?

Some institutions are just beginning to provide supportive resources to LGBTQIA+ students and a Safe Zone program may stand out from resources already available to students of color, women, differently abled, international students, etc. This does not mean the program should not intersect these other identities.

Safe Zone programs make visible the issues and identities of the LGBTQIA+ community. They can encourage dialogue instead of keeping it hidden. LGBTQIA+ people or those questioning their sexual orientation or gender identity will often assume a space is not safe until shown otherwise. Some campuses, such as UC Riverside, are recognizing the need to offer specific programs to develop allies and advocates for other hidden populations, including veterans, students with disabilities, and undocumented students.

Prejudice and discrimination based on sexual orientation or gender identity oftentimes go unchallenged. Because a person may not be recognizable as LGBTQIA+, they may hear heterosexist, biphobic, or transphobic comments from people who are not aware of whom they offend. Furthermore, potential LGBTQIA+ mentors may be hidden within a hostile climate. Safe Zone placards specifically reaching out to LGBTQIA+ people help them connect with advocates on campus.

SHOULDN'T WE FOCUS ON THINGS THAT BRING US TOGETHER, RATHER THAN SUPPORT SPECIAL PROGRAMS THAT DIVIDE US?

Allies Safe Zone programs actually do bring people together as advocates for social justice and support of a marginalized community. LGBTQIA+ people are often rendered invisible by heterosexism and cissexism, in which everyone is assumed to be heterosexual and cisgender. Their experiences ignored, LGBTQIA+ people may be excluded consciously or unconsciously from activities, programs, and public conversations. By acknowledging the unique experiences of LGBTQIA+ people, Safe Zone programs promote mutual understanding and enrich the cultural experiences of all people.

OUR CAMPUS SHOULD SUPPORT ALL PEOPLE, AND NOT JUST LGBTQIA+ PEOPLE. WON'T ALLIES SAFE ZONE PROGRAMS MAKE OTHERS FEEL EXCLUDED?

While some people may be upset by efforts to show visible support for LGBTQIA+ people, supporting one group of people does not mean excluding others. Valuing diversity is not a pie in which one group's slice of respect reduces the slice of respect for another group. Instead, people of all sexual orientations and gender identities are invited to think about their experiences more deeply, as well as how we show respect and understanding across differences. Efforts to welcome LGBTQIA+ people is not the same thing as excluding heterosexual or cisgender people.

SHOULDN'T WE OFFER A SAFE ZONE PROGRAM FOR HETEROSEXUAL PEOPLE, TOO, IF WE TRULY WANT TO TREAT PEOPLE EQUALLY?

Actually, due to institutionalized homophobia, biphobia, and transphobia, campus resources are already set up to support heterosexual and cisgender people. Also, heterosexual and cisgender people do not experience the bias, harassment, and discrimination that LGBTQIA+ people suffer based on prejudice against their sexual orientation or gender identity.

OUR CAMPUS SHOULDN'T BE IN THE BUSINESS OF ENDORSING THE "GAY LIFESTYLE" OR PROMOTING HOMOSEXUALITY. DON'T LGBTQIA+ SAFE ZONE PROGRAMS LEAD PEOPLE TO EXPERIMENT WITH A HARMFUL SEXUALITY?

Safe Zone programs promote a safe learning environment on our campus for all people, including LGBTQIA+ people. Allies affirm the right of people of all sexual orientations and gender identities to live free from bias, harassment, and discrimination. Rather than "promoting homosexuality," Allies Safe Zone programs affirm and accept LGBTQIA+ people and promote understanding and dialogue across differences.

WHY SHOULD WE DISCUSS PERSONAL ISSUES LIKE OUR SEXUAL ORIENTATION OR GENDER IDENTITY IN THE CLASSROOM OR WORKPLACE?

Heterosexual people "out" themselves every day by displaying photos of their spouses, sharing information about their home life, bringing their spouses to work events, etc. Many non-heterosexual people cannot safely share similar details about their personal life, because of the fear of bias or discrimination in the workplace. Likewise, heterosexual faculty and students share personal stories in class discussion and in assignments without the fear of negative reactions. In addition, cisgender people take for granted their gender identity being validated by others using their preferred names and pronouns without resistance or hesitation. Many LGBTQIA+ people simply wish to share their lives as easily as heterosexual and cisgender people do already.

DON'T LGBTQIA+ SAFE ZONE PROGRAMS DISCRIMINATE AGAINST PEOPLE WHO OPPOSE HOMOSEXUALITY BASED ON MORAL OBJECTIONS?

Safe Zone programs exist to educate anyone willing to learn about sexual orientation and gender identity; to create a network of supportive people on campus to affirm LGBTQIA+ people; and to provide resources and a listening ear to anyone with questions about sexual orientation or gender identity.

The intention of these programs is not to make others look bad if they do not participate but to identify support and active affirmation on campus. No one should be pressured to be a member and participation should be voluntary. An assessment at Duke University found that "members did not join the program because they were required or pressured" (Poynter & Lewis, 2003, p. 1), which contradicted earlier criticism that people would feel pressured to join.

MEMBERSHIP

Membership in LGBTQIA+ Safe Space Ally programs varies from campus to campus. Additionally, it is likely that there are a number of allies on campus that are just not ready to identify publicly.

Organizers of these programs must emphasize that not all allies to the LGBTQIA+ community are members of their program. Many potential members of the program—individuals supportive of the LGBTQIA+ community on a daily basis who may have great knowledge of issues and resources—never participate. They may not have the opportunity to attend a training or feel unsafe participating in the program for professional reasons.

Assuming that those with negative attitudes toward LGBTQIA+ people will not get involved, we can then predict membership characteristics based on research on negative attitudes toward LGBTQIA+ people. Characteristics of those that may not become involved include heterosexuals with traditional gender role values, conservative religious people, men categorically, and introverts with low self-esteem (D'Augelli, 1989; D'Augelli & Rose, 1990; Herek, 1998; Herek & Glunt, 1993; Mohr & Sedlacek, 2000; Patel, Long, McCammon, & Wuensch, 1995; Simoni, 1996).

Characteristics of those that are affirming and thus may get involved include women, people with previous interpersonal contact with LGBTQIA+ people, those with an advanced education, friends that have similar views, and those with prior involvement in social justice activities for other traditionally underrepresented groups (Herek & Capitanio, 1995, 1996; Herek & Glunt, 1993). These characteristics show that specific outreach may be needed to reach those that would not typically get involved.

ONGOING ACTIVITIES

Most LGBTQIA+ Safe Space Ally programs only require that members attend an initial training, display a sticker or sign, and provide a "safe" environment. While a mandatory training provides a strong foundation, members require ongoing educational opportunities to better understand and provide appropriate resources for a complex and diverse LGBTQIA+ community. While this book explains a series of ongoing advanced sessions, some programs provide additional components or ongoing voluntary activities. These components or activities include social events, focused educational workshops, brown-bag lunch discussions, train the trainer workshops, social events, social media pages, newspaper ads and web pages featuring the names of members across campus, and invitations to LGBTQIA+ events. Some workshops, discussions, or panels may also be open to the wider campus community while others are only open to current program members.

CONCLUSION

The examples and topics covered here represent the experiences of individuals working in a higher education environment in the United States of America. Although this is not intended as the only model of implementing or coordinating an LGBTQIA+ Safe Zone program, it is hoped that the information here is transferable to other educational institutions such as high schools, private schools, religiously affiliated institutions, and various models of education worldwide.

Prospective members must critically think about how hanging a sign that indicates affirmation toward LGBTQIA+ students will potentially affect their work or learning environment. Attendance at workshop sessions that allow for this, a self-assessment of knowledge or skills sets, and review of campus operating procedures can ensure a stronger presence of allies and further a more inclusive institution. Workshops must move beyond limiting "coming out" narratives and embrace the totality of sexualities and gender expressions present in the LGBTQIA+ community. Integrating topics that intersect multiple identities around race, ethnicity, culture, and faith beliefs (or lack thereof) will support ongoing development of these allies among other communities.

"I would argue that the change we initiated as a community, this is community building, was very much supported by the educational piece. You need to have the educational piece to build the capacity to make the allies to make the (institutional policy) changes" (D. A. Dirks, personal communication). Programs of this nature cannot be the sole response to creating an inclusive campus climate at a college, university, or any institution of learning. A multifaceted approach that considers policies, operating procedures, and educational interventions (such as a Safe Zone program) is but one of the approaches. Administrators, faculty, and decision makers must not rely on the visible presence of LGBTQIA+ students as the sole answer to creating a diverse campus.

Parts of this chapter appear in "Safe Zones: Creating LGBT Safe Space Ally Programs" (2007) by Kerry Poynter and Nancy Jean Tubbs in the *Journal of LGBT Youth*. Reprinted by permission of Taylor & Francis LLC (http://www.tandfonline.com).

REFERENCES

Alvarez, S. D., & Schneider, J. (2008). One college campus' need for a safe zone: A case study. *Journal of Gender Studies, 17*(1), 71–74.

Ballard, S. L., Bartle, E., & Masequesmay, G. (2008). *Finding queer allies: The impact of ally training and safe zone stickers on campus climate.* Retrieved from http://files.eric.ed.gov/fulltext/ED517219.pdf.

Bowen, A. M., & Bourgeois, M. J. (2001). Attitudes toward lesbian, gay, and bisexual college students: The contributions of pluralistic ignorance, dynamic social impact, and contact theories [Electronic Version] *Journal of American College Health, 50*(2), 91–96.

Bresciani, M. J. (2003, March). The updated outline for assessment plans. Netresults. Retrieved August 27, 2003, from http://www.naspa.org/netresults/article.cfm?id=996.

Broido, E. (2000). Ways of being an ally to lesbian, gay and bisexual students. In V. Wall & N. Evans (Eds.), *Toward acceptance: Sexual orientation and today's college campus* (pp. 345–69). ACPA Media.

Bullard, M. A. (2004). *Working with heterosexual allies on campus: A qualitative exploration of experiences among LGBT campus resource center directors.* Unpublished doctoral dissertation, Western Michigan University, Kalamazoo.

D'Augelli, A. R. (1989). Homophobia in a university community: Views of perspective resident assistants. *Journal of College Student Development, 30,* 546–52.

D'Augelli, A. R., & Rose, M. L. (1990). Homophobia in a university community: Attitudes and experiences of heterosexual freshmen. *Journal of College Student Development, 31,* 484–91.

Draughn, T., Elkins, B., & Roy, R. (2002). Allies in the struggle: Eradicating homophobia and heterosexism on campus. In E. P. Cramer (Eds), *Addressing homophobia and heterosexism on college campuses* (pp. 9–20). Binghamton, NY: Harrington Park Press.

Devine, P. G., Evett, S. R., & Vasquez-Suson, K. A. (1996). Exploring the interpersonal dynamics of intergroup contact. In R. M. Sorrentine & E. T. Higgins (Eds.), *Handbook of motivation and cognition: vol 3. The interpersonal context* (pp. 423–64). New York: Guilford Press.

Duke University. (2003). *Train the trainer.* SAFE on campus facilitator training manuals. Retrieved July 19, 2004. from http://lgbt.studentaffairs.duke.edu/programs/safe/dvddownloads.html.

Evans, N. (2002). The impact of an LGBT safe zone project on campus climate. *Journal of College Student Development, 43*(4), 522–39.

Evans, N., & Broido, E. (2005). Encouraging the development of social justice attitudes and actions in heterosexual students. In R. D. Reason, E. M. Broido, T. L. Davis, & N.J. Evans (Eds.) *Developing social justice allies (New Directions for Student Services,* No. 110). San Francisco: Jossey-Bass.

Finkel, M. J., Storaasli, R. D., Bandele, A., & Schaefer, V. (2003). Diversity training in graduate school: An exploratory evaluation of the Safe Zone project. *Professional Psychology: Research and Practice 34,* (5), 555–61.

Franklin, K. (1998). Unassuming motivations: Contextualizing the narratives of antigay assailants. In G. M. Herek (Ed.), *Stigma and sexual orientation: Understanding prejudice against lesbians, gay men, and bisexuals* (pp. 1–23). Thousand Oaks, CA: Sage.

Gelberg, S., & Chojnacki, J. T. (1995). Development transitions of gay/lesbian/bisexual affirmative, heterosexual career counselors. *The Career Development Quarterly, 43,* 267–73.

Goldstein, S. B., & Davis, D. S. (2010). Heterosexual allies: A descriptive profile. *Equity & Excellence in Education, 43*(4), 478–94.

Henquinet, J., Phibbs, A., & Skoglund, B. (2000 November–December). Supporting our gay, lesbian, bisexual, and transgender students. *About Campus,* 5(5), 24–26.

Herek, G. M. (1988). Heterosexuals' attitudes toward lesbians and gay men: Correlates and gender differences. *The Journal of Sex Research, 25,* 451–77.

Herek, G. M., & Capitanio, J. P. (1995). Black heterosexuals' attitudes toward lesbians and gay men in the United States. *The Journal of Sex Research, 32*(2), 95–105.

Herek, G. M., & Capitanio, J. P. (1996). Some of my best friends: Intergroup contact, concealable stigma, and heterosexuals' attitudes toward gay men and lesbians. *Personality & Social Psychology Bulletin, 22*(4), 412–24.

Herek, G. M., & Glunt, E. K. (1993). Interpersonal contact and heterosexuals' attitudes toward gay men: Results from a national survey. *The Journal of Sex Research, 30*(3), 239–44.

Hothem, K. B., & Keene C. D. (1998). Creating a safe zone project at a small private college: How hate galvanized a community. In R. Sanlo (Ed.) *Working with lesbian, gay, bisexual, and transgender college students: A handbook for faculty and administrators* (pp. 363–69). Westport, CT: Greenwood Press.

Lesbian, Bisexual and Gay Student Association (LBGSA). (1992). *Safe on campus informational manual.* Ball State University, Muncie, IN.

Lewis, T., & Purcell, C. (2015). The top 10 things we need to stop doing in LGBTQ+ programming. NASPA GLBT KC Blog Series. Accessed July 28, 2015, at https://www.naspa.org/constituent-groups/posts/the-top-10-things-we-need-to-stop-doing-in-lgbtq-programming.

Mohr, J., (2002). Heterosexual identity and the heterosexual therapist: An identity perspective on sexual orientation dynamics in psychotherapy. *The Counseling Psychologist, 30,* 532–66.

Mohr, J. & Sedlacek, W. (2000). Perceived barriers to friendship with lesbians and gay men among university students. *Journal of College Student Development, 41,* 70–80.

Patel, S., Long, T. E., McCammon, S. L., & Wuensch, K. L. (1995). Personality and emotional correlates of self-reported antigay behaviors. *Journal of Interpersonal Violence, 10*(3), 354–66.

Pearlman, S. F. (1991). Mothers' acceptance of daughters' lesbianism: A parallel process to identity formation. (Doctoral dissertation, Antioch University). *Dissertation Abstracts International, 52,* 287.

Poynter, K., (1999, March). *Heterosexual allies: Their role in the learning community.* Paper presented at the annual conference of the American College Personnel Association, Atlanta, GA.

Poynter, K., & Barnett, D. (n.d.). National Consortium of Directors of LGBT Resources in Higher Education. *How do I start or implement a safe zone program at my college or university?* Frequently asked question. Retrieved July 20, 2004, from http://www.lgbtcampus.org/faq/safe_zone.html.

Poynter, K. & Lewis, E. (2003). *SAFE on campus assessment report.* Durham, NC: Duke University, Center for LGBT Life. Retrieved February 21, 2005.

Poynter, K., & Schroer, S. (1999). Safe on campus: A program for allies of lesbian, gay, and bisexual students. *Michigan Journal of College Student Development, 3*(1), 6–8.

Poynter, K. J., & Tubbs, N. J. (2008). Safe zones: Creating LGBT safe space ally programs. *Journal of LGBT Youth, 5*(1), 121–32.

Poynter, K. (Producer), & Wang, C. (Director). (2003). *SAFE on campus dvd: A free training and development resource for LGBT safe space ally programs* [Digital Video Case Studies]. (Available from Duke University Center for LGBT Life: Durham, NC, http://lgbt.studentaffairs.duke.edu/programs/safe/dvd.html.)

Riddle, D. (1994). The Riddle scale. *Alone no more: Developing a school support system for gay, lesbian and bisexual youth.* St Paul: Minnesota State Department. ERIC Number: ED409411

Ryan, M., Broad, K. L., Walsh, C. F., & Nutter, K. L. (2013). Professional allies: The storying of allies to LGBTQ students on a college campus. *Journal of Homosexuality, 10,* (1), 83–104.

Sanlo, R., Rankin, S., & Schoenberg, R. (Eds.). (2002). *Our place on campus: Lesbian, gay, bisexual, transgender services and programs in higher education.* Westport, CT: Greenwood Press.

Simoni, J. M. (1996). Pathways to prejudice: Predicting students' heterosexist attitudes with demographics, self-esteem, and contact with lesbians and gay men. *Journal of College Student Development, 37,* 68–78.

Texas A&M University. (2000). ALLIES membership survey. *Student Life Studies.* Retrieved September 5, 2003, from http://stls.tamu.edu/survey/15070/15070.asp.

Tubbs, N. (2003) Campuses which offer safe zone or allies programs. *Consortium of LGBT Directors in Higher Education.* Retrieved August, 6, 2003 from http://www.lgbtcampus.org/faq/safe_zone_roster.html.

Tubbs, N., Bliss, L., Cook, M., Poynter, K., & Viento, W. (2000, November). *Training and programming for campus safe space programs: A roundtable discussion.* Creating Change Conference, National Lesbian and Gay Task Force, Atlanta, GA.

University of California Riverside Allies Contract. (n.d.). Retrieved January 31, 2005, from http://out.ucr.edu/allies.html.

Upcraft, M. L., & Schuh, J. H. (1996). *Assessment in student affairs: A guide for practitioners.* San Francisco: Jossey-Bass.

Washington, J., Evans, N. J. (1991). Becoming an ally. In N. J. Evans & V. A. Wall (Eds.), *Beyond tolerance: Gays, lesbians and bisexuals on campus* (pp. 195–204). Alexandria, VA: American College Personnel Association.

Woodford, M. R., Kolb, C. L., Durocher-Radeka, G., & Javier, G. (2014). Lesbian, gay, bisexual, and transgender ally training programs on campus: Current variations and future directions. *Journal of College Student Development, 55*(3), 317–22.

Worthen, M. G. (2011). College student experiences with an LGBTQ ally training program: A mixed methods study at a university in the southern United States. *Journal of LGBT Youth, 8*(4), 332–77.

Worthington, R. L., Savoy, H. B., Dillon, F. R., & Vernaglia, E. R. (2002). Heterosexual identity development: A multidimensional model of individual and social identity. *The Counseling Psychologist, 30*(4), 496–531.

Young, S. L., & McKibban, A. R. (2013). Creating safe places: A collaborative autoethnography on LGBT social activism. *Sexuality & Culture, 18,* 361–84.

CHAPTER 3

The Wisdom Is in the Room: Safe Zone Workshops Are Most Effective When They Are Experiential

EVANGELINE WEISS

INTRODUCTION: SAFE ZONE TRAINING IS ABOUT ADVOCACY AND POWER

THIS CHAPTER BUILDS THE CASE FOR USING ADULT LEARNING THEORY AND EXPERIENTIAL EDUCATION BEST practices to deliver the most effective Safe Zone training possible. By developing curriculum that recognizes the values and assumptions embedded in Safe Zone training, staff and students will achieve more community building and inclusivity on their college campuses than ever before. When we utilize constructivist pedagogy, we tap the wisdom of peers, our classrooms become incubators for critical thinking, and we inspire a form of inclusion, which is more than mechanical political correctness, but is instead a form of inclusion that is founded on justice, self-awareness, and accountability.

HOW DOES THIS PEDAGOGY INSPIRE CHANGE?

We implement Safe Zone programs on our college and university campuses to inspire change—to create more balance between the experiences of LGBTQIA+ students and their heterosexual peers. Embedded in our work is the notion that power dynamics impact our LGBTQIA+ students' experiences and that most (if not all) campuses continue to perpetuate heteronormative cultures, and spaces that communicate that heterosexuality is the norm.

We must be prepared for these power dynamics in our classrooms; as we leverage the beliefs and assumptions that learners bring to the Safe Zone process, we have a tremendous opportunity to productively tap those dynamics for the sake of the learning. Traditional, more passive forms of teaching (such as lectures and film screenings) are successful in engaging learners in deep self-reflection and inspiring open dialogue, and can even reinforce heterosexist beliefs or power dynamics.

Across the country, more and more institutions of higher education are addressing heterosexism, homophobia, and transphobia by launching LGBT centers, creating gender-neutral restrooms, adopting inclusive policies of non-discrimination and inclusive operating procedures, among other strategies. We are seeing much progress and the demand for Safe Zone trainings, curricula, and training of the Safe Zone facilitators has increased proportionally.

In the case of Safe Zone training (where staff, faculty, and students are trained to support LGBTQIA+ students through their exploration of their sexual and/or gender identities, coming out, or day-to-day lived experiences on campus) we consistently aim to develop the awareness and skills of Safe Zone allies so that they can:

1. adapt better and more effective strategies for creating fair and safer policies, practices, and space for LGBTQIA+ campus community members;
2. build more empathic, inclusive, and affirming classrooms, offices, student organizations, and residence halls;
3. ensure that they have the skills and awareness to consistently resist or interrupt micro-aggressions (usually unintended slights that have the effect of disparaging a group or person) or negative comments when needed.

Safe Zone training is an opportunity for learners to explore their values about sexuality and gender, to recognize some of the unique challenges that LGBTQIA+ people face, and to hone their skills as advocates, allies, and advisors. For example, during our gender continuum activity (discussed in chapter 7 of this volume), we describe an activity where participants are invited to reflect on their ideas about masculinity and femininity on a deeply personal level.

Giving Safe Zone trainees the chance to actively explore, discuss, and share their ideas about their gender expression helps to strengthen the overall climate on campus, in ways a static lecture about gender expression being relative would not. By engaging with each other, participants share their beliefs and come to understand that others may or may not have similar ideas about gender, and why.

This opportunity for critical thinking and collective self-reflection affords Safe Zone attendees the chance to gain a new perspective on their campus and peer group, which is more easily transferred into their everyday lives than more abstract discussions of these issues would be. The meanings that they make in the classroom are applicable right away, as they can immediately bring the insights that they gain from discussing masculinity and femininity with their fellow Safe Zone trainees to their interactions with their peers, professors, and staff members.

This type of activity, which aims to change attitudes and transform behavior, focuses on helping learners explore ideas which are often beyond their usual comfort zone, and as such is most successful when active adult learning principles (such as personal reflection and active engagement and discussion) are applied.

ADULT LEARNING AND CONSTRUCTIVISM

Adult learning theory posits that engaging adults in their own learning process is most effective for retention of new information, increases the likelihood that a behavior change will last, and is more respectful of diversity in the classroom. When it comes to teaching about gender expression and sexual orientation and asking learners to practice interrupting a bias statement, we can turn to interactive, engaging pedagogical principles to ensure that learning objectives make it out of our training rooms and onto our campuses.

We cannot effectively facilitate attitude changes or help to clarify values through passive modes of learning such as lectures. Safe Zone training curriculum thus requires us to think about participatory activities, and to facilitate these activities, as clearly and effectively as possible. For some trainers, this is a challenge, as we may or may not have considerable experience in or comfort with group facilitation.

Working to support volunteer programs in HIV/AIDS awareness, prevention, and education, and in diversity programs in higher education, experiential education invites learners to think critically about the concepts being discussed in immediate and real-world terms. This is vitally important, as notions of safety and inclusion for LGBTQIA+ students are not abstract. Rather, we are building safer spaces in our classrooms and residential halls by helping Safe Zone allies to develop specific communication skills that we know will create more inclusion. And we know that the failure to listen and to effectively and consistently use these communication skills and counseling tools can result in further excluding marginalized students.

FACILITATOR ROLE

Ultimately, a terrific Safe Zone trainer *will use the dynamics in the room* (people, their thoughts, and experiences) and to help the group see how they may be replicating outside power dynamics. And the only way to achieve this is to generate dialogue and discussion in the room. This dialogue needs to be structured through a series of activities, designed to help trainers clarify their values and beliefs around issues of sexuality and gender.

Most activities include a debrief section, designed to give participants the chance to talk through their feelings about and experiences in these activities. It is during this vitally important time that Safe Zone trainers make sure that they focus on asking thoughtful questions of participants, rather than "talking at them" with predetermined lecture points.

The purpose of the activities throughout this volume is to inspire reflection, ideas about practice, the sharing of beliefs or perspectives, and any other kinds of learning which has taken place. And it is in the unpacking of these activities that we as facilitators have the opportunity to check in with learners about their process.

We should identify learning points that have been successfully transferred to our participants, stir the group to deepen their awareness and analysis by anticipating how it relates to their own experience, pose hypothetical situations for them to consider, or simply challenge them to reflect upon the activity's learning objectives more seriously. For twenty years, I have trained trainers to manage group dynamics, design interactive and engaging workshops, and to master the attitude and skills that are essential for excellent experiential training. A fundamental skill for experiential trainers is the ability to gauge the group's learning, and to ask the right question at the right time.

QUESTIONS ARE KEY

In order to assess how a group is doing with the information we are teaching, we need to consistently ask both fact-checking and opinion questions. At the beginning of a session, after each activity, and at the end of the session, it is the trainers' task to assess the learning in the room. Is the group where we need them to be? Think, for example, of the difference between these two questions about the social construction of gender:

A: How is gender socially constructed?
B: What are three social institutions that inform our understanding of masculinity and femininity?

Both questions are good. However, question A requires the group to 1) know what we mean by "gender" and 2) understand the concept that gender is socially constructed. Therefore, question A is better as an evaluation question at the end of an activity. Question B is a solid assessment question for the early stage of a workshop, and should give trainer information about the specific learners in the room, and where they are in their process. The group is set up early on for success with question B and later should be able to answer question A.

Questions that ask others to reflect on a specific facet of the topic under discussion spark better discussions and better facilitate participant learning than questions that are too broad and open, such as "What is gender?" There may be times when this type of question is helpful, but one should exercise caution against overuse of these broad questions, because they can lead to a feeling in the room that there are "insiders" and "outsiders"—people in the room who already "know what they are talking about" and others who do not.

By asking a question about masculinity and femininity and then, in your reflections, making the point that this is what we mean by "gender," you are able to mirror to the group that although we are in different stages of our learning process, we all have access to this knowledge. By using such a framework, we create less friction and any sense of shame, embarrassment, or a feeling of "ignorance" for the newer learners, which helps to keep the process open and engaging for all participants.

Take the gender continuum activity from chapter 7 of this volume, in which we ask questions that support participants to reflect on their own curiosity and assumptions about each other's gender expression and identity. In that activity, we ask participants to reflect on the following questions:

What assumptions did you find yourself making about others in the lineup [in the exercise, participants are asked to line up from "most masculine" to "most feminine," and engage in discussions with one another to determine this lineup]? What do you believe your assumptions were based on?
How did it feel to be asked questions about your gender expression or identity?
Did you at any point feel misunderstood, or like assumptions were being made about you?

This is a rich direction for the conversation to go in, because it allows participants to unpack assumptions and stereotypes openly, and thus to begin to correct misinformation and reduce stereotyping. In addition, this line of questioning models for the group how they might solicit this kind of thinking from their students or peers when they perceive that stereotypes or assumptions are actively interfering with a group's learning process or dynamic.

When leading trainings, consider communicating that most people are worried about what they are going to say. Instead, suggest focusing on what questions you are going to ask. If that statement makes perfect sense to you, please feel free to skip the next section of this chapter. If you are puzzled or curious about why you would say such a thing, then please do continue reading.

DEVELOPING SHARED MEANING

In order for Safe Zone training to be effective, it is strategically and culturally important that allies and advocates develop shared meaning about the Safe Zone program, about the value of an LGBTQIA+-inclusive campus overall, and about the particular content of the specific training in question (such as the needs of transgender students, or how to hold multiple identities at once). When it comes to building a culture of inclusion and emotional safety on our campuses, there is much to discuss and many nuances to contain. Building shared meaning is a process that encourages exploration and reflection by individuals in order for learners to evolve a group understanding of the content.

Learners, for example, may come to the Bisexuality & Pansexuality session (please see the curriculum in chapter 5 of this volume for this session) possessing a wide range of ideas about sexuality over the life span that have been informed by their specific lived experiences and beliefs, and with different degrees of knowledge and familiarity with bisexuality and pansexuality. Once the session on Bisexuality & Pansexuality has been completed, however, the trainer must confirm that there is now a shared meaning—a new normal—for participants. This is key to true cultural change to be effective. Transforming a campus from a place where it is scary to come out and reveal an LGBTQIA+ identity to a place where students, staff, and faculty feel welcomed and affirmed is a powerful form of cultural change. And in order for this type of cultural transformation to succeed, we need shared meaning.

The basic principle of constructivism or adult learning theory is that the trainer's main responsibility is to help the learners access their own experience. In order for trainers to verify that this process is active, that we are succeeding, we must engage with all the participants actively. Not all learners will share out loud to an equal degree, and we are not suggesting you force people to participate out loud.

There are many tools for reality testing (are they understanding?) our work in the room. We cannot overstate the importance of drawing the learners out, helping them engage with each other and creating a learning environment that honors their own experience and questions. We are there to facilitate a learning experience for them, not to prove to them how smart we are. In order to manage the task of engagement successfully, we train using a curriculum which provides learners with a series of thoughtfully arranged and timed activities in order to solicit their opinions and beliefs.

PARALLEL PROCESSES

Recognizing the parallel process and using it to meet our learning objectives is one of the most essential elements that trainers need who work in the field of values clarification. What happens in the room is a parallel process to what happens out on the campus, in academic classrooms, and in the residence halls. We will meet learners who have varying degrees of compassion and knowledge, some allies who come in with less knowledge and receptivity about what they know, and some who are wonderful and fierce. We discover some LGBTQIA+ advisors who are still closeted or so quiet they may as well be, some who are so outspoken and angry that they can be ineffective, and, of course, we still meet a handful of deeply judgmental people who turn up surprisingly to "save" or "counsel" the queerness away.

At the same time, when we uncover a participant who is pushing our buttons, we discover where our own learning curve is, and are reminded that this is true for all of us. When Safe Zone attendees experience a challenging person in the session, it is such a gift to use that challenge as a learning moment—to invite all the learners to imagine what this means in the context of an academic advising session or a student leadership meeting. For example, a learner makes a comment that lands on a participant as offensive to transgender people. There is a back-and-forth about the comment and a desire for clarity and reconciliation. As the process unfolds, we might seek opportunities to explore how this could look in a classroom—would the professor be able to tolerate letting the students talk it out? What skills or support would a professor need to support this interaction and who has the influence to make that happen?

As trainers learn to work with experiential content, as opposed to PowerPoint slides and Q&As, they discover the seemingly endless opportunities for pointing out "how is this discussion similar to one you might hear in the residence hall or in the dining hall?"

MANAGING DEBRIEFS

As we mentioned earlier, our questions are pivotal to learning and this is evident during the debrief of an activity. The questions we ask direct the conversation. For example, yes-or-no questions are minimally useful in a debrief section, unless you want to do some straw polling. "Did you enjoy that?" or "Was that hard for you?" a not as effective questions as "What was surprising about this activity?" or "What did you learn about yourself?" Questions get at the heart of the learner experience. When we allow the group the space and time to bring their learning out, we are able to encourage them to reflect on and analyze the content and the process of their own learning.

CHALLENGING BEHAVIORS/WHAT TO DO

Sometimes, when faced with challenging material or discomfort, participants will push back with silence, frustration, or personal attacks on the facilitator. The gender spectrum activity has led to learners saying things like "*This activity is insulting,*" or "*Why are you making us do this?*," or "*Are you gay?*"

Quiet Groups

When we are faced with quiet groups, it's helpful to stagger the debrief, beginning in pairs of two and then moving to small-group discussions and ultimately a large-group closing conversation that transitions the group to the next activity. This unfolding of debrief methods demands a lot of time; however, it's worth it. Often, inexperienced facilitators will respond to a silent room by filling in the process points via a mini-lecture. This is disrespectful and ultimately gives the trainer no idea where the group is.

Later, a trainer might be surprised to discover that the group was stuck or an individual said something offensive we didn't catch, or something in the activity was confusing which we failed to clarify. These challenges are normal, and nothing to panic about. However, if we meet silence with lecture notes, we fail to improve as a trainer, and the group will retain far less of the content.

Personal Questions/Attention

On the one hand, groups need to see modeled for them people who hold and value multiple social identities. It's inspiring and sets a tone of vulnerability and safety when trainers are willing to tell their own coming out stories or to impart some wisdom from their personal experience as allies or members of the LGBTQ community. On the other hand, it can become very distracting when a training becomes about the social identities and beliefs of the facilitator(s). Think before you disclose any part of your story. Don't use coming out as a cheat to gain the respect of the group. Our social identities are not why we have credibility as trainers—it's our smarts and our passion for educating people about LGBTQ inclusion.

Working with Co-Facilitators

Many of us work alone and are at times given a chance to co-facilitate. Some of us co-facilitate regularly. There are many reasons to have a two- or three-person training team. Variety of identities and styles are the two biggest reasons. If a training is all day long, it is especially good to mix up the voices from the front of the room. And when we work on issues of identity, having an out LGBTQ person and a team that is multiracial is pivotal. If all the trainers are White or straight, the impact on LGBTQ and people of color participants is considerable.

When working with other trainers, prepping the training with your co-facilitators is key; the group will pick up on your lack of coordination and it will be distracting for everyone. Build in the time to make flip charts together, review the curricula, practice introducing yourselves and the transition points throughout the training. A solid team spends as much time preparing a training as they will spend in the training. Once you have trained with someone on the same content several times, it will become less pivotal to invest as much time and effort into preparation.

TIPS FOR FACILITATORS

In a training of the trainer, I use a zine (see figure 3.1) to review best practices with new learners. This page provides quick visual hints that can go a long way to creating a useful workshop session:

- **Smile**: Engage participants as they arrive. Have the flip charts and tech figured out ahead of time so that you can welcome people with a smile!
- **Eyeball**: Be reading your face all the time—be aware of your facial expressions! The group is watching you.
- **Clock:** You are responsible for managing time and you don't need to speak out loud about it all the time. It's not the group's problem or concern. Keep your stress about time management to yourself.
- **People:** When a disagreement arises, ask yourself, Does resolving this here and now serve the whole group or am I managing this one person? Only address things in the room that serve the group.
- **Glass of Water:** When you are stumped and you need a minute, that's a great time to have a drink of water. You don't need to answer every question or address every point immediately. You can also ask the group, "What do you think about this?"

Figure 3.1. Tips for Facilitators.
Source: Created by Evangeline Weiss

- **Yin/Yang:** Paradox is when an event or statement has both merit and challenge. It is helpful as a facilitator to remember that so much of what happens in the room is paradoxical.

SUMMARY

Using training methods that engage participants actively is the most effective way to support LGBTQ-affirming campuses. Pedagogy that actively inspires learners to reflect, listen, practice, and dialogue is likely to lead to behaviors in the college culture that are also about reflection and dialogue. When we work with adults, we can assume they bring all of themselves into the room—their beliefs, their experiences, and their personalities. Adult learning accepts and leverages this truth out of respect for the myriad of ways in which our communities hold difference.

In addition, as facilitators we can support the group to develop shared meaning about LGBTQIA+ needs which can easily be transferred to the campus environment and reinforced through other types of programming. Using the concepts and tips in this chapter need not be limited to Safe Zone training as these ideas are easily applicable to other workshops and more formal learning environments.

ANNOTATED BIBLIOGRAPHY

- Adams, M., Bell, L., & Griffin, P. (Eds.). (2007). *Teaching for diversity and social justice: A sourcebook* (2nd ed.). New York, NY: Routledge.

  For nearly a decade, *Teaching for Diversity and Social Justice* has been the definitive sourcebook of theoretical foundations and curricular frameworks for social justice teaching practice. This thoroughly revised second edition continues to provide teachers and facilitators with an accessible pedagogical approach to issues of oppression in classrooms. Building on the groundswell of interest in social justice education, the second edition offers coverage of current issues and controversies while preserving the hands-on format and inclusive content of the original. *Teaching for Diversity and Social Justice* presents a well-constructed foundation for engaging the complex and often daunting problems of discrimination and inequality in American society. This book includes a CD-ROM with extensive appendices for participant handouts and facilitator preparation. Safe Zone facilitators are part of a larger community of social justice educators and this book is a clear example of how this work fits into this.

- Landreman, L. M. (2013). *The art of effective facilitation: Reflections from social justice educators* (1st ed.). Sterling, VA: Stylus Publishing.

  The authors illuminate the art and complexity of facilitation, describe multiple approaches, and discuss the necessary and ongoing reflection process. What sets this book apart is how the authors illustrate these practices through personal narratives of challenges encountered, and by admitting to their struggles and mistakes.

  They emphasize the need to prepare by taking into account such considerations as the developmental readiness of the participants, and the particular issues and historical context of the campus, before designing and facilitating a social justice training or selecting specific exercises.

  The book is informed by the recognition that "the magic is almost never in the exercise or the handout but, instead, is in the facilitation," and by the authors' commitment to help educators identify and analyze dehumanizing processes on their campuses and in society at large, reflect on their own socialization, and engage in proactive strategies to dismantle oppression.

  Facilitators will find chapter 6 useful when facilitating across identities, chapter 9 on triggering, chapter 10 on multipartiality, and chapter 11 on interactive dialogues.

- Mindell, A. (1995). *Sitting in the fire: Large group transformation using conflict and diversity* (1st ed.). Portland, OR: Lao Tse Press.

  Arnold Mindell, Ph.D., shows how working with power, rank, revenge, and abuse helps build sustainable communities. Mindell is the co-founder of Processwork and author of numerous books, including *Quantum Mind*, *The Deep Democracy of Open Forums*, and *The Leader as Martial Artist*. He has appeared on national radio and television and works internationally with multiracial and highly conflicted groups.

- Roberts, J. W. (2016). *Experiential education in the college context: What it is, how it works, and why it matters.* New York, NY: Routledge.

  Experiential Education in the College Context provides college and university faculty with pedagogical approaches that engage students and support high-impact learning. Organized around four essential categories—active learning, integrated learning, project-based learning, and community-based learning—this resource offers examples from across disciplines to illustrate principles and best practices for designing and implementing experiential curriculum in the college and university setting.

  Framed by theory, this book provides practical guidance on a range of experiential teaching and learning approaches, including internships, civic engagement, project-based research, service learning, game-based learning, and inquiry learning. At a time when rising tuition, consumer-driven models, and e-learning have challenged the idea of traditional liberal education, this book provides a compelling discussion of the purposes of higher education and the role experiential education plays in sustaining and broadening notions of democratic citizenship.

- Stanchfield, J. (2007). *Tips & tools: The art of experiential group facilitation* (1st ed.). Oklahoma City, OK: Wood 'N' Barnes Publishing.

  This book treats facilitation as an art. By its very nature, group facilitation is an experiential practice, an ever-dynamic process of give-and-take, learning, and development. Jennifer Stanchfield's book *Tips & Tools: The Art of Experiential Group Facilitation* explores the facilitator's role in groups of all kinds and offers creative tools and activities to enhance group experience. *Tips & Tools* serves as a guide and an inspiration for educators and group facilitators looking to spark their creativity and enhance their own unique style.

  Tips & Tools offers practical ideas and key ingredients for enhancing group facilitation including:

  - Ideas for setting the tone and creating a positive environment for learning
  - Strategies and activities to engage groups from the beginning of a program
  - Ways to facilitate ownership and involvement in the group experience
  - Ideas for cultivating teachable moments throughout the learning experience
  - Experiential learning philosophy and methods

- Engaging processing/reflection tools and techniques
- Exploration of the role of a facilitator and the experiential approach to facilitation
- Techniques for becoming a "participant-centered" facilitator and empowering participants to take control of their learning
- Methods for tapping into your own creativity and unique style as a facilitator
- Reflective activities to tie it all together and create meaning and opportunities for future learning

CHAPTER 4

Safe Zone Fundamentals Workshop: Basic Awareness & Knowledge Acquisition

Kerry John Poynter

"Allyship . . . It's not supposed to be about you . . . your feelings . . . of glorifying yourself at the expense of the folks you claim to be an ally to. It's not supposed to be a performance. It's supposed to be a way of living your life that doesn't reinforce the same oppressive behaviors you're claiming to be against. . . . Actions count, labels don't. The work of an ally is never ceasing. (Allyship) is not an identity, it's a practice. Sounds exhausting . . . because the people who experience racism, misogyny, ableism, queerphobia, transphobia, classism, etc. are exhausted. So, why shouldn't their allies be? Maybe how exhausted you are is a good measure of how well you're doing the work."

—*Mia Mckenzie,* Black Girl Dangerous, *pp. 138–41*

This chapter references handouts (available as a single PDF formatted for easy and clear printing on 8.5" × 11") that supplement the curriculum and assessment pieces of this book. Please email resourcematerial@rowman.com to request the PDF, providing both the title and editor of this book along with proof of purchase (receipt).

DESCRIPTION

A BASIC AWARENESS AND KNOWLEDGE SESSION THAT PREPARES PARTICIPANTS FOR THE FIVE ADVANCED SESsions. This introductory three-hour session includes a guided imagery, interactive terminology game that also introduces sexuality and gender as a continuum, an introduction to the coming-out process, and an LGBTQIA+ historical icon's game with an emphasis on multiple identities. Student peer educators conclude with an engaging activity and interactive panel.

CONTEXTUALIZATION

Learning to be a better ally to LGBTQIA+ people will encompass more than one training session or a series of them. It is an ongoing pursuit of knowledge acquisition and skills practice. The fundamentals of this knowledge will include immersing oneself in the LGBTQIA+ community, understanding contemporary terminology, realizing that the coming-out process is not a one time event but ongoing, understanding the state of politics in your country, and understanding how concerns for other marginalized communities intersect the LGBTQIA+ community. A general outline for an introductory Safe Zone session can be found in chapter 2; explained here is an example of those elements.

Understanding the vast array of terms used in the LGBTQIA+ community seems to be the element of knowledge acquisition that is a barrier to further growth and it should not be. The ability to cite definitions to terms, word by word, is not the end goal of becoming a great ally to LGBTQIA+ people or young adults. It is okay to make a mistake, pick yourself up, learn from it, and try again.

A good ally should know the difference between sex (male, female, intersex) and gender (woman, genderqueer, trans, man) or sexual orientation (gay, lesbian, bisexual, pansexual, asexual, heterosexual) and how each of these falls on a continuum instead of a binary. Within those continuums there are specific terms and they do morph over time as individuals ever explain the vast diversity of human biology and expression. The human species is not a cookie-cutter mold that everyone fits into. The exhaustive list of terms with definitions provided here is a snapshot of those commonly used.

Similarly, the coming-out process, or revealing a sexual identity or gender identity, is not the same experience for everyone. It is not just a post on social media or an excuse to throw a party. The coming-out process for a White cisgender male will be demonstrably different for a Latina lesbian that is undocumented or an African American transwoman that grew up in the Black Church. Becoming a better ally needs to include an understanding of sexual/gender identity development over the life span that considers how multiple oppressions intersect.

Numerous theorists have proposed models of sexual and gender identity development (Bilodeau & Renn, 2005) over the past few decades. Life span approaches that allow for situational context, as opposed to solely linear stage models, are attempting to reflect contemporary thinking that is more inclusive of fluid and racial identities. A guided imagery and a group scenario are used in this Fundamentals session to introduce these concepts and ready participants for advanced work in continuing sessions.

Attending these sessions and joining a Safe Zone program for LGBTQIA+ young adults can be a gateway to social justice work for other marginalized groups. Social justice ally development in college, as explained by Broido (Broido & Reason, 2005), occurs with some patterns. These include precollege attitudes that everyone should be treated fairly and equally, acquiring information from various sources inside and outside the classroom, and making meaning of new information by employing three strategies: discussion, self-reflection, and perspective taking. "These students did not just passively absorb information; they talked about it with others; reflected on their own experiences, thoughts, and feelings; and tried to see the world through others' eyes" (Broido & Reason, 2005, p. 22).

Developing confidence in themselves and the knowledge they are gaining play a role in taking action as an ally. This confidence comes from being able to develop skills with other allies and finding the available tools. A model Safe Zone program, by putting theory into practice, can cultivate these patterns of ally work. When offered early in an academic career or uniquely situated within the institutional structure, these programs could be the chance to recruit a student or employee to becoming a better ally and thus improve campus climate.

Although these programs focus on gender and sexual minorities, an intersectional lens should be found throughout the workshop sessions. Create opportunities for critical thinking about how the LGBTQIA+ community is diverse in not only sexuality and gender, but by race, ethnicity, faith beliefs, etc. In an introductory session that provides fundamental information, interject opportunities for "aha!" moments that whet the appetite for advanced work that crosses borders, includes people of color, and includes gender expressions that are not just cisgender.

A history of icons that were not heterosexual can be a unique way to do this. Consider mentioning historical icons such as James Baldwin, Audre Lorde, Weiwha, and Harvey Milk. This has the bonus of providing support to LGBTQIA+ youth and young adults since they likely have not been taught this part of their history.

The homophobia and transphobia that put these icons in the closet continues in policies, laws, and attitudes found today. Reviewing the status of LGBTQIA+ people in society, law, and governance should give an overview of the lay of the land. Ask students from your institution to share their thoughts about these issues, their stories, as well as the aforementioned topics of terminology and the coming-out process. This panel of students should personalize these topics without solely relying on them to be the educators.

READINGS FOR FACILITATORS
The following annotated readings are intended as starting points for new learners on these fundamental topics. They support the learning goals of the curriculum explained in this section. Facilitators should use them as a means of self-learning and reference for those participants inquiring for additional information. They will also be beneficial to group discussion among co-facilitators before practicing and especially in facilitating the activities contained in this curriculum.

- Bilodeau, B. L., & Renn, K. A. (2005). Analysis of LGBT identity development models and implications for practice. In R. L. Sanlo (Ed.), *Sexual orientation and gender identity: New directions for student services* (Vol. 111, pp. 25–40). San Francisco: Jossey-Bass.

The authors review and analyze sexual identity development models with a critical look at how they apply to fluid and transgender identities as well as women and people of color. These theories include stage models and life span approach models, and Postmodern/Feminist/Queer theory perspectives. Particular attention should be given to the life span approach as well as the Feminist perspective as they are crucial elements found in brief in this session but are the underlying theories that guide the Gender & Transgender Session, Bisexuality & Pansexuality Session, and the Multiple Identities Session.

- Evans, N. J., & Broido, E. M. (2005) Encouraging the development of social justice attitudes and actions: An overview of current understandings. In R. D. Reason, E. M. Broido, T. L. Davis, & N. J. Evans (Eds.), *Developing social justice and allies: New directions for student services*, (Vol. 110, pp. 17–28). San Francisco: Jossey-Bass.
  The authors review the theoretical understandings that develop social justice attitudes in college students. Models of ally development (Bishop, Hardiman & Jackson, Broido) that attempt to explain the process of becoming a better ally to various marginalized groups. The patterns explained in this model, particularly "acquiring information," "meaning making," and "skill development," can be used to theorize the usefulness of a Safe Zone program with a series of comprehensive workshops. The chapter concludes with explanations of college impacts (also applicable to a model Safe Zone program) and recommendations for campus environments. Safe Zone program coordinators and facilitators will find this chapter useful by putting these theories and concepts into practice.

- Green, E. R., & Peterson, E. N. (2014). *LGBTQI terminology*. University of California Riverside LGBT Office, retrieved from http://out.ucr.edu/docs/terminology.pdf.
  This online resource is a comprehensive listing of terms used by LGBTQIA+ people and their allies. The list encompasses a vast array of genders, sexualities, and sexes. In rare cases, some terms can be understood as a pejorative and thus caution should be used. This list is used during the dominoes activity in the Fundamentals session.

- Keith, S. (2009). *Queers in history: The comprehensive encyclopedia of historical gays, lesbians and bisexuals*. Dallas, TX: BenBella Books.

- Killermann, S. (2013). Using the genderbread person. In *The social justice advocate's handbook: A guide to gender* (pp. 60–67). Austin, TX: Impetus Books.
  The author provides a visual aid that helps to explain the differences between gender, gender expression, biological sex, and sexual orientation. These categories are succinctly explained in a casual prose written for new learners. A required reading for facilitators as this visual aid is used in the Fundamentals as well as Gender & Transgender curriculum in order to explain these categories. This is an updated version of design concepts that owes itself to educators and the thinking of feminists that are decades in the making.

- Russel, P. (1995). *The gay 100: A ranking of the most influential gay men and lesbians, past and present*. Secaucus, NJ: Carol Publishing Group.
  These two history books, *Queers in History* and *The Gay 100*, meant for mass consumption and not necessarily academically rigorous, are not meant to replace a more researched history of these historical figures. Nevertheless, they do provide an introduction to these histories for a novice learner. The icons bingo game during this session utilizes this information.

Tips for Facilitators
- Use the readings to familiarize yourself with the topics covered during this introductory session before learning how to facilitate the session.
- Take time to discuss the point of each reading with your co-facilitators. Seek out faculty or staff with expertise in psychology, sexuality, and gender studies to help lead discussions.
- Assign roles for each facilitator in the session.
- Arrange a practice session with knowledgeable and interested members of the community. Ask for feedback.
- Use the facilitator and session evaluation forms (chapter 10) to receive feedback from the practice session. Incorporate feedback into the next session.
- Example process statements and questions are provided below to help provide context to that particular section of the curriculum. Use these as examples to learn from and not exactly to read verbatim. Use your own words and ways of communicating the same concepts.

CURRICULUM—2 HOURS

Curriculum Outline
- Introductions, Welcome, Goals, What Is Safe Zone, Explain Safe Zone Sign, Intros & PGPs, Ground Rules—15 Minutes
- Stars Activity: Guided Imagery—20 minutes
- Dominoes Terminology Activity—20 minutes
- Debrief from Terminology—15 minutes
- Prezi: Human Sexuality Continuum/Coming-Out Process—20 minutes
- Break—5–10 minutes
- ICON's Bingo Game: Multiple Identities & LGBT Icons in History—20 minutes
- Crossing the Line Activity and Student Panel Q&A (Student Peer Educators)—45 minutes
- Evaluation, Closing, & Sign up for Advanced Sessions—15 minutes

Editor's Note
This curriculum is made available as an online quiz. Participants can test out so as to pass to advanced workshops. The 35 multiple-choice questions are made available in a PDF by sending an email to resourcematerial@row man.com. Alternately, schools that utilize the Moodle platform can download an export of the test at UIS.EDU/Programs/SafeZone. Ninety percent or above accuracy was considered proficiency for passing the Fundamentals Workshop session.

Learning Outcomes
- Introduce fundamental topics such as terms, gender/sex/sexual orientation on a continuum, coming-out process, intersection of identities, and status of sexual and gender minorities in the country.
- Explain the Safe Zone program and give examples of the learning style used in the advanced sessions.
- Meet and hear about experiences on campus from current LGBTQIA+ students.

Materials
- Blue, yellow, red, and white paper stars; and golf pencils for each participant
- Preprinted sets of 8.5" × 11" sheets with terms and definitions.
- Prezi (http://prezi.com/svr0q7xy6416/?utm_campaign=share&utm_medium=copy)
- Test projector in advance and screen
- "ICONS" bingo sheets (five versions)
- Tape
- TRUE and FALSE signs
- Index cards

Handouts
- Genderbread Person handout
- "Joanne" case study
- Consider providing terms as an online download for later perusal.

INTRODUCTIONS, DISCLAIMER, & GROUND RULES—15 MINUTES

A. Welcome
- Explain Safe Zone and the process to becoming a member. Use a graphic of the sign projected on a screen. Mention the rainbow flag and its meaning.
- Briefly run through the agenda for the session. Mention each activity and section by name.

B. Introductions
- Ask each Safe Zone Coordinating Committee member and Facilitation Team member to introduce themselves and share their PGPs (preferred gender pronouns). Briefly explain PGPs. **The use of they, their, ze, or hir will be new concepts for most participants. Allow some time to fully describe the use of these terms and for participants to ask questions.**

PROCESS STATEMENT: *"As you may have learned in the Gender and Transgender Safe Zone session, gender is fluid and many genders exist. Therefore, we cannot assume the gender of everyone in the room. Sharing our preferred gender pronouns, such as he, him, she, her, they, their, ze, or hir, allows us to understand and communicate with each other respectfully."*

- Go around the room and ask everyone to introduce themselves by sharing their name, department (as relevant), major (as relevant), title (as relevant), and PGPs.

C. Ground Rules

PROCESS STATEMENT: *"We want to as much as possible make this the safest place to ask questions and share thoughts and stories. This session, like all Safe Zone sessions, is incredibly participatory and reliant on you being able to engage with each other. With this in mind, let's brainstorm a few suggested operating principles for this session."*

- Confidentiality (What is shared here stays here.)
- Respect (Don't interrupt.)
- Step Up! Step Back! (Be willing to step up and share your own ideas, while also being sure to share the floor with others.)
- Use "I" statements ("I feel like this." "This is my experience.")
- Don't use names of people not present in the room or make generalizations.
- Take a risk! (No question is a bad question.)
- Safe Word: "Ouch!" PROCESS STATEMENT: *"Use this to indicate that something you've heard or experienced during this session seems offensive, hurtful, or different from your experience. Allows you to be recognized and provides an opportunity for discussion after the current person is finished speaking."*
- Keep an open mind. Be willing to learn from others' viewpoints and experiences.

D. Parking Lot
- Directions: Write "Parking Lot" on a dry erase board/chalkboard, or large sheet of paper affixed to the wall. Write topics or ideas that come up during discussion but do not pertain to the topic at hand. This recognizes the topic was heard, understood, but will be addressed another time. This can be an important time management device.

PROCESS STATEMENT: *"The Parking Lot is a way for us to recognize thoughts and items of discussion that may not be pertinent to the topic we are discussing. It helps us manage our time in this session when topics of discussion get off track. We want to make sure we recognize these topics at another time, after the session is over, or will include it in a different session."*

Tips for Facilitators
- Some participants will make light of PGP use during the introduction. Make sure to request that everyone respect the process, take it seriously, and share accurate pronouns. Do not be afraid to interrupt casual joking and laughing for those that are new to this idea.
- It can be easy to gloss over this introductory process particularly if you are running late. Always set up early and be ready to welcome people when they arrive. Proper introductions, ground rules setting, and a welcoming attitude will set the tone for the session.
- Always start on time! Create a reputation that your sessions begin promptly and that participants need to show up a few minutes early to find a seat. Time is valuable to you and those that agreed to attend. Starting late means you may not get to all of your content.

COMING-OUT STARS ACTIVITY—20 MINUTES
Created by Jeffrey Pierce, used with permission of the LGBT Resource Center at the University of Southern California. Adapted by Kerry John Poynter.

A. Goal
- Introduce how experiential activities are the learning style for these Safe Zone workshops. This activity will elicit emotions that will mimic some of the experiences of a LGBTQIA+ young adult and thus a desire for personal change that eliminates actions that replicate these feelings.

B. Directions

• Give each person either a BLUE, YELLOW, RED, or WHITE star.

PROCESS STATEMENTS: *"Imagine that this star represents your world with you in the center and those things or people most important to you at each point of the star. So we'll begin by writing your name in the center of the star making it your very own star! Now, pick a side of the star to begin with. Choose a friend who is very close to you. Someone you care about very much. A best friend or a close friend, it doesn't matter. Write their name on this side of the star."*

"Next, think of a community that you belong to. It could be a religious community, your neighborhood, a fraternity or sorority, or just a group of friends. Take the name of this group that you are a part of and write it on the next side of the star moving clockwise."

"Now, think of a specific friend or family member. Someone that you have always turned to for advice or maybe who knows how to cheer you up when you're sad. A mother, father, aunt, or uncle . . . any family member who has made a large impact in your life. Please write their name on the next side of the star."

"What job would you most like to have? It could be anything from president to dentist. Whatever your career aspiration is, write it on the next side."

"Lastly, what are some of your hopes and dreams? Maybe you want to be a millionaire, maybe you want the perfect family. Think of a few of your hopes and dreams and write them on the last side of your star."

"As previously explained a majority of our activities are experiential. Everyone with a start is now gay, lesbian, bisexual, or transgender and each is about to begin their coming-out process. No one will talk for the rest of this activity; just listen to the narration and think about your communities you've written on your stars."

Friends/Support

PROCESS STATEMENTS: *"You decide that it will be easiest to tell your friends first, since they have always been there for you in the past and you feel they need to know. If you have a BLUE star, your friend says that they "have no problem with it." They have suspected it for some time now and thank you for being honest with them. Luckily, they act no different toward you and accept you for who you are."*
(pause for effect)

"If you have a YELLOW or WHITE star, your friends are kind of hesitant. They are a little irritated that you have waited so long to tell them, but you are confident that soon they will understand that being gay or lesbian is just a part of who you are. . . . In passing they jokingly say, 'I'm glad you're not one of those femmy guys or lesbos wanting to look like guys.' You realize you just need to give them some time. When you bring your boyfriend or girlfriend over to your room, your roommate seems uncomfortable with small displays of affection. You don't feel accepted, but tolerated. Please fold back this side of your star."
(pause for effect)

"If you have a RED star, you are met with anger and disgust. This friend who has been by your side in the past tells you that being gay or lesbian is wrong and they can't associate with anyone like that. Their background is that they come from a small town within Illinois and have transferred from a small private Christian college. They tell you the Bible says homosexuality is wrong and they just can't approve. If you have a red star, please tear off this side and drop it to the ground; this friend is no longer a part of your life."
(pause for effect)

Family/Support

PROCESS STATEMENTS: *"With most of you having such good luck (or haven't) with your friends, you decide that your family probably deserves to know. So, you turn to your closest family member first so that it will be a little*

easier. If you have a WHITE star, the conversation does not go exactly how you planned. Several questions are asked as to how this could have happened, but after some lengthy discussion this person who is close to you seems a little more at ease with it. Fold this side of your star back, as they will be an ally, but only with time."
(pause for effect)

"If you have a BLUE star, you are embraced by this family member. They are proud that you have decided to come out and let you know that they will always be there to support you."
(pause for effect)

"If you have a YELLOW or RED star, your family member rejects the thought of being related to a person who is gay or lesbian. Much like some of your friends, they are disgusted and some of you are thrown out of your house or even disowned. Your family consults your pastor that you have known all your life and other members of your church who also don't approve. You are now part of the 42 percent homeless youth who identify as trans, gay, lesbian, or bi. If you have a yellow or red star, please tear off this side and drop it to the ground."
(pause for effect)

Community/Support

PROCESS STATEMENTS: "Having told your friends and family, the wheels have started to turn and soon members of your community begin to become aware of your sexual orientation or gender identity. If you have a WHITE star, your sexual orientation or gender identity seems to be accepted by your community. They continue to embrace you like anyone else and together you celebrate the growing diversity in your community."
(pause for effect)

"If you have a BLUE star, your sexual orientation or gender is tolerated by your community, coworkers, and friends. The topic is rarely, if ever, discussed or acknowledged. However, you are now contemplating a move to another city or region in order to find acceptance."
(pause for effect)

"If you have a YELLOW star, you are met with a mixed response. Some accept you and some don't know what to think. You find that you have to compartmentalize your racial identity and your sexual identity with different communities. You got the message from some of your friends at the Black Student Union (BSU) that you were a part of that you had to choose between being gay or being in the group. You remain in the community, and with time, you hope that you will fit in as you once did. If you have a yellow star, please fold back this side."
(pause for effect)

"If you have a RED star, your community reacts with indifference, misunderstanding, and in some cases with hatred because you have also begun to come out as transgender. It is your experience that the gay community may love drag queens but many view the world in a binary where there is just men and women. Many of your heterosexual friends have drifted away. You feel like you don't belong in your community. Those who had supported you in your times of need no longer speak to you or even acknowledge you. If you have a red star, tear this side off and drop it to the ground."
(pause for effect)

"You have heard that rumors have started circulating at work regarding your sexual orientation or gender identity. In the past, you have made it a point to confront these rumors as soon as they began, but now you're not sure if that will do more harm than good. But, unfortunately, you don't have the chance."
(pause for effect)

"If you have a BLUE star, your coworkers begin to approach you and let you know that they have heard the rumors and that they don't care, they will support you. Your bosses react the same way letting you know that you do good work and that's all that matters."
(pause for effect)

"If you have a WHITE star, your workplace has become quite interesting. Everyone seems to think that you are gay or lesbian, even though you haven't mentioned it to anyone or confirmed any of the rumors. Some people speak to you less, but the environment has not seemed to change too drastically. If you have a white star, please fold back this side."
(pause for effect)

"*If you have a RED or YELLOW star, you continue to work as though nothing is happening, ignoring the rumors that have spread throughout your workplace. One day, you come in to find that your office has been packed up. You are called into your boss's office and she explains that you are being fired. When you ask why, she tells you that lately your work has been less than satisfactory and that she had to make some cutbacks in your area. If you have a red or yellow star, please tear off this side and drop it to the ground.*"

Dreams/Hope for the Future

PROCESS STATEMENTS: "*Now, your future lies ahead of you as a gay man or lesbian, bisexual, or transgender person. Your hopes and dreams, your wishes for the perfect life . . . for some of you these are all that remain. If you have a WHITE, BLUE, or YELLOW star, these hopes and dreams are what keep you going. Most of you have been met with some sort of rejection since beginning your coming-out process, but you have managed to continue to live a happy and healthy life. Or have you? Your personal hopes and dreams become a reality.*"
(pause for effect)

"*If you have a RED star, you fall into despair. You have been met with rejection after rejection and you find it impossible to accomplish your lifelong goals without the support and love of your friends and family. You become depressed and with nowhere else to turn, many of you begin to abuse drugs and alcohol. Eventually, you feel that your life is no longer worth living. If you have a red star, please tear it up and drop the pieces to the ground. You are now part of the 40 percent of suicide victims who are gay or lesbian, bisexual, or transgender.*"

C. Activity Processing Discussion

PROCESS QUESTIONS:
- How did it feel to fold back or tear off part of your star?
- Look on the ground. What do these torn pieces represent?
- What was it like to have a blue star? A red star? A white star?
- Do you know someone that has had similar situations? Please share.

Tips for Facilitators
- Keep a slow pace while reading the activity. Do not do this lightly and instead take your time. Use a pronounced voice that everyone can hear.
- Put emphasis on "tearing" and "ripping" the stars. Use pauses.
- Help to process the difference between the stars. Some forms of bias, homophobia, and transphobia can be more subtle in the blue or white stars. Make mention of this subtlety.
- Consider editing the guided imagery to include recognizable terms, programs, and locations at your educational institution.

TERMINOLOGY: DOMINOES ACTIVITY—30 MINUTES

A. Goals
- Create awareness of various terms.
- Gauge the room on terms that are well known and those that are not.
- Gender, sex, and sexual orientation are each a continuum, not a binary. Many terms fall on these continuums.

B. Directions

- Prepare adequate space to move about in the room so groups can place dominoes on the floor. Use adjacent rooms if needed.
- Gender Bread Person on screen for large-group processing of the activity.
- Test projector and screen in advance.
- Split participants into groups of four or five depending on the size. Have them count off by fours.
- Have each group meet in designated areas in the room.
  - Explain that we are going to engage in an activity that exposes them to multiple terms and definitions by matching terms with definitions like they would with domino pieces. Use floor space to form a shape with the 8.5" $\times$ 11" pieces. Do this for 15 minutes.
- Process the activity for another 15 minutes while also using the Gender Bread Person to introduce gender, sex, and sexual orientation as nonbinary.

PROCESS STATEMENTS: "*Much like dominoes, you need to match the correct term with the correct definition. Place each 8.5" $\times$ 11" domino sheet on the floor and create a shape of your choosing. Feel free to discuss as a group, ask questions, and change your matches when you make a mistake. When you are done, we all will discuss this together.*"

NOTE: The main idea for this activity is for people to ponder what meanings these names can carry. There are always questions of what these words do commonly mean. Use the terms available as a download with this book. Consider updating the list as other terms come more into use.

C. Small-Group Discussion

PROCESS QUESTIONS:
- What was the most challenging part of this activity?
- Did you learn anything by participating in this?
- Which terms were you already familiar with?
- Which terms were new to you? Please be specific.

Directions: Project Gender Bread Person on a screen (Available as a download).

PROCESS STATEMENT: "*Terms about gender tend to be the most confusing. 'Trans' is an umbrella term for many possible genders and expressions just like sexual orientation can be a number of identities including gay, lesbian, bisexual, pansexual, asexual, and heterosexual. However, gender is not our sex. Sex (female, intersex, male) refers to a combination of biological and anatomical features including genitalia and chromosomes. Gender is socially constructed. Here is a visual of a Gender Bread Person that explains these continuums. We will use this in the Gender & Transgender as well as Bisexuality & Pansexuality advanced sessions.*"

PROCESS POINTS:
- Trans/transgender terms will likely be mentioned most as unfamiliar so stress attending the Trans Advanced Session! Gender is a continuum of possible expressions.
- Sexual identities are more than just a binary of heterosexual and lesbian/gay. Sexuality can even manifest in various ways over the life span. Encourage attendance at the Bisexuality & Pansexuality advanced session.
- It is easy to get caught up in being concerned about using the wrong words. These terms can even change over time as identities develop or communities change. Listen to the person you are communicating with rather than trying to give them a label they are not using or familiar with.
- Being able to remember these definitions word for word does not make a good ally! There is more work to do beyond mere memorization of terminology.

Tips for Facilitators
- Have multiple facilitators ready to help with this activity. A helpful guide or cheat sheet is provided with this book for facilitators to use.

- Encourage questions during the activity while in small groups but keep the game moving along as there should be time built in afterward to process it with everyone in the room.
- Some participants will want to discuss the terms related to gender at length. However, the learning objective here is to define "trans" and help realize this issue is complex. Thank them for their interest and encourage them to attend the trans advanced session to better understand. Use the "Parking Lot" to recognize this need.

COMING-OUT PROCESS CASE STUDY—20 MINUTES

A. Goals
- Coming out is an ongoing and sometimes fluid process.
- Location, space, community, and people affect how someone experiences their sexual or gender identity.
- Other identities (race, religion, etc.) need to be considered.

B. Directions
- Pass out "Joanne" case study.

PROCESS STATEMENT: *"What do you think these statements mean, like 'Coming out is an ongoing process'?"* (Cass, 1979, 1984)

PROCESS POINT: *Cass is an example of a linear stage model that builds from one state to another such as a lack of awareness, immersion into the community, and integration of a sexual identity as one facet of a full identity. It illustrates that the coming-out process is more than a onetime event but an ongoing process.*

- *"Some sexual minorities discover their individual emotional identity or how they feel about their sexuality due to a significant relationship with someone of the same gender"* (Fassinger & Miller, 1997).

PROCESS POINT: *"Although it is quite possible to express feelings for people of the same sex without a significant emotional or sexual relationship with someone of the same sex, it can confirm these previously held feelings. This can be true for bisexuals as well as lesbian and gay men."*

- *"Social environments (peers, family, social groups) have a big impact. How individuals experience their sexual identity or gender identity can be fluid over time and place"* (D'Augelli, 1994; Klein, Sepekoff, & Wolf, 1985).

PROCESS POINT: *"Growth as a sexual or gender minority can be fluid and influenced by environmental and biological realities. They may be not out to family but could be out to an LGBTQIA+ social group. This can and will change."*

TRANSITIONAL PROCESS STATEMENT: *"These are generalities based in accepted theory. Now let's experience some of this with Joanne, an example student at our institution."*

Joanne Case Study

Joanne is an 18-year-old first-year student. She is really excited to be at college! In high school, Joanne was quite successful academically and seems to have an aptitude for science. She is African American and comes from a strong religious faith that believes that "homosexuality" is "an abomination." While this has been somewhat painful for Joanne, she values her faith and wishes to maintain her strong faith base. As an only child, Joanne is very close with her parents and extended family.

During high school, Joanne started to notice that she was different from her peers who were expressing attractions and dating. At age 15, she started to talk to her dad about some of the differences that she was noticing and subsequently came out to him. Dad is very supportive of Joanne, but encouraged her not to share her sexual identity with her mother at this time.

During orientation, Joanne was intrigued by a skit on gay coming-out issues; however, she has decided to keep this to herself. As a new student, she is privately assessing the culture and climate at our university and really doesn't know if it is okay for her to come out. Currently residing in the residence hall for first-year students, Joanne did tell her roommate that she was not interested in dating men. Although she came out to her roommate, they do not talk about it.

While Joanne has a few close friends who are very supportive, they decided to attend other universities and are currently out of touch. Joanne knows about the Gender & Sexuality resources on campus, but is reluctant to go right now for fear that it is "too gay." Given that Joanne is new to campus, she wants to be very intentional about the reputation she forms on campus.

PROCESS QUESTIONS:
- How did this case study show coming out as an ongoing process?
- How were Joanne's multiple identities shaping her experience? What were they?
- When she visits the cafeteria for the first time, what decisions is she making about where to eat her lunch? Where are all the student communities sitting?
- When she is in class and discussions about sexuality, race, or gender occur, what decisions does she make?
- This case study is primarily about sexual identity. How might it be different if this were a trans student?

Tips for Facilitators
- Consider creating identity development statements to use in your own workshop session that mirror the student population at your school. Use real-life examples to bring theory into practice.
- Consider using a Prezi campus map to create a unique journey using images and stories from your institution such as classrooms, cafeterias, and residence halls.
- Use questions about the intersections of faith, race, and gender to encourage participation in the continuing education advanced sessions explained in this book.
- Recruit staff or faculty that have a background in psychology, counseling psychology, or student development to facilitate this section.
- Consider offering a 5-minute break at this point in the session.

ICONS IN HISTORY BINGO: MULTIPLE IDENTITIES—20 MINUTES

A. Goals
- A basic understanding that sexual and gender minorities are diverse in race, gender, and religion.
- An overview of terms and words used in various cultures that describe sexual and gender minorities.
- A multicultural and gender-inclusive understanding of some historical icons that are not heterosexual.

B. Directions
- We do not have permission to share the original PowerPoint images, but one can be created easily with these directions and images easily found from a number of resources. Become familiar with the icons listed here by going to the University of Illinois Springfield LGBTQA Resource Office website at http://www.uis.edu/lgbtq/programs/lounge/.
- Split participants into groups of four or five depending on the size. Have them count off by fours or fives. If already at tables, then each table serves as a group.
- Pass out ICONS sheets (available as a download). Make sure each group gets a different sheet.

PROCESS STATEMENT: "*Not all LGBTQ people are White, Atheist, easily fit into the gender binary, or identify with common labels in the LGBTQIA+ community. Also, history has set the record a little too straight. For example, Barbara Smith wrote in her essay 'Blacks and Gays Healing the Great Divide,' 'Perhaps the most maddening question anyone can ask me is, "Which do you put first: being Black or being a woman, being Black or being Gay? The underlying assumption is that I should prioritize one of my identities because one of them is actually more important than the rest or that I must arbitrarily choose one of them over the others for the sake of acceptance in one particular community."*"

Audre Lorde: This person won international acclaim for her poetry and prose and was poet laureate of New York state from 1990 to 1991.

Barbara Jordan: This person was a Texas Congress member from 1973 to 1979 and was the first African American woman from a southern state in the House. After winning re-election in 1974, she made an influential televised speech before the House Judiciary Committee in support of the impeachment of President Richard Nixon. Her speech at the 1976 Democratic Convention is considered by many historians to have been the best convention keynote speech in modern history.

Bayard Rustin: This person was a Quaker and a pacificist who spent his life advocating for civil rights. He worked with Martin Luther King Jr. to organize the Montgomery bus boycott and other important demonstrations.

Bessie Smith: This person was born in Tennessee and became the most successful Black vocalist of the 1900s–1920s. Responsible for introducing the blues into mainstream American popular music.

Billie Holiday: This person was a prominent jazz vocalist and song stylist of the 1930s whose career started in Harlem nightclubs but soon grew widespread.

Down-low: This term refers to a subculture of Black men who have sex with other Black men but who identify exclusively as heterosexual.

Eleanor Roosevelt: This person served as First Lady for an unprecedented 12 years. She used her behind-the-scenes influence to promote humanitarian causes for African Americans, youth, the poor, and others in need. She was appointed in 1945 by President Truman to the U.S. delegation to the United Nations, and she chaired the committee that produced the Universal Declaration of Human Rights in 1948.

Gender: This term refers to a person's sense of being masculine, feminine, or other.

Glenn Burke: This person was a born ballplayer who spent several years as an outfielder with the Los Angeles Dodgers and the Oakland A's before the pressures of living a double life with his teammates forced him into early retirement— and an honored place on San Francisco's gay softball teams.

Harvey Milk: This person became the first openly gay city commissioner in the country when he was appointed by the San Francisco mayor in 1976. In 1977, he became the first openly gay candidate to be elected in any big city in the United States when he won a supervisor election in San Francisco. He was assassinated in 1978, and he has been called the Martin Luther King Jr. of the gay and lesbian civil rights movement.

Hijra: This Indian term refers to individuals who are an alternative gender, neither man nor woman. They are viewed as an in-between gender, impotent, and thus not men or women. Individuals must renounce sexual desire and activity, even having their genitals cut off to achieve such a status. India legally recognizes them as a third gender.

James Baldwin: Born in Harlem, New York in 1924, this person suffered verbal abuse and discrimination based on his African American and gay male identities. At the age of 24, he moved to France to escape these experiences. There, he became an avid writer and poet. Aside from literature, he was against the Vietnam War and an outspoken advocate of gay and lesbian rights. He also made valuable contributions to the African American civil rights movement.

Kathoey: A Thai gender variant sometimes historically referred to as a third sex but due to effects of colonialization, now refers to transgender males.

Langston Hughes: This person was the author of African American–themed poetry, short stories, and the novel *Not Without Laughter*.

Michelangelo: The most important artist of the Italian High Renaissance, whose output spanned over seven decades, and a key figure within European art history.

Same-gender-loving: A term sometimes used by members of the African American/Black community to express an alternative sexual orientation without relying on terms and symbols of European descent. The term emerged in the early 1990s with the intention of offering Black women who love women and Black men who love men a voice, a way of identifying and being that resonated with the uniqueness of Black culture in life.

Sex: A medical term designating a certain combination of gonads, chromosomes, external gender organs, secondary sex characteristics, and hormonal balances. Because usually subdivided into "male" and "female," this category does not always recognize the existence of intersexed bodies.

Spoiled masculinity: This term is based in Black men's experiences in society as criminals and their pronounced economic disadvantage compared to White men. Homosexuality represents an additional sense of devastation and inferiority, another element of this term.

Stud: This term refers to an African American and/or Latina masculine lesbian. Also known as "butch" or "aggressive."

Two-spirit: This Native American term refers to alternatively gendered people of any sex.

Virginia Woolf: Born in London into a large family of rather eminent Victorians, she wrote 10 novels, in addition to copious essays and short stories, which have secured her a place in the modernist canon afforded few other women writers. Her essay "A Room of One's Own" (1929) has become a feminist classic; from that essay, the sentence "Chloe liked Olivia" has become shorthand for lesbianism. Nearly all of her novels and many of her short stories have been interpreted from a variety of feminist, lesbian feminist, and queer critical perspectives.

Weiwha: This person was a Native American Two-Spirit who was recognized for her many contributions to her village and the Zuni culture. She visited Washington in 1866.

Walt Whitman: This person is considered one of the premiere U.S. poets, especially his *Leaves of Grass* collection of poems. He wrote his last great poem, "When Lilacs Last in the Dooryard Bloom'd," to memorialize Abraham Lincoln after his assassination.

Willa Cather: This person was an American writer who focused on the American heartland and those who immigrated and settled there in the late nineteenth and early twentieth centuries.

PROCESS STATEMENT: *"We just had some fun learning about some icons in history that were not heterosexual or did not fit a binary of gender. We also introduced or reintroduced some terms used to explain sexual or gender minorities in various cultures. Want to learn more? Attend the Multiple Identities and/or Gender & Transgender advanced sessions."*

CROSSING THE LINE ACTIVITY & STUDENT PANEL—45 MINUTES

A. Goals
- Highlight and educate about common issues about LGBTQIA+ people.
- Share stories from students that are LGBTQIA+ to personalize these issues and others.

B. Directions

PROCESS STATEMENT: *"In this, the presenters engage with students in an activity called Crossing the Line and a student panel. Crossing the Line highlights contemporary and historical information about LGBTQIA+ people and topics by asking participants to move across a line in the middle of the room to express the answer they believe is correct. After each question, a brief facilitated discussion ensues that also includes information to better inform. The activity is followed by the presenters sharing personal stories in a panel format and concludes with a question-and-answer session for the audience. Estimated time: 45–60 minutes."*

C. Overview of Program
- Brief coming-out stories (5 minutes each)
- Crossing the Line Activity (20 minutes)
- Question & Answer period student panel
  - Setup: Lay down a line of tape on the floor, put up TRUE and FALSE signs or write on the board, one on either end of the room. Write names, contact info on board.
  - Hand out index cards for anonymous questions.

PROCESS STATEMENT: *"We are about to engage in an activity called Crossing the Line which is to highlight some basic information and issues about the LGBTQIA+ community. Choose the true side or false side by crossing the line on the floor. Do your best; it is okay if you get it wrong, as we just want you to consider some issues and encourage further questions during our dialogue afterward.*

When answering the true/false questions, pick the true or false side of the room to indicate your answer; it is okay if you pick the wrong side so please do your best. If you are not able to stand, please let us know and we will stand for you. There is NO TALKING when deciding on which side of the line to stand, but there will be an opportunity for a few people to share their thoughts after each question.

The terms we have passed out may be unfamiliar to some, so if at any time we use a term that you are unfamiliar with or do not understand, just ask. We have a few operating guidelines to try to make this a good place to have this conversation: Be courteous of everyone in this room. Respect the opinions, beliefs, and ideas of everyone in this room, even if you do not agree; just discuss your thoughts, feelings, and opinions. It is important that what we say here, the stories, ideas, beliefs, and opinions expressed by all, should remain confidential, and should not be used against anyone when we leave."

- Each presenter takes turns reading the questions. Read each TWICE slowly. Do not read the answers off the sheet; just use bullet points and engage the audience. While another presenter is talking, prepare your response for your next question.
- When possible, please write statistics on the board so students can see them during the discussion portion. It will help them to answer questions if they can see and remember the numbers. Make sure to provide the handout with the answers after the activity.
- Coming-Out Stories (10 minutes)
  ○ Pass out answers page.
- Anonymous Questions (5 minutes)
  ○ Pass out index cards or scrap paper.
- Speaker Panel Format (15 minutes)

D. Activity Questions

Directions: After each question, get responses and encourage discussion of reasons for answers **before** providing the correct answer and sharing the process points.

QUESTION 1: "True or False: It is legal to fire someone in the United States based on their sexual orientation or gender identity."

*ANSWER: "The answer is **True**."*

PROCESS POINTS:
- Thirty-one states offer some protection for sexual orientation.
- Nine of those offer protection for state employees.
- Only 23 states offer protection for gender identity.
- Five of those offer protection for state employees.

QUESTION 2: "A majority of states in the union ban insurance exclusions for transgender healthcare. This means insurance companies must cover healthcare for transgender people in these states."
  Get responses.
  Encourage discussion of reasons for answers.

*ANSWER: "The answer is **False**. It is still a small minority of states."*

PROCESS POINTS:
- Eleven states ban insurance exclusions.
- Eight of those also provide health benefits for state employees.
- Two states do not ban exclusions but do provide insurance for state employees.
- Illinois only bans insurance exclusions.
- This means that the vast majority of states do not provide any sort of insurance coverage! (Source: http://www.hrc.org/state_maps)

QUESTION 3: *"True or False: The Christian Bible condemns homosexuality."*
    Get responses.
    Encourage discussion of reasons for answers.

*ANSWER: "The answer is **False**."*

PROCESS POINTS:
- The Bible has also been translated many times into many different languages; the earlier versions, or most closely translated versions, read quite differently than others.
- The quotes and stories commonly used against the LGBTQIA+ community are usually taken out of context.
- The story of Sodom and Gomorrah, when read in the context of the time period, can be interpreted as a story about inhospitality and rape, rather than about homosexuality. The word "homosexual" was not coined until the late nineteenth century. The Bible does not refer to loving same-sex relationships as we know them today.

QUESTION 4: *"True or False: It is possible to change someone's sexual orientation through reparative therapy."*
    Get responses.
    Encourage discussion of reasons for answers.

*ANSWER: "The answer is **False**."*

PROCESS POINTS:
- Although sexuality is more fluid for some, it is not possible to change one's innate sexual orientation.
- The American Psychiatric Association urges ethical practitioners to refrain from this practice as it is detrimental to an individual's well-being.
- Three states plus the District of Columbia (DC) ban this practice: California, New Jersey, and Oregon. It is now illegal for persons under the age of 18.

QUESTION 5: *"True or False: Homosexuality's classification as a mental disorder was removed from the* Diagnostic and Statistical Manual of Mental Disorders *(DSM) by the end of 1973."*
    Get responses.
    Encourage discussion of reasons for answers.

*ANSWER: "The answer is **True**."*

PROCESS POINTS:
- Homosexuality was removed in 1973.
- Due to empirical data along with changing social norms and growing gay communities, the American Psychiatric Association removed it from the DSM.

QUESTION 6: *"True or False: Less than 20 states allow same-sex adoption."*
    Get responses.
    Encourage discussion of reasons for answers.

*ANSWER: "The answer is **True**."*

PROCESS POINTS:
- In most states, whether gay adoption is legal is made on a case-by-case basis by a judge. However, there are 16 states that definitely allow joint gay adoptions.
- Nine states have some form of law against discrimination of placement into homes.
- Illinois allows joint adoption and single adoption. (Source: http://www.lifelongadoptions.com/lgbt-adoption/lgbt-adoption-statistics; Source: http://www.hrc.org/state_maps).

QUESTION 7: "True or False: It is illegal to remove a trans* individual from a restroom that is consistent with their gender identity."
    Get responses.
    Encourage discussion of reasons for answers.

*ANSWER: "The answer is **True**."*

PROCESS POINTS:
- According to Title IX and the Occupational Safety and Health Administration (OSHA), trans students and employees have the same rights as everyone else to the use of facilities that are consistent with their gender identity.
- Title IX works toward gender equality in 10 key areas: Access to Higher Education, Career Education, Employment, Math and Science, Standardized Testing, Athletics, Education for Pregnant and Parenting Students, Learning Environment, Sexual Harassment, and Technology.
- Gender equality is for all men, women, fluid, queer, or otherwise identifying individuals whether the chosen gender identity is the same as their assigned gender at birth or not.

QUESTION 8: "True or False: LGBTQA people or same-sex couples who raise children influence the children to sexually identify as gay or lesbian."
    Get responses.
    Encourage discussion of reasons for answers.

*ANSWER: "The answer is **False**."*

PROCESS POINTS:
- Studies show that children raised by same-sex couples or LGBTQ individuals are more accepting.
- They understand and embrace individuals of different social classes, backgrounds, nationalities, races, and religious beliefs.
- There is no correlation between same-sex couples and their children sharing the same sexual identity.
- The children of same-sex couples or LGBTQA individuals are usually never forced to be "straight" or forced to be anything other than what they choose to express.
- Nature versus nurture argument.
- Mention homeless LGBTQA youth.

QUESTION 9: "True or False: Asexuality is basically another form of celibacy."
    Get responses.
    Encourage discussion of reasons for answers.

*ANSWER: "The answer is **False**."*

PROCESS POINTS:
- Asexuality is the lack of sexual attraction. Celibacy is a person not having sex.
- Someone who is celibate could be asexual, or they could be any other sexuality. They simply do not engage in sex.
- Asexuals are capable of having a sex drive (libido), but simply do not feel sexual attraction to someone else.
- ***ASEXUAL IS NOT EQUAL TO AROMANTIC***. People who do not feel sexual attraction are still capable of romantic attraction (given they are not aromantic). (Source: http://www.asexualityarchive.com/asexuality-and-celibacy-whats-the-difference/.)

QUESTION 10: "True or False: The term 'queer' is used by some people as all encompassing that includes a number of possible sexual orientations and/or gender identities that are not cisgender."
    Get responses.
    Encourage discussion of reasons for answers.

*ANSWER: "The answer is **True**."*

PROCESS POINTS:
- The term "queer" has historically been used as a negative word of hate. Some people in the LGBTQIA+ community still view it this way.
- Others, particularly Queer Theory academics and activists, have reappropriated the term to move away from conformist labels such as "gay" so as to describe non-normative genders and sexualities.

QUESTION 11: *"True or False: The FBI's 2013 report puts sexual orientation as the FOURTH leading motivation for hate crimes out of race, ethnicity, religious bias, disability, and of course sexual orientation."*
  Get responses.
  Encourage discussion of reasons for answers.

*ANSWER: "The answer is **False**."*

PROCESS POINTS:
- Sexual orientation was the second leading motivation for hate crimes in the United States.
- In 2012, 19.6 percent of hate crimes were based on sexual orientation.
- The number one motivation for hate crimes is race (48.3 percent).
- Consider that the statistics rely on what the victim is willing to disclose. If they are not out, they may not tell their crime to anyone.
- It also depends on the police as to whether the crime is termed a "hate" crime or just a violent offense.

QUESTION 12: *"True or False: Gender identity disorder was removed from the* Diagnostic and Statistical Manual of Mental Disorders *(DSM)."*
  Get responses.
  Encourage discussion of reasons for answers.

*ANSWER: "The answer is **True**."*

PROCESS POINTS:
- The American Psychiatric Association (APA) now uses "gender dysphoria" to erase the stigma that transgender people have a disorder. They are distressed. This is brought on by a society that is largely transphobic and continues to allow for only a strict binary of gender/expression.
- Many transgender individuals do not feel like their true selves without hormone therapy and may include some medical procedures typically called gender confirmation surgery.
- Gender dysphoria: Gender at birth is contrary to the one they identify with and there is the presence of clinically significant distress associated with the condition.

E. Activity Process Discussion

PROCESS STATEMENT: *"Okay, you can all return back to your seats. As we tell our coming-out stories to you, please take a minute to write an anonymous question related to our stories or the topics from the Crossing the Line activity."*

- FURTHER INSTRUCTIONS:
  - Have students return to seats.
  - Share your coming-out stories!
  - Have students write anonymous questions on the sheets and then collect them; only give them about a minute, and collect them ALL before you start answering the written questions.
  - While waiting, open the floor for any verbal questions.
  - While one presenter is answering a question, another needs to quietly sort through the questions and divide them up to pass out.
  - Answer all questions with "I" statements, or "In my opinion. . . ." In my experience you can't speak for everyone.

- End with advertising how to get involved—"If you want to be a peer educator or would like to have a presentation for your class or organization, please contact the LGBTQA Resource Office." Hand out peer education info sheets.
- Clean up tape and signs. Erase the board.

EVALUATION & TAKEAWAY CLOSING ACTIVITY—15 MINUTES

A. Goals:
- Provide a brief overview of the contents of the session by allowing participants to voice their personal experience.
- Close the session on a high point.
- Allow for evaluation and feedback.

B. Directions
- Pass out Evaluation Sheet and allow a couple of minutes to begin to complete.
- Closing Activity: *"What are you leaving here and what are you taking with you? Perhaps it's a myth or new piece of information or a story you heard. Think about this while completing your evaluation. Does anyone want to go first?"*
- Have each person briefly share their answers to the question above.
- Thank them for participating in the session. Sign the Safe Zone pledge if this is their third session (second advanced session).

Tips for Facilitators
- Emphasize how important participant feedback is to facilitators, how seriously they take it, and how useful it is for them in crafting future sessions. Strongly encourage participants to leave specific, written feedback about what they thought worked especially well during the session, and what they felt needed improvement. (It can sometimes be a challenge to get participants to leave this extensive feedback, as the evaluation portion comes at the end of the session, and participants can sometimes feel rushed for time. So be sure to allot sufficient time for participants to share their thoughts. Start evaluations before you begin with the closing activity.)
- Please note to participants that facilitators are always available if participants have more questions or concerns they want to discuss after the session is over, and that the end of the session does not need to mean the end of the discussions which the session raised.

REFERENCES

Cass, V. C. (1979). Homosexual identity formation: A theoretical model. *Journal of Homosexuality*, 4, 219–35.

Cass, V. C. (1984). Homosexual identity formation: Testing a theoretical model. *Journal of Homosexuality, 20*(2), 143–67.

D'Augelli, A. R. (1994) Identity development and sexual orientation: Toward a model of Lesbian, Gay, and Bisexual development. In E. J. Trickett, R. J. Watts, and D. Birman (eds.), *Human diversity: Perspectives on people in context.* San Francisco: Josssey-Bass.

Fassinger, R. E., & Miller, B. A. (1997). Validation of an inclusive model of sexual minority identity formation on a sample of gay men. *Journal of Homosexuality*, 32(2), 53–78.

Klein, F., Sepekoff, B., & Wolf, T. J. (1985). Sexual orientation: A multi-variable dynamic process. *Journal of Homosexuality, 11*, 35–49.

CHAPTER 5

Bisexuality & Pansexuality Workshop

KERRY JOHN POYNTER

"Only the human mind invents categories and tries to force facts into separated pigeonholes. The living world is a continuum in each and every one of its aspects. The sooner we learn this concerning human sexual behavior, the sooner we shall reach a sound understanding of the realities of sex."

—*Alfred Kinsey*

This chapter references handouts (available as a single PDF formatted for easy and clear printing on 8.5" × 11") that supplement the curriculum and assessment pieces of this book. Please email resourcematerial@rowman.com to request the PDF, providing both the title and editor of this book along with proof of purchase (receipt).

CONTEXTUALIZATION

Current socialization processes presuppose very specific ideas of normality when it comes to sexual orientation. Specifically, society teaches that two distinctive sexes exist (male and female), and one sexual orientation (heterosexual) is acceptable. Narrow views of sex, gender, and sexuality serve to promote an oversimplification of these remarkably complex constructs (Thompson, 2015).

Bisexuality is often the invisible "B" in the acronym LGBTQIA+. This is due to Western society operating under a binary of only heterosexual versus homosexual or gay versus straight. Such binary thinking does not allow for a sexual orientation that is fluid with sexuality falling on a spectrum of identity, experiences, and attraction. Those that do identify as bisexual or pansexual endure a pervasive biphobia within the LGBTQIA+ and heterosexual communities. Many myths and stereotypes exist that serve to enforce this binary and create the invisibility of bisexual identities.

A bisexual person (sometimes called "fluid") is emotionally, physically, and/or sexually attracted to males/men and females/women. This attraction does not have to be equally split between genders, can be fluid over time, and there may be a preference for one gender over others. Some people prefer to define themselves as pansexual because gender is not the determining factor for attraction to a person and thus are capable of being attracted to all or many gender expressions.

Science has been attempting to study human sexual behavior for decades. Perhaps the best-known scientist is Alfred Kinsey, who studied thousands of men and women in the 1940s and 1950s. His groundbreaking research unveiled the sexual behaviors and fantasies of people living in the United States as not limited to just heterosexual contact (Kinsey, Pomeroy, & Martin, 1948; Kinsey, Pomeroy, Martin, & Gebhard, 1953). In fact, his work brought homosexuality and bisexuality to the public discourse by revealing that many humans were attracted to both men and women and fell on a scale from 0 to 6 with 0 = exclusively heterosexual and 6 = exclusively homosexual (Nye, 1999). Forty-six percent of the population fell within the 1–5 range indicating attraction and sexual experiences with both men and women (Klein, Sepekof, & Wolf, 1985).

However, someone may have attractions to people of any gender but not identify as bisexual. Likewise, someone can identify as bisexual with or without dating or sexual experiences. Klein et al. (1985) explains how a bisexual orientation (or any sexual orientation) should be explained using multiple variables that include sexual attraction, fantasies, behavior, emotional attraction, and self-identification (among others).

Some examples: A man married to a woman identifies as heterosexual, has children, is involved with a male lover, but does not identify as "gay" or "bi." A woman that is involved with a woman identifies as "lesbian" among a women's community and is emotionally connected to her partner, yet still has fantasies about men or a particular man. A teenager comes out as bisexual because he/she has attractions and fantasies about people of any gender but has not engaged in any sexual behaviors with anyone.

The self-identification of any of these examples could change over time depending on the gender of the person they are involved with and/or the community they are associating with. Although it is completely possible for people to experience an attraction for someone of the same gender at some point in their lives (Fox, 1995), the myth that everyone is bisexual confuses fantasy/attraction for experience and identity. For most people these feelings pass or change over time without the person ever questioning or redefining their sexual orientations.

As explained above, not everyone identifies as bisexual and thus statistics attempting to explain and document the percentage of bisexuals are skewed to favor smaller numbers. However, we do know that bisexuals can outnumber those that identify as exclusively "gay" or "lesbian." Data shows that bisexuals make up the largest group within the LGB community, with 1/3 of men and 2/3 of women (Cahill, 2005).

According to the National Survey of Family Growth (CDC, 2005), 2.8 percent of women ages 18 to 44 identify as bisexual. In comparison, 1.3 percent identify as lesbian. These numbers show a bisexual majority among the LGBTQIA+ community and refute the invisibility of these individuals as real. Contributing to an invisibility is the notion that bisexuality is a phase and thus not real. Diamond (2008) found that 92 percent of people who identified as "bisexual" still do 10 years later.

While in an opposite-gender relationship, bisexuals may not be viewed as bisexual, thus contributing to an invisibility. Whether in same-gender and opposite-gender relationships, a bisexual or pansexual orientation does not change. This invisibility may confuse others and form the basis of the myth that bisexuals need more than one partner or partners at the same time.

The capacity to form attractions to either gender does not necessarily equal a need for two partners at once. In fact, private polyamorous (more than two) arrangements have been found among married heterosexuals (15–28 percent), cohabitating couples (28 percent), lesbian couples (29 percent), and gay male couples (65 percent) (Weitzman, 2006). Most bisexuals do not have to be involved with more than one gender at a time in order to feel fulfilled (Cahill, 2005).

The myth of having multiple partners at once contributes to one of the more pervasive myths in that bisexuals transmit sexually transmitted diseases. Who a person is (bisexual, heterosexual, homosexual) does not determine likelihood of disease. What a person does, the sexual practices of a person, in particular, and how well a person protects themselves during sexual activities is more determinative (Miller, Andre, Ebin, & Bessonova, 2007; Berkowitz, Callen, & Dworkin, 1983).

These myths, misinformation, and biphobic attitudes are prevalent among heterosexual as well as lesbian, gay, and trans people (Welzer-Lang, 2008). Heterosexual people may consider bisexuals and pansexuals as "confused" while lesbian and gay people will not see bisexuality as a valid sexual orientation due to stigma around sexual "preference" as a choice.

READINGS FOR FACILITATORS

The following annotated readings are intended as starting points on bisexuality for new learners. They support the learning goals of the curriculum explained in this section. Facilitators should use them as a means of self-learning. They also will be beneficial to group discussion among co-facilitators before practicing and ultimately facilitating the activities contained in this curriculum.

- Cahill, S. (2005). Bisexuality: Dispelling the myths. National Gay and Lesbian Task Force Policy Institute: Washington, DC. Accessed on July 18, 2012: http://www.thetaskforce.org/downloads/reports/BisexualityDispelngtheMyths.pdf.

This white paper from The Task Force is an excellent first read for new facilitators. Some of the data cited here is detailed in later readings and used to debunk myths and stereotypes in the session. The paper defines bisexuality, shares statistics, and broaches a few myths. The statistics lay bare the difference between identity and attraction among men and women.

- Diamond, L. M. (2008). Female bisexuality from adolescence to adulthood: Results from a 10-year longitudinal study. *Developmental Psychology, 44* (1).
  A comprehensive longitudinal study explains how sexual attractions, behaviors, and identities may change over time (alternating between a same-sex relationship or other-sex partner or describing one's sexual identity) among bisexual women. The results support a model of bisexuality that is stable rather than transitional. Bisexuality is supported as a valid third sexual orientation. Facilitators will need this research to explain bisexuality as a sexual orientation and counter stereotypes of it as a "phase."

- Fox, R. (1995). Bisexual identities. in A. D'Augelli & C. Patterson. (Eds.) *Lesbian, gay and bisexual identities over the lifespan: Psychological perspectives.* New York: Oxford University Press.
  This chapter by Ronald Fox is an overview of how bisexuality has "appeared in the literature as a concept, a descriptive term, a sexual orientation category, and a sexual identity" (p. 49). Notable is how it takes a historical view of the literature from early evolutionary theory in the late nineteenth century (including Freud), anthropological incidence, sexual orientation theory (including Kinsey), and concluding with psychological perspectives. The psychological perspectives describe identity versus behavior, bisexuality in marriage, and milestones in identity formation (first attractions, behavior, relationships, and gender differences). This chapter will prove useful for new facilitators looking to understand these concepts and works well with the Cahill (2005) white paper by The Task Force.

- Klein, F., Sepekoff, B., & Wolf, T. J. (1985). Sexual orientation: A multi-variable dynamic process. *Journal of Homosexuality, 11*, 35–49.
  The Klein Sexual Orientation Grid (KSOG) is explained and supported by a research project that builds from the knowledge of Kinsey. KSOG goes further than Kinsey by explaining sexual orientation as beyond a binary process that includes life situations that change over time. These variables include attraction, behavior, fantasy, lifestyle, emotional preference, social preference, and self-identification. Sexuality beyond the heterosexual/homosexual dichotomy should be explained using these variables. Facilitators for this session need to understand these variables when explaining sexuality on a spectrum and while conducting the Beyond Binaries activity.

- Nye, R. A. (1999). Kinsey's seven-point scale of sexual identity. In *Sexuality* (pp. 345–47). Oxford: Oxford University Press.
  Robert Nye succinctly explains the Kinsey seven-point scale of sexual identity. The model explains that there are those that are exclusively heterosexual or homosexual but the vast majority of the population has both heterosexual and homosexual experiences or "psychic responses" in their history. Where you fall on the scale can be dependent on the period in your life. The scale (in brief): 0 = exclusively heterosexual; 1 = incidental homosexual contact; 2 = more than incidental contact; 3 = equally homosexual & heterosexual; 4 = more overt homosexuality yet maintains heterosexuality; 5 = entirely homosexual, incidental heterosexuality; 6 = exclusively homosexual. It is the basis for the scale used in the Beyond Binaries activity.

- Rust, P. (2001). Two many and not enough: The meanings of bisexual identities. *Journal of Bisexuality, 31*, 58.
  Paula Rust attempts to give meaning to how various people construct a bisexual identity. These identity labels can also have compound identities or "multiple sexual identities" to complete a more accurate picture of their sexual attractions such as "bisexual-lesbian." People that use the compound identities describe their potential bisexuality (attraction) and/or behavioral bisexuality (sexual experiences or partners). This article provides an in-depth understanding of the complexity of describing oneself as bisexual and should be required reading for a facilitator looking to better understand and explain this complexity to others.

- Sell, R. L. (2007). Defining and measuring sexual orientation for research. In I. H. Meyer & M. E. Northridge (Eds.) *The health of sexual minorities: Public health perspectives on lesbian, gay, bisexual, and transgender populations.* New York: Springer.
  Randall Sell explains measures of sexual orientation for researchers. These measures include Kinsey and Klein, who are both integral parts of this session explained later in this section. Although facilitators will not be measuring the sexualities of anyone in the session, this article is none the less important to understand when considering the differences between

identity, behavior, fantasies, and attraction. These are important factors when facilitating the Beyond Binaries activity during the session.

- Sumpter, S. F. (1991). Myths/realities of bisexuality. In L. Hutchins & L. Kaahumanu (Eds.) *Bi any other name: Bisexual people speak out* (pp. 12–13). Boston: Alyson Pub.
  This is a good primer on the many myths and stereotypes surrounding bisexual and fluid people. This brief overview responds to each myth in a succinct fashion. Any facilitator wanting to learn how to respond to these myths and stereotypes will find useful language and examples to adapt to their own use.

- Weitzman, G. (2006). Therapy with clients who are bisexual and polyamorous. *Journal of Bisexuality, 6*(1/2), 137–64.
  Geri Wietzman advocates for an increased understanding of polyamorous relationships for therapists working with these clients. She provides a detailed overview of polyamory, types of polyamorous relationships, as well as the ethical and psychological benefits. The overview provides statistics of the prevalence of nonmonogamy in all relationship types (gay, lesbian, and heterosexual couples). Stereotypes such as a need to date two genders simultaneously and spreading sexually transmitted diseases are also debunked using statistical data. Facilitators should have an understanding of polyamory as this question may arise during the session and this article is effective at debunking myths. Although this session is not about polyamory, the information contained here would be useful in responding to students and others in polyamorous relationships.

- Welzer-Lang, D. (2008). Speaking out loud about bisexuality: Biphobia in the gay and lesbian community. *Journal of Bisexuality, 8*, 81–95.
  The authors surveyed activists at a national LGBTQIA+ conference to better understand biphobia and how bisexuals are represented in the LGBTQIA+ community. Responses are ordered in numerous categories such as most biphobic to most bipositive. This gradation scale is explained with numerous quotes from the survey. These quotes prove useful to new facilitators in need of understanding biphobia in the LGBTQ community.

SUGGESTED READINGS

Hutchins, L., & Kaahumanu, L. (1991). *Bi any other name: Bisexual people speak out*. Boston: Alyson Pub.
Ochs, R., & Rowley, S. E. (2005). *Getting bi: Voices of bisexuals around the world*. Boston, MA: Bisexual Resource Center.
Weinberg, M. S., Williams, C. J., & Pryor, D. W. (1994). *Dual attraction: Understanding bisexuality*. New York: Oxford University Press.

TIPS FOR FACILITATORS

- Use the readings to familiarize yourself with the topic of bisexuality before learning how to facilitate the session.
- Take time to discuss the point of each reading with your co-facilitators. Seek out faculty or staff with expertise in psychology and/or sexuality studies to help lead discussions.
- Assign roles for each facilitator in the session.
- Arrange a practice session with knowledgeable and interested members of the community. Ask for feedback.
- Use the facilitator and session evaluation forms (chapter 5) to receive feedback from the practice session. Incorporate feedback into the next session.
- Example process statements and questions are provided below to help provide context to that particular section of the curriculum. Use these as examples to learn from and not exactly to read verbatim. Use your own words and ways of communicating the same concepts.

CURRICULUM—2 Hours

Curriculum Outline
- Introductions and Ground Rules—15 minutes
- Some Terminology & Definitions, Pansexuality Graphic, Quotes—10 minutes
- Kinsey Scale/Klein (handout)—10 minutes
- Robin Ochs Beyond Binaries Sexuality Spectrum Activity—30 minutes
- Bisexuality Myths Matching Game—20 minutes
- Bi the Dice Role-Play Game—20 minutes
- Evaluation and Takeaway Closing Activity—15 minutes

Learning Outcomes
- Greater awareness and visibility of bisexuality and pansexuality as a valid sexual orientation.
- Not everyone fits into a binary of exclusively heterosexual/straight or gay/lesbian.
- Break down common stereotypes and myths.
- Biphobia and prejudice is present among heterosexual and LGBTQ populations.

Materials
Bi the Dice Role Play:

- Name tags for Bi the Dice role play (Alex, Sam, Chris, and Pat)
- Big fuzzy dice
- Notes with responses for role players (four copies)

Handouts
- Pansexuality Graphic (without arrows)
- Quotes: What is Pansexuality?
- Continuum of Sexuality (Kinsey/Klein)
- Robyn Ochs Beyond Binaries Activity
- What Does Biphobia Look Like?
- Bisexual/Pansexuality Myths Matching Game
- Advocates for Youth Brochure: I Think I Might Be Bisexual (download from Advocates for Youth)
- Bi the Dice Role Play Descriptions

INTRODUCTIONS: PGPs, GROUND RULES—15 MINUTES
Use the introductions section explained in chapter 4 Fundamentals on page 28. Include introductions, PGPs, Ground Rules, Parking Lot, and review of the Safe Zone program.

TERMINOLOGY, PANSEXUALITY GRAPHIC, QUOTES—10 MINUTES

A. Terminology & Definitions
Goals

- Remind participants of pertinent terms from the initial Fundamentals session.
- Explain differences between bisexuality and pansexuality.

Directions

- Write the following terms on the dry erase board or chalkboard in the room or project on a screen.
- Ask participants if they remember these terms from the initial Fundamentals session and if they can define them.

PROCESS STATEMENT: *"Let's review a few terms from the Fundamentals session in order to refresh our memory. Can we get a few volunteers to define these?"*

Bisexual/Fluid—A person emotionally, physically, and/or sexually attracted to males/men and females/women. This attraction does not have to be equally split between genders, can be fluid over time, and there may be a preference for one gender over others.

Pansexual—Gender is not the determining factor for attraction to a person. Capable of being attracted to all or many gender expressions.

Biphobia—The fear of, discrimination against, or hatred of bisexuals, which is oftentimes related to the current binary standard. Biphobia can be seen within the LGBTQIA+ community, as well as in general society.

Gender Identity—A person's sense of being masculine, feminine, or other gendered. Possible gender identities include female, male, genderqueer, transwoman, transman, transgender, transsexual, gender fluid, two-spirit, etc.

Sexual Orientation—The desire for intimate emotional and/or sexual relationships with people of the same gender/sex, another gender/sex, or multiple genders/sexes.

B. Pansexuality Graphic (by Kerry Poynter & Ryan McConville, used with permission)
Directions

- Project graphic without arrows (Fig. 5.1) on a screen.
- Ask participants to draw arrows to the correct gender using their handout. Give them 1 minute.
- Reveal the graphic with arrows (Fig. 5.2).
- Discuss the graphic: Mention the gender binary. Mention how even some "bisexuals" will also say they are attracted to many genders as well.
- Make mention of the Pansexuals Define Pansexuality handout. Read a couple of examples.

Figure 5.1. Pansexuality Diagram (no arrows).
Source: Created by Kerry Poynter and Ryan McConville.

What genders are a bisexual or pansexual potentially attracted to?

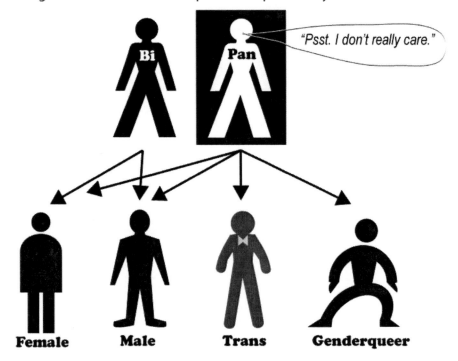

Figure 5.2. Pansexuality Diagram.
Source: Created by Kerry Poynter and Ryan McConville

PROCESS STATEMENT: *"Understanding the subtle differences between bisexuals and pansexuals can be confusing for some. Please take out the Pansexuality Graphic and draw arrows to the persons that a bisexual and a pansexual may be attracted to."*

PROCESS QUESTIONS:
- Show of hands: Who figured this out and was correct?
- Does this graphic provide a better understanding of pansexuality?
- What is still confusing? Does understanding gender as not a binary but a continuum help?

C. Pansexuals Define Pansexuality (handout)
By Bonny Albo, About.com

"Pansexual is the opposite of bisexual because bisexual means when a person is attractive to both male and female but pansexual means when a person is sexually attractive no matter the gender." —Wisdom

"I am pansexual because I want to love a person for who they are, underneath the layers of needless behaviors that have been beaten into us since birth." —Ash

"This is going to sound odd, so bear with me. I used to be very confused. I've typically only dated men, but I have been with a couple women. Everyone I told this to would identify me as bisexual, but I wouldn't accept it for some reason. I don't like men and women. I like people. I thought I was the only one until I started watching this show called Doctor Who. There's this character who hits on anyone, any gender, race, aliens or humans. . . . I thought that was sooo cool and fell in love with him because he's so much like me. People on the show would ask what his orientation was and he'd say ohh you 21st century humans are so stuck on genders. . . . And it's true!! He didn't care who they were, if they were gorgeous, they were gorgeous. And I agree." —Lyra

"I have a sexual attraction toward all genders, but I feel the presence of a person, I don't only look at their body parts." —Maria

"Well, first of all, I'm 14 and a dude, and well, all my life I said love is love, no matter what gender. I always respected other people's preferences, and just recently I knew I was pansexual, because, some time ago I fell in love with a friend of mine, I didn't mind that he was a dude, it was just that he's straight and a friend, so yeah. I don't see why people focus on gender, it's the same person." —Indifferent

"I've always been confused as to why I had feelings for people that were of the opposite and same gender as myself. I am glad that there is finally a definition of orientation that I can identify with. I have always developed feelings for people despite their looks and have been criticized for it but I'm happy with who I am, and I don't think anyone should judge you for it." —Ashley

"I knew I was pansexual when I met this great guy on campus . . . purple hair and very nineties punk . . . like my dream date. We started hanging out and getting to know one another. . . . He told me he was transgender. . . . He helped me to fully understand the whole concept of transgender and I realized, he's still going to be him regardless of his gender. I love him." —Dani

"Well like everyone else has said, liking someone for what's on the inside, not out. I knew I was pansexual when I fell for this geeky guy and we started dating. After about a week he told me he was transgender, and my feeling didn't change at all. To me he would still be who he was. Whether he was a guy or a girl." —Wolf

"Pansexual is when you love someone for what is in their heart, NOT what is in their pants :)" —MB

"The definition of pansexual to me is when you love someone for who they are and not what they have and the word pan is derived from Greek meaning all so you have love for all no matter if they are male, female or transgender." —Forever_young81

"Pansexuality, especially in the way that I use it in reference to my own sexual orientation, means to be emotionally and spiritually inclined towards dating members of all genders. Note the use of the word 'genders' and not 'sexes.'" —Christa

- Albo, B. (n.d.). *Readers respond: Readers share their definition of a pansexual.* About.com, accessed October 10, 2013, from http://dating.about.com/u/ua/glossarywordspq/readerdefinitionofpansexual.01.htm.

Common Participant Questions

- What is genderqueer?
- Can a bisexual person also be attracted to any gender such as a trans person?
- I still don't quite understand pansexuality. If gender isn't what determines attraction, does it mean their personality?

Tips for Facilitators

- Some participants will be confused about the subtle difference between bisexuals and pansexuals. Repetition of these definitions early on and later in the session will be useful.
- Be prepared to remind participants of the difference between gender and sexuality. You may need to define *transgender* and *genderqueer*, from the Fundamentals session, while using the Pansexuality Graphic.

CONTINUUM OF SEXUALITY—KINSEY SCALE & KLEIN—10 MINUTES

Originally created by Dr. Holly Thompson. Used with permission.

Goals

- Introduce Kinsey and Klein to explain sexuality as a spectrum that includes bisexuals and pansexuals.
- Understand that this spectrum includes behavior, attraction, fantasy, and identity.
- Sexuality can be fluid for some and change over time.

Directions

- Point out the Continuum of Sexuality handout.
- This is not a participatory section and will rely on a brief verbal introduction.

PROCESS QUESTIONS:

- Have any of you heard of the Kinsey Scale before? Would you like to explain in your own words?

PROCESS STATEMENT: "***Sexual Orientation*** *exists along a continuum that ranges from exclusive homosexuality to exclusive heterosexuality and includes various forms of bisexuality. Bisexual persons can experience sexual, emotional and affectional attraction to both their own sex and the opposite sex. Persons with a homosexual orientation are sometimes referred to as gay (both men and women) or as lesbian (women only).*

"***Sexual Orientation*** *is different from sexual behavior because it refers to feelings and self-concept. Persons may or may not express their sexual orientation in their behaviors."*

The Sexuality Continuum: An Introduction

Kinsey

PROCESS STATEMENT: "*During the 1940's, Alfred Kinsey and associates shocked Americans when he first published his work on male sexuality. His controversial research challenged traditional notions of sexuality as a one-dimensional construct. Through extensive research, Kinsey et al. pioneered the first comprehensive continuum of sexuality.*"

Heterosexual-Homosexual Rating Scale Criteria

0—Exclusively heterosexual with no homosexual
1—Predominantly heterosexual, only incidentally homosexual
2—Predominantly heterosexual, but more than incidentally homosexual
3—Equally heterosexual and homosexual
4—Predominantly homosexual, but more than incidentally heterosexual
5—Predominantly homosexual, only incidentally heterosexual
6—Exclusively homosexual

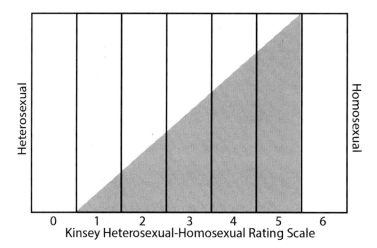

Figure 5.3.   Kinsey Scale.

Klein

PROCESS STATEMENT: *"Building on the work [of] Kinsey, Dr. Fritz Klein viewed sexual orientation as a 'dynamic, multi-variable process.' In an attempt to measure his hypotheses, he created the Klein Sexual Orientation Grid. Klein's work was significant because he attended to sexual and non-sexual variables, which fluctuate with time. Three factors address sexual self (attraction, fantasies, behavior), three variables focus on critical aspects of sexual orientation (emotional preference, social preference, heterosexual or homosexual lifestyle), and the final factor assesses self-identification."*

Klein Sexual Orientation Grid

VARIABLE	PAST	PRESENT	FUTURE	IDEAL
A. Sexual Attraction				
B. Sexual Behavior				
C. Sexual Fantasies				
D. Emotional Preference				
E. Social Preference				
F. Self Identification				
G. Hetero/Homo lifestyle				

Figure 5.4.   Klein Sexual Orientation Grid.

BEYOND BINARIES—30 MINUTES
By Robyn Ochs. Used with permission.

NOTE: In order to facilitate this activity, attain the full Beyond Binaries activity in Murphy and Ribarsky's (2013) *Activities for Teaching Gender & Sexuality in the University Classroom*, Rowman & Littlefield Publishers. The up-to-date handout is available as a download with this book.

Goals
- Participants will put theory to practice and experience sexuality as fluid over time.
- Sexual orientation includes experiences, behavior, fantasies, and identity.

Directions

- Post the numbers 0–6 on a wall with plenty of room for participants to stand by each number.
- Ask participants to anonymously complete the Beyond Binaries handout for about 5 minutes in length.
- Explain to complete the handout by using the scale 0 to 6 (similar to Kinsey).
- Ask participants to not provide any identifying information such as name or other signifiers.
- Point to the place in the room with the numbers posted on the wall and ask participants to stand at the number corresponding to the first question on their anonymous Ochs Activity sheet.

Tips for Facilitators

- If a small group of less than 10 people is in attendance, consider providing the participants copies of previously completed handouts in order to keep this activity as anonymous as possible.
- This activity requires participants to stand and walk along the continuum. If you have someone with a physical disability, offer to have a facilitator stand for them while they engage in conversation.
- Occasionally ask how pansexuality is applicable to the activity or experiences during the activity.

BEYOND BINARIES

Robyn Ochs

This is an *anonymous* exercise. Please keep your answers to yourself and respect others' privacy. If you don't fit into the framework of a question, remember that the limitation lies with the tool, not with you, and place an "X" instead of a number in the circle provided. Answer questions asking about the past based upon how you understood yourself then. Questions referring to sexual experiences refer only to *consensual* experiences.

speaker teacher writer activist

I AM ORIENTED TOWARD PEOPLE WHOSE GENDER IDENTITY IS...

| 1 | 2 | 3 | 4 | 5 | 6 | 7 |

DIFFERENT FROM MINE   SIMILAR TO MINE

Consider the scale above. Write a number in below that represents your experience.

| 1A | ____ | Your sexual orientation overall? |
| 1B | ____ | Your romantic orientation overall? |

2A	____	Your sexual attractions before age 16?
2B	____	During the past year?
2C	____	In the past month?

3A	____	Your romantic attractions (crushes) before age 16?
3B	____	During the past year?
3C	____	In the past month?

4A	____	Your sexual experiences before age 16?
4B	____	During the past year?
4C	____	In the past month?

5A	____	Your fantasies before age 16?
5B	____	During the past year?
5C	____	In the past month?

| 6A | ____ | Where do most of your friends think you are? |
| 6B | ____ | Your closest family members? |

7 What words do you currently use–privately or publicly– to describe your sexual orientation (i.e. straight, bisexual, queer, lesbian, asexual, etc.)**?**

The following questions reference how you understand yourself, and not necessarily your experience or current behavior.

8 I experience sexual desire...

| 1 | 2 | 3 | 4 | 5 | 6 | 7 |

NEVER (ASEXUAL)   ALWAYS

9 I prefer relationships that are...

| 1 | 2 | 3 | 4 | 5 | 6 | 7 |

MONOGAMOUS   NON-MONOGAMOUS

10	____	How old were you when you had your first major romantic crush?
11	____	How old were you when you had your first sexual crush?
12	____	How old were you when you first used a sexual orientation label to describe yourself?

Note: This exercise was designed by Robyn Ochs (www.robynochs.com , robyn@robynochs.com). You may use and adapt this exercise providing you give credit to the author and inform her when you do so. Suggestions/feedback welcome. **V. 9/2015-U**

Figure 5.5. Beyond Binaries.
Source: Created by Robyn Ochs. Used with permission of Rowman & Littlefield. This is chapter 8 in the Rowman & Littlefield book *Activities for Teaching Gender & Sexuality in the University Classroom* by Murphy and Ribarsky.

Created by Kerry Poynter.

Goals

- Debunk common myths and stereotypes about bisexuals and pansexuals.
- Provide data and research that supports the knowledge gained while playing the game.

Directions

- Split into small groups of 3–5 people.
- Pass out matching game sheet with references on back.
- Ask each group to discuss the myth and match the correct reality.
- Do this for 5 minutes.
- Provide correct answers and ask for a show of hands for correct answers.

Bisexuality & Pansexuality Myths—Matching Game Results for Facilitators

By Kerry Poynter

- **Myth #1: Bisexuality or Pansexuality is just a phase. Nobody stays bisexual.**
  Reality D: 92 percent of people who identified as "bisexual" still do 10 years later (Diamond, 2008).
- **Myth #2: Bisexuals and Pansexuals are greedy and need to be with a man and woman at once.**
  Reality C: The capacity to form attractions to either gender does not necessarily equal a need for two partners at once. In fact, private polyamorous arrangements have been found among married heterosexuals (15–28 percent), cohabiting couples (28 percent), lesbian couples (29 percent), and gay male couples (65 percent) (Weitzman, 2006). Most bisexuals do not have to be involved with more than one gender at a time in order to feel fulfilled (Cahill, 2005).
- **Myth #3: Bisexuals and Pansexuals don't exist.**
  Reality F: Alfred Kinsey's work in the 1940's (Kinsey, 1998) would disagree. More recent data shows that bisexuals make up the largest group within the LGB community with 1/3 of men and 2/3 of women (Cahill, 2005). According to the National Survey of Family Growth (CDC, 2005), 2.8 percent of women ages 18 to 44 identify as bisexual. In comparison, 1.3 percent identify as lesbian.
- **Myth #4: Bisexuals and Pansexuals are promiscuous.**
  Reality A: It is a mistake to assume that because someone has the potential to be attracted to all genders, they must have twice as many sex partners (Rust, 2001). Bisexuality or pansexuality is a sexual orientation independent of any cultural definition of what is moral behavior.
- **Myth #5: Bisexuals and Pansexuals are more likely to have sexually transmitted diseases.**
  Reality G: Who a person is does not determine likelihood of disease. What a person **does**, the sexual practices of a person, in particular, and how well a person protects themselves during sexual activities is more determinative (Miller, Andre, Ebin, & Bessonova, 2007; Berkowitz, Callen, & Dworkin, 1983).
- **Myth #6: Bisexuals and Pansexuals are accepted within the gay and lesbian community.**
  Reality B: Lesbian, gay, trans, and heterosexual people harbor misinformation and biphobia (Welzer-Lang, 2008). Heterosexual people may consider bisexuals and pansexuals as "confused" while lesbian and gay people will not see bisexuality as a valid sexual orientation due to stigma around sexual "preference" as a choice.
- **Myth #7: Everybody is Bisexual.**
  Reality E: Although it is completely possible for people to experience an attraction for someone of the same gender at some point in their lives (Fox, 1995), this myth confuses fantasy/attraction for experience and identity. For most people these feelings pass or change over time without the person ever questioning or redefining their sexual orientations.

Bisexuality & Pansexuality Myths & Realities Matching Game

Myth #1:
Bisexuality & pansexuality is just a phase.

Myth #2:
Bisexuals & pansexuals are greedy and need to be with a man and woman at once.

Myth #3:
Bisexuals & pansexuals don't exist.

Myth #4:
Bisexuals & pansexuals are promiscuous.

Myth #5:
Bisexuals & pansexuals are more likely to have sexually transmitted diseases.

Myth #6:
Bisexuals & pansexuals are accepted within the gay and lesbian community.

Myth #7:
Everybody is bisexual.

Reality A: It is a mistake to assume that because someone has the potential to be attracted to all genders, they must have twice as many sex partners (Rust, 2001). Bisexuality and pansexuality are sexual orientations independent of any cultural definition of what is moral sexual behaviour.

Reality B: Lesbian, gay, trans, and heterosexual people harbor misinformation and biphobia (Welzer-Lang, 2008). Heterosexual people may consider bisexuals as "confused" while lesbian and gay people will not see bisexuality or pansexuality as a valid sexual orientation due to stigma around sexual "preference" as a choice.

Reality C: The capacity to form attractions to any gender does not necessarily equal a need for two partners at once. In fact, private polyamorous arrangements have been found among married heterosexuals (15-28%), cohabitating couples (28%), lesbian couples (29%), and gay male couples (65%) (Weitzman, Davidson, & Phillips, 2009). Most bisexuals or pansexuals do not have to be involved with more than one gender at a time in order to feel fulfilled (Cahill, 2005).

Reality D: 92% of people who identified as bisexual or pansexual still do 10 years later (Diamond, 2008).

Reality E: Although it is completely possible for people to experience an attraction for someone of the same gender at some point in their lives (Cahill, 2005), this myth confuses fantasy/attraction for experience and identity. For most people these feelings pass or change over time without the person ever questioning or redefining their sexual orientations.

Reality F: Alfred Kinsey's work in the 1940's (Kinsey, 1998) would disagree. More recent data shows that bisexuals and pansexuals make up the largest group within the LGB community with 1/3 of men and 2/3 of women (Cahill, 2008). According to the National Survey of Family Growth (CDC, 2005), 2.8 percent of women ages 18 to 44 identify as bisexual. In comparison, 1.3 percent identify as lesbian.

Reality G: Who a person is does not determine likelihood of disease. What a person DOES, the sexual practices of a person, in particular, and how well a person protects themselves during sexual activities is more determinative. (Miller, Andre, Ebin, & Bessonova, 2007).

Figure 5.6.   Bisexuality & Pansexuality Myths Matching Game.
Source: Created by Kerry Poynter

PROCESS QUESTIONS:
- Have you heard of any of these myths before?
- Where did you learn them?
- Did you learn anything new during this activity?

Tips for Facilitators
- Encourage each group or person in the group to explain the meaning of the reality in their own words after reading it aloud. This will help allow the information to be more easily digested.
- Provide encouragement to the group that finishes first since you initially set the activity up as a competition; however do the same when soliciting responses from each group during the answer session.

Common Questions
- The data says bisexuals and pansexuals are the majority in the LGB community. Why is that not my experience?
- I'm surprised at the statistics on polyamorous arrangements. What does that mean and how does it apply to this session?

Bi the Dice—Bisexuality Role Play—20 minutes
Created by Abigail Francis, MIT; Revised by Dr. Michele Miller, University of Illinois Springfield

Goal
- An understanding of how biphobia can manifest in casual conversation.

Directions
- Include the die rolls and corresponding responses as handouts in session packet.
- Ask for 2 volunteers to begin (2 more will be requested later).
- Assign each volunteer a role to play (Chris and Pat).
- Facilitators will play the roles of Alex and Sam for the first scenario, 2 new volunteers will replace the facilitators for scenarios two and three (4 total volunteers).
- Facilitator playing Alex will act as a narrator and guide for first scenario.
- Instruct/guide volunteers in rolling the dice to determine the responses to act out.
- A total of three scenarios will be played out at random (as determined by the dice).

*Do not assign specific genders to the actors.

Materials
- Dice (large fuzzy dice are recommended)
- Role Play Descriptions based on number rolled

Role Play Script

Facilitator: We are going to perform a "choose your own adventure" role play and need two volunteers to start. We will ask for two more people to help out after the first scenario has been acted out. If there are no volunteers we will pick people!"

Let me set the scene for you. I will be playing the role of Alex, who is meeting friends Sam *(played by the other facilitator)* and Chris *(played by volunteer's name)* for lunch on campus. Alex has also invited Pat *(played by volunteer's name)* to join them for lunch. [TO START, PAT WILL STAND OFF TO THE SIDE] At various points in our story, Sam, Chris, and Pat will each roll a die to determine their specific reactions and responses to act out.

Alex (played 1st by facilitator): (to Sam and Chris) Hey it's great to see you! I wonder what is being served for lunch.

[**Sam** and **Chris** respond.]

Alex: I hope you don't mind, but I invited my new partner Pat to join us for lunch.

[**Sam** and **Chris** respond with approval.]
By the way, Pat is a different gender than my previous partner.

Sam and Chris each roll the dice to determine their individual reactions to this news.

    If they roll . . .

        1 = (Negative) Oh, so now you're "gay"/"straight"?

        2 = (Positive/still offensive) Congrats and welcome to the other side!

        3 = (Negative) Switching it up for a while because you got bored?

        4 = (Positive) I support whoever you choose to be with as long as you are happy.

        5 = (Negative/Denial) So, how long is this experimenting going to last?

        6 = (Neutral) Cool, I look forward to meeting Pat.

Alex: I've always been bisexual. This doesn't change who I am, I've always liked both genders. Pat is walking over here now.

    [All exchange greetings]

Sam (played 1st by facilitator): Pat we were just talking about you. Specifically that you are a different gender than Alex's previous partner.

Pat rolls the dice to determine her reaction to this news.

    If Pat rolls . . .

    2, 4, or 6 = Pat was aware of this news and has a positive/supportive reaction.

    1 = Pat was not aware of the news but has no problem with it.

    3 = Pat was not aware of the news and asks for time to think about it.

    5 = Pat was not aware of the news and tells Alex that the relationship is over.

    Repeat the role play 2 more times, having 2 additional volunteers replace the facilitators for the roles of Alex and Sam.

Process Questions for Group Discussion:

- What occurred during this role play (various combinations of acceptance/indifference/fear/disapproval)?
- If you could re-create the scene, what would you change?
- For Alex: What was it like to receive those responses from your friends? What if the friends' reactions are very different and they do not agree with one another?
- What will you take away from this activity?

NOTE: Since this activity is about biphobia, this is a good time to pass out or draw attention to the "What Does Biphobia Look Like?" handout.

What Does Biphobia Look Like?

Directions: If time permits, have a few participants point out a number that is salient, interesting, or new to them. Briefly discuss.

- Assuming that everyone you meet is either heterosexual or homosexual.
- Supporting and understanding a bisexual identity for young people because you identified "that way" before you came to your "real" lesbian/gay/heterosexual identity.
- Expecting a bisexual to identify as heterosexual when coupled with the "opposite" gender/sex.
- Believing bisexual men spread AIDS/HIV and other STDs to heterosexuals.
- Thinking bisexual people haven't made up their minds.
- Assuming a bisexual person would want to fulfill your sexual fantasies or curiosities.
- Assuming bisexuals would be willing to "pass" as anything other than bisexual.
- Feeling that bisexual people are too outspoken and pushy about their visibility and rights.
- Automatically assuming romantic couplings of two women are lesbian, or two men are gay, or a man and a woman are heterosexual.
- Expecting bisexual people to get services, information, and education from heterosexual service agencies for their "heterosexual side" and then go to gay and/or lesbian service agencies for their "homosexual side" (sic).
- Feeling bisexuals just want to have their cake and eat it too.
- Believing that bisexual women spread AIDS/HIV and other STDs to lesbians.
- Using the terms "phase" or "stage" or "confused" or "fence-sitter" or "bisexual" or "AC/DC" or "switchhitter" as slurs or in an accusatory way.

- Thinking bisexuals only have committed relationships with "opposite" sex/gender partners.
- Looking at a bisexual person and automatically thinking of their sexuality rather than seeing them as a whole, complete person.
- Believing bisexuals are confused about their sexuality.
- Assuming that bisexuals, if given the choice, would prefer to be within an "opposite" gender/sex coupling to reap the social benefits of a "heterosexual" pairing.
- Not confronting a biphobic remark or joke for fear of being identified as bisexual.
- Assuming bisexual means "available."
- Thinking that bisexual people will experience inclusion when lesbian and gay people experience it.
- Being gay or lesbian and asking your bisexual friend about their lover only when that lover is the same sex/gender.
- Feeling that you can't trust a bisexual because they aren't really gay or lesbian, or aren't really heterosexual.
- Thinking that people identify as bisexual because it's "trendy."
- Expecting a bisexual to identify as gay or lesbian when coupled with the "same" sex/gender.
- Expecting bisexual activists and organizers to minimize bisexual issues (i.e. HIV/AIDS, violence, basic civil rights, fighting the Right, military, same sex marriage, child custody, adoption, etc.) and to prioritize the visibility of "lesbian and/or gay" issues.
- Avoid mentioning to friends that you are involved with a bisexual or working with a bisexual group because you are afraid they will think you are a bisexual.

EVALUATION AND TAKEAWAY CLOSING ACTIVITY—15 MINUTES

A. Goals
- Provide a brief overview of the contents of the session by allowing participants to voice their personal experience.
- Close the session on a high point.
- Allow for evaluation and feedback.

B. Directions
- Pass out Evaluation Sheet and allow a few minutes to complete.
- Closing Activity: *"What are you leaving here and what are you taking with you? Perhaps it's a myth or new piece of information or a story you heard. Think about this while completing your evaluation. Does anyone want to go first?"*
- Have each person briefly share their answers to the question above.
- Thank them for participating in the session. Sign the Safe Zone pledge if this is their third session (second advanced session).

Tips for Facilitators
- Please emphasize how important participant feedback is to facilitators, how seriously they take it, and how useful it is for them in crafting future sessions. Strongly encourage participants to leave specific, written feedback about what they thought worked especially well during the session, and what they felt needed improvement. (It can sometimes be a challenge to get participants to leave this extensive feedback, as the evaluation portion comes at the end of the session, and participants can sometimes feel rushed for time. So be sure to allot sufficient time for participants to share their thoughts. Start evaluations before you begin with the closing activity.)
- Please note to participants that facilitators are always available if participants have more questions or concerns they want to discuss after the session is over, and that the end of the session does not need to mean the end of the discussions which the session raised.

REFERENCES

Berkowitz, R., Callen, M., & Dworkin, R. (1983). *How to have sex in an epidemic.* News From the Front Publications (Brochure), New York: Tower Press. Retrieved March 3, 2014, from http://richardberkowitz.com/.

Cahill, S. (2005). *Bisexuality: Dispelling the myths. National Gay and Lesbian Task Force Policy Institute Washington, DC:* Accessed on July 18, 2012, at http://www.thetaskforce.org/downloads/reports/BisexualityDispellingtheMyths.pdf.

Centers for Disease Control. (2005). *National Survey of Family Growth: Sexual behavior and selected health measures: Men and women 15–44 years of age, United States, 2002.* Retrieved July 19, 2012, from www.cdc.gov/nchs/data/ad/ad377.pdf.

Diamond, Lisa M. (2008). Female bisexuality from adolescence to adulthood: Results from a 10-year longitudinal study. *Developmental Psychology, 44* (1).

Fox, R. (1995). Bisexual identities, in A. D'Augelli & C. Patterson (Eds.) *Lesbian, gay and bisexual identities over the lifespan: Psychological perspectives.* New York: Oxford University Press.

Kinsey, A. (1998). *Sexual behavior in the human male.* Bloomington, IN: Indiana University Press.

Klein, F., Sepekoff, B., & Wolf, T. J. (1985). Sexual orientation: A multi-variable dynamic process. *Journal of Homosexuality*, 11, 35–49.

Miller, M., Andre, A., Ebin, J., & Bessonova, L. (2007). *Bisexual health: An introduction and model practices for HIV/STI prevention programming.* National Gay and Lesbian Task Force Policy Institute, The Fenway Institute at Fenway Community Health, BINET USA. Accessed July 19, 2012, from http://www.thetaskforce.org/reports_and_research/bisexual_health.

Mosher, W., Chandra, A., & Jones, J. (2005, September 15). *Sexual behavior and selected health measures: Men and women 15–44 years of age, United States, 2002.* Advance Data from Vital Health and Statistics. Number 362. Hyattsville, MD: U.S. Department of Health and Human Services, Centers for Disease Control and Prevention, National Center for Health Statistics. Accessed July 19, 2012, from http://www.cdc.gov/nchs/products/pubs/pubd/ad/361-370/ad362.htm.

Rust, P. (2001). Two many and not enough: The meanings of bisexual identities. *Journal of Bisexuality, 31*, 58.

Thompson, T. (2015). Continuum of sexuality: Kinsey & Klein. *University of Illinois Springfield Safe Zone program.*

Weitzman, G. (2006). Therapy with clients who are bisexual and polyamorous. *Journal of Bisexuality, 6*(1/2), 137–64.

Weitzman, G., Davidson, J., & Philips, R. (2009) *What psychology professionals should know about polyamory.* Baltimore, MD: National Coalition for Sexual Freedom, inc. Accessed August 31, 2016, from https://ncsfreedom.org/images/stories/pdfs/KAP/2010_poly_web.pdf.

Welzer-Lang, D. (2008). Speaking out loud about bisexuality: Biphobia in the gay and lesbian community. *Journal of Bisexuality, 8*, 81–95.

CHAPTER 6

Religion & Faith Workshop

HOLLY KENT, KERRY JOHN POYNTER, AND BRADY SULLIVAN

"Liberation theology is a distinct way of talking about God. Liberation theology works from within religious traditions to stand against the drive to power of patriarchal and priestly elites who speak for those traditions. Liberation theology tries to restore the courage of those who are oppressed, confident that those who suffer truly understand God's message and, in standing against such injustice, embody God's will in this world."

—Kugle, 10, p. 37

This chapter references handouts (available as a single PDF formatted for easy and clear printing on 8.5" × 11") that supplement the curriculum and assessment pieces of this book. Please email resourcematerial@rowman.com to request the PDF, providing both the title and editor of this book along with proof of purchase (receipt).

DESCRIPTION

This session allows for participants to engage in discussion about the intersections of LGBTQIA+ people and religion while also introducing key challenges for people seeking to balance both identities. Participants will gain information and LGBTQIA+-supportive resources in an Abrahamic religious context, as well as thoughtful, respectful language and strategies to engage with LGBTQIA+ people of faith. Recommended for any potential Safe Zone member that may be struggling with this issue or in need of information to support LGBTQIA+ students of faith.

CONTEXTUALIZATION

Allies to LGBTQIA+ people as well as those doing social justice work often do not broach the topic of religion with non-normative sexualities and genders. There are good reasons for this reluctance: a fear of controversy with people of faith, a lack of affirming resources, personal wariness about delving into a topic with which they are personally unfamiliar (especially for agnostic and atheist facilitators), and the real possibility that they too have been mentally and emotionally damaged by organized religion or people of faith. This reluctance has the effect of further marginalizing LGBTQIA+ people who are struggling with reconciling their faith with their sexuality or gender identity.

There are thousands of religions and faith beliefs worldwide. A recent study of religious beliefs in the United States by the Pew Research Center found that 48 percent of gay, lesbian, and bisexual respondents identified as Christian; 11 percent identify with another faith (Jewish, Muslim, Buddhist, Hindu, and others); and 41 percent as atheist, agnostic, or nothing in particular (Smith, 2015). This particular workshop session uses the Abrahamic religions (Christianity, Islam, Judaism) as contextual examples.

However, the framework set out here in this workshop can be adapted for any religious or faith background, and this session is deliberately structured to be open to participants from all (or no) faith traditions to be able to share their insights, and to be adapted as facilitators may find it useful to focus on other faith communities, depending on the specific demographics of the institution where the session is being held.

The dual intent of this workshop session is to explain how LGBTQIA+ people can (if they choose to do so), reconcile their faith with a liberation theology viewpoint, and provide them with examples to support them as (and if) they choose to reconcile their LGBTQIA+ and religious identities. It avoids the trap of debating scriptural interpretation that is rarely a fruitful enterprise and usually fraught with disrespect.

This session offers strategies, tactics, and resources for LGBTQIA+ people wishing to reconcile their religious identities with their sexual orientations and/or gender identities. We emphasize throughout our session that such reconciliation is possible, while that process may take time and will definitely take different forms for different people. Although our emphasis throughout is on the ways that religion and spirituality can be positive and affirming for LGBTQIA+ people, we are also very much aware of the extensive suffering and hurt which has been suffered historically (and continues to be suffered currently) by many LGBTQIA+ people, because of intolerant religious institutions, ideologies, and members of religious communities. Our session therefore works to strike a balance between acknowledging this very deep, extensive pain, and offering productive, healing models for future religious and spiritual growth and community, for those who wish to pursue it.

Many LGBTQIA+ people of faith face intolerance, discrimination, and bias within religious institutions. This intolerance can take a variety of forms. Among those frequently articulated in previous sessions of this curriculum, the following themes have emerged. Some LGBTQIA+ people are frustrated to not find themselves reflected or represented in the sacred texts of their faith, ordination, or in its religious leadership. Others find that particular members of their religious community are accepting and loving, but nonetheless experience pain and frustration because their larger faith tradition refuses to affirm LGBTQIA+ people.

Some religious communities will welcome LGBTQIA+ people as members, but will still refuse to allow them access to specific sacraments, rituals, or ceremonies (such as communion, confirmation, or marriage), or the process of becoming ordained. LGBTQIA+ people of faith may be told that God loves them (but only if they remain celibate), or that God does not and cannot love them, unless they conform to the "right" gender identity and/or sexual orientation. If they choose to come out, they may risk rejection from religious family members and friends, and marginalization within (or rejection from) their religious community.

Given these realities, it is perhaps unsurprising that many LGBTQIA+ people of faith who are part of non-affirming communities internalize homophobic, biphobic, and transphobic ideas, and experience feelings of shame and self-hatred about their sexual orientation and/or gender identity. In fact, LGBTQIA+ individuals of faith who feel they are cut off from a sense of spirituality or belonging are more at risk to experience alienation, low self-esteem, and depression (Kocet, Sanabria, & Smith, 2011). Fears of rejection from religious loved ones, religious leaders, and from God, are also common.

For many LGBTQIA+ people of faith, making the decision to come out is often a challenging one, as they may risk losing support from family and friends within their religious community, and even losing that entire community itself. LGBTQIA+ people in non-affirming religious institutions face difficult decisions about whether to remain within those communities, seek to find a new religious community, or move away from organized religion altogether. This session offers allies resources to help them be supportive as LGBTQIA+ people of faith who are working through these difficult emotions and grappling with these challenging choices.

This session has its roots in liberation theology, an approach to religious faith that emphasizes social injustice as a sin. Liberation theology originates largely from Catholic churches and thinkers of the Global South in Central and South America, in response to the economic concerns of the poor and oppressed during the 1950s and 1960s (Enns, 1989). Since then, liberation theology has also been applied to racial, sexual, and gender minorities, broadening out to include Black theology, feminist theology, and womanist (women of color) theology. While many of its early proponents were Christian, people of faith in numerous different religious traditions embrace contemporary liberation theology.

LGBTQIA+ Muslims draw on liberation theology as a means of protesting systems of oppression. A noted scholar of Islam, Scott Siraj al-Haqq Kugle (2010) notes, "The liberation theology approach of (LGBTQIA+) Muslims provides a profound interpretation of the Qur'an. Its central principle—striving for justice in solidarity with the oppressed—lets (LGBTQIA+) Muslims join a wider coalition of reformers. It lets them join all women, youth, racial minorities, and others who are marginalized or disempowered by the political-religious system that rules them.

"From the position of being an oppressed minority, they hear the Qur'an's voice from a particularly sensitive position, when it insistently asks Muslims, *Why don't you struggle in the way of God and on behalf of those who are oppressed? On behalf of those men, women and youth who say 'O Lord! Help us to escape from this town whose people oppress us, give us a guardian appointed by you, and grant us aid from one close to you'* (Q. 4:74)" (p. 35).

LGBTQIA+ Muslims who follow liberation theology read the Qur'an with a sexuality-sensitive interpretation. While this interpretation, much like those of Christian scripture, does not clearly address LGBTQIA+ Muslims or the issue of homosexuality (as no term in the Qur'an corresponds to contemporary definitions of homosexuality), it is nonetheless explicitly non-patriarchal, does not assume male supremacy, does not presume all readers are heterosexual, and avoids imposing restrictive and oppressive ideas about gender and sexuality (Kugle, 2010). As Muhsin Hendrix, the founder of the South African organization Inner Circle, writes, "I believe that just because I am gay does not mean I can't practice Islam or be a Muslim and I've used the Qur'an to back up this belief" (Kugle, 2010, p. 34).

Although we do not recommend a debate on scripture or religious texts, it is helpful to understand how LGBTQIA+ people reconcile several of the key texts commonly used to support anti-LGBTQIA+ ideas. The story of Lot, for example, appears both in the Bible, Torah, and Qur'an, and is often used to justify discrimination against gay men specifically, and all LGBTQIA+ people generally.

As Kugle (2010) writes in his text, *Homosexuality in Islam*, "Sexuality-sensitive Muslims contend that the Prophet Lot condemned same-sex rape and denounced the use of sex as coercion against the vulnerable, and that the men of Sodom and Gomorrah attempted to commit lustful violence against Lot's guests not out of sexual appetite but in order to deny Lot's prophetic mission by denying him the authority and dignity of giving hospitality to guests and strangers" (p. 39). In the era, culture, and region within which the story of Lot takes place, people lived in an agrarian culture. In this culture, it was considered sinful to not offer shelter to a fellow herder.

This hospitality was commonplace, and an important facet of the culture that is the crux of Lot's story. Lot was providing shelter to strangers, but the townspeople wished to both deny these strangers shelter and to sexually assault them. The story of Lot, therefore, is not about consensual same-gender-loving relationships, and the sin of Sodom was not about homosexuality but rather inhospitality and the threat of rape. This sexuality-sensitive interpretation is one example of how LGBTQIA+ people can reconcile passages from sacred texts from the Abrahamic faiths with their own gender identity and/or sexual orientation. However, providing alternative readings of harmful scripture is not enough for many LGBTQIA+ people of faith. It is also important that they have access to a wider support system, and resources to help them think through how (or whether) they wish to seek out a religious or spiritual community.

One useful way for allies to support LGTBQ people of faith through this process is the GRACE model. The GRACE model was developed by Bozard and Sanders (2011) as a means to help counselors and mental health professions address the complicated relationship between spiritual and sexual identity for LGBTQIA+ individuals. Within this model, religion and spirituality are recognized as a potent potential source of support for LGBTQIA+ people. Unfortunately for sexual minorities, many avenues to spirituality are blocked and inaccessible for them, because of institutional barriers, personal prejudice, and other factors.

Not only does this lack of access to desired spiritual and religious resources inflict negative psychological trauma on LGBTQIA+ people of faith, it also bars these individuals from much-needed sources of support. The GRACE model works to heal these wounds by addressing the shame and the pain, which individuals may have experienced after having been rejected from religious institutions. The model then works to help individuals rebuild a new, healthy sense of spirituality that they themselves create.

This session includes the GRACE model for a number of reasons. Our audience feedback for this session indicated that there was a lack of understanding about how LGBTQIA+ people (who wished to do so) could integrate their sexual identity/gender identity with their faith or religion. By including this model, we are pulling away from the "religion versus sexuality" debate, because we have discovered that such debates are damaging to individuals who are LGBTQIA+, and do not help to enhance session attendees' understandings of spirituality. The GRACE model thus emphasizes working with LGBTQIA+ people interested in integrating their faith with their sexual and/or gender identity, as opposed to using the session to engage in debates about whether or not such integration is possible.

The model moves through five phases. The first phase is **G**oals. In this phase, the individual discusses what they want out of their spiritual life and how they would like to enhance it or change it. It is during this phase that the ally would collect a religious history of the individual, and learn about the individual's religion of origin and any feelings they have about that religion.

The next phase is **R**enewal of Hope. In this phase, the ally will address any feelings of shame or rejection that were identified during the Goals phase. It is in this phase that the ally would offer new interpretations of religious texts or scripture. The individual can then use these interpretations as a means of recognizing that other opinions exist on sexual orientation and sexual minorities within different religions and communities of faith.

The third phase is **A**ction. In this phase, the individual is presented with three options: remain, renew, or create. If the individual chooses to remain, they stay in their current spiritual situation at their current spiritual institution, and make no changes in their spiritual life. If the individual chooses to renew, they make some changes within their current spiritual situation. For example, they may remain within the Baptist denomination, but decide to change churches. If the individual decides to create, they try on a completely new form of spirituality from what they were previously ascribing to.

The fourth phase is **C**onnection. It is during this phase that the ally focuses on internal conflicts within the individual. This phase takes time. The individual will address how their sexuality and/or gender identity blends with their spirituality. An example of this is some individuals may believe that God is a perfect being who does not make mistakes, and that their sexual orientation and/or gender identity is consequently part of God's design.

Others may struggle with previously held beliefs about the inherent "sinfulness" of their sexual orientation and/or gender identity, and may consequently struggle to believe in a god who loves them just as they are. It is also during this phase that the individual will discern between different types of discrimination that occur within their spiritual institution. Not all discrimination within the institution is spiritually based. Many acts of discrimination find their roots in homophobia, heterosexist privilege, and inaccurate stereotypes.

In the final stage, **E**mpowerment, the ally will meet with the individual after they have attended a service at their new spiritual institution and process the experience with them. It is here that the ally will address any discrimination or shame that the individual may have experienced in this process. This stage will also encourage them to not give up on integrating their spiritual and sexual identities, if they wish to continue to pursue it. The concepts in this introductory section relate to the readings for facilitators and are directly connected to the goals of the session and will be referenced in the curriculum.

READINGS FOR FACILITATORS

The following annotated readings are intended as starting points on religion and faith for new learners. They support the learning goals of the curriculum explained in this section. Facilitators should use them as a means of self-learning. They also will be beneficial to group discussion among co-facilitators before practicing and ultimately facilitating the activities contained in this curriculum.

- Bozard, R. L., & Sanders, C. J. (2011). Helping Christian lesbian, gay, and bisexual clients recover religion as a source of strength: Developing a model for assessment and integration of religious identity in counseling. *Journal of LGBT Issues in Counseling, 5,* 47–74.
  This article describes a five-step method for addressing the topic of spiritual identity for the LGBTQIA+ community. The steps are Goals, Renewal of Hope, Action, Connection, and Empowerment. These steps are used to help an individual grow in both their faith identity as well as their sexual identity without sacrificing one or the other. This source is incredibly enlightening in that it not only gives a framework to help an individual who is struggling with their spiritual and sexual identities. It also moves at a pace the client is comfortable with as they are the ones who are in control of their progression through the model. This article is an answer to the difficult question: "How do we successfully integrate a spiritual identity with a sexual one?"

- Cannon, J. R. (2009). *The Bible, Christianity, & homosexuality*. Lexington, KY: Author.
  This book is a concise review of the Bible's interpretations of homosexuality. It reviews translations of scripture from a historical-critical perspective commonly used against LGBT people. New learners will find it an accessible read and a good

starting point for considering the Bible and LGBTQIA+ issues. This book pairs nicely with the Helmniak reading on the city of Sodom.

- Dworkin, Sari (1997). Female, lesbian, and Jewish. In B. Greene (Ed.), *Ethnic and cultural diversity among lesbians and gay men* (pp. 63–87). Thousand Oaks, CA: Sage Publications.
  This chapter, written for therapists working with lesbian, Jewish clients, contains information of use to the general reader. The author provides an overview of the history of anti-Semitism, and the ways in which the sacred scriptures of Judaism have been used to condemn gay and lesbian people. The author also provides a useful summary of the ways in which the different branches of Judaism have thought about homosexuality, and the place of gay and lesbian people within the Jewish faith.

- Enns, P. P. (1989). Socialist theologies. In *The Moody handbook of theology*. Chicago, IL: Moody Press.
  A handbook compilation of the various forms of theology found in Christianity. Part five: Contemporary Theology, chapter 43, Socialist Theology is a primer on liberation theology. The chapter summarizes the major theological viewpoints beginning with Moltmann's theology of hope, the five liberation theology viewpoints, and concludes with the critical reservations of conservative Christians. Facilitators of this curriculum will find this chapter useful when explaining liberation theology.

- Helminiak, D. A. (1994). The sin of Sodom: Inhospitality. In *What the Bible really says about homosexuality* (pp. 35–41). San Francisco, CA: Alamo Square Press.
  This book, written by a theologian and Catholic priest, is a summary of research from various scholars on how the Bible does not condemn homosexuality. The strength of this text is the accessibility of content for new readers to this subject. It covers a number of topics including a review of the biblical texts that are used to justify prejudice against LGBTQIA+ people, interpreting words from a literal or historical-critical approach, and a review of same-sex relationships found in the Bible. Pay particular attention to chapter 3 on the sin of Sodom, as it is used as a brief example during the session.

- Karslake, D., Mendoza, H., Kennedy, N. C., Suozzo, M., VisionQuest (Firm), Atticus Group (Firm), & First-Run Features (Firm). (2007). *For the Bible tells me so.* New York, NY: First Run Features.
  This film looks at how the Bible has been used to condemn gay and lesbian people, and explores the flaws in these scriptural interpretations. Featuring scholars and leaders from a diverse assortment of faith traditions, the documentary tackles the "Clobber Passages" often used to denounce homosexuality. The film clearly analyzes the historical and cultural context of these passages, and demonstrates how they do not condemn LGBT people.
      The documentary also profiles families about how they reconcile their beliefs about religion and homosexuality with their love for their gay and lesbian family members. This film gives viewers a useful perspective on how liberation theology can operate in the lives of Jewish and Christian LGBTQIA+ people. A short section from this documentary is used during the session.

- Kocet, M., Sanabria S., & Smith M. R. (2011). Finding the spirit within: Religion, spirituality, and faith development in lesbian, gay, and bisexual individuals. *Journal of LGBT Issues in Counseling, 5*, 163–79.
  This article addresses the struggle that can occur when members of the LGBTQIA+ community attempt to address their spiritual identity. It sheds light on how mental health professionals can go about addressing this topic and helping their LGBTQIA+ clients explore their spiritual self. This article also provides a counseling framework that can be used as a guide when addressing this topic. This article flows well and begins by stating the negative effects that a lack of spirituality and religion can have on an individual, and then moves into how to address these issues by providing a four-part counseling framework to address the issue. This source provides support for the idea that spiritual or religious rejection leads to negative mental health effects.

- Kraig, B. (1998). Exploring sexual orientation issues at colleges and universities with religious affiliations. In R. L. Sanlo (Ed.), *Working with lesbian, gay, bisexual, and transgender college students: A handbook for faculty and administrators.* Westport, CT: Greenwood Press.
  This chapter provides helpful suggestions on how to begin to engage a religiously affiliated community in conversation about religion and LGBTQIA+ people. Particularly useful are tables 14–16, which provide example guidelines, helpful discussion questions, and lists of affirming religious groups by denomination. This chapter could be a helpful reflection piece for the organizer in preparation for this session, particularly if they are situated at a religiously affiliated institution.

- Kugle, S. (2010.) *Homosexuality in Islam: Critical reflection on gay, lesbian, and transgender Muslims.* Oxford, UK: One World Publications.

  This text considers how the sacred laws of Islam have represented gay, lesbian, and transgender people. Noting that it is often claimed that the Qur'an condemns homosexuality, Kugle makes the case for liberation theology readings of the Qur'an as affirming of all people, regardless of their gender identity and/or sexual orientation.

  Kugle analyzes Islamic scripture, contending that neither the Prophet Muhammad nor the Qur'an condemns homosexuality. He discusses Islamic religious law, how it has been interpreted to discriminate against gay, lesbian, and transgender people, but persuasively argues that this discrimination misinterprets these laws' intent. Kugle also includes case studies, demonstrating how these arguments impact LGT Muslims' lives.

- Kugle, S. (2014). *Living out Islam: Voices of gay, lesbian, and transgender Muslims.* New York, NY: New York University Press.

  These interviews with gay, lesbian, and transgender Muslims from secular, democratic countries offer the opportunity to hear the voices of LGT Muslims about their experiences. These interviews consider how women and men think about the intersections between religious traditions and their identities as LGT people, and their experiences coming out to their families and in their communities. This volume would be especially useful for those seeking narratives about different paths to reconciling religious and LGT identities.

- Miner, J., & Connoley, J. T. (2002). The Clobber Passages. In *The children are free: Reexamining the biblical evidence on same-sex relationships* (pp. 141–45). Indianapolis, IN: Jesus Metropolitan Community Church.

  This chapter reviews the six passages in the Bible used to "clobber" LGBTQIA+ people. These include Sodom and Gomorrah (Genesis 19), which is probably the most used when justifying prejudice against LGBTQIA+ people; trading natural relations for unnatural (Romans 1:21–28); and no fems no fairies (1 Corinthians 6:9–10 and 1 Timothy 1:10). In chapter 2, this book also describes affirming scripture in the stories of David and Jonathan, and Naomi and Ruth. These two chapters are the basis for the Clobber Passages handout used in this session.

- Tigert, L. M., & Brown, T. (2001). *Coming out young and faithful.* Cleveland, OH: The Pilgrim Press.

  This book addresses the issue of coming out as LGBTQIA+ within a religious community. Individuals share the reactions that occurred when they came out in institutions of faith. Readers can find support in knowing that there are others out there attempting to find acceptance within communities of faith. These stories reinforce the need to inform others of systems such as the GRACE model utilized in this chapter. When these sources are coupled together they provide a source of comfort and guidance for individuals struggling to integrate their spiritual and sexual identities.

SUGGESTED READINGS

Boswell, J. (1980). *Christianity, social tolerance, and homosexuality.* Chicago: University of Chicago Press.

Boswell, J. (1994). *Same-sex unions in premodern Europe.* New York: Villard Books.

Scanzoni, L., & Mollenkott, V. R. (1990). *Is the homosexual my neighbor? Another Christian view.* San Francisco: Harper & Row.

Smith, G. (2015, May 12). *America's changing religious landscape: Christians decline sharply as share of population; Unaffiliated and other faiths continue to grow* (Rep. p. 87). Retrieved May 13, 2015, from Pew Research Center website: http://www.pewforum.org/files/2015/05/RLS-05-08-full-report.pdf.

Tips for Facilitators

- Use the readings to familiarize yourself with the topic of religion and LGBTQIA+ issues before learning how to facilitate the session.
- Take time to discuss the point of each reading with your co-facilitators. Seek out faculty, staff, or community leaders with expertise in religious studies for additional discussion and clarification of any points about which you have questions.
- Assign roles for each facilitator in the session.
- Arrange a practice session with knowledgeable and interested members of the community. For this session, it can be useful to receive feedback both from those currently part of religious institutions, as well as those who are not (as in your sessions, you will be working with those who identify as religious, and those who do not). Ask for feedback.
- Use the facilitator and session evaluation forms (chapter 5 of this volume) to receive feedback from the practice session. Incorporate feedback into next session.

- Example process statements and questions are provided below to help provide context to that particular section of the curriculum. Use these as examples to learn from and not exactly to read verbatim. Use your own words and ways of communicating the same concepts.
- Be aware that this topic is often a distinctly fraught and challenging one for participants, and that participants will likely come into the session with strong feelings about the subject. Be sure to emphasize the need for respectful language, and the need for the session to respectfully include a diverse assortment of perspectives at the beginning of the session and throughout.
- Research and create an affirming resource list specific to your local community. We have included our own resource list for an example of a potential template, and facilitators may find some of the websites, texts, and resources listed useful for them, regardless of region. When it comes to local religious institutions and leaders, we strongly recommend that facilitators vet recommended affirming and accepting institutions before listing a religious organization or leader on their resource sheet, as we have discovered through such vetting that some institutions which claim to be affirming are, in fact, not supporters of LGBTQIA+ people or rights.
- Ask participants to put away phones and electronic devices before the session starts.

<h1 style="text-align:center">CURRICULUM—2 HOURS</h1>

Curriculum Outline
- Introductions, PGPs, What is Safe Zone?—10 minutes
- Laying of ground rules for discussion and activities—5 minutes
- Notecard Activity and Discussion: Personal experiences and beliefs regarding religion and LGBTQIA+ issues—30 minutes
- Film clip from *For the Bible Tells Me So* and discussion—15 minutes
- Grace Model—Role Play Scenario: Having a discussion with a faculty or staff member and student—30 minutes
- Debrief and Discussion—15 minutes
- Concluding Discussion Resource Distribution, Closing Activity—15 minutes

Learning Outcomes
- Introduce some of the key challenges facing LGBTQIA+ people of faith seeking to balance both identities.
- Provide participants with information and resources regarding LGBTQIA+ issues primarily in an Abrahamic religious context.
- Provide participants with information about how to be allies to LGBTQIA+ people struggling with religious concerns.

Materials
- Note cards
- Writing utensils

Handouts
- Ground Rules and Guidelines
- Safe Zone Clobber Passages: Finding Affirmation in Scripture
- Homosexuality Is Not a Biblical Concern handout by Daniel Helmniak
- Liberating Qur'an handout
- GRACE model
- Resource List and Local Affirming Resources (customize your own)
- Evaluation Sheet

<h2 style="text-align:center">INTRODUCTIONS: PGP'S, GROUND RULES—15 MINUTES</h2>

Use the introductions section explained in chapter 4 Fundamentals on page 28. Include introductions, PGPs, Ground Rules, Parking Lot, and review of the Safe Zone program.

Disclaimer Section
Directions

- After introducing the session topic, pass out ground rules handout to participants as they join the session.

PROCESS STATEMENT: *"The purpose of this module is to open discussions and provide information about LGBTQIA+ issues and how they intersect with religious faith and belief—it is not to try to question participants' faith (or lack thereof), but rather to ensure that UIS allies (regardless of their personal religious views, or lack thereof) have information and resources to give to LGBTQIA+ students about religious issues, and have information about how to have productive conversations about these issues on campus.*

"This session is open and affirming to all participants, regardless of what their own personal faith (or lack thereof) might be. We are aware that the issues that we will be grappling with today are complex, challenging, and difficult. The material that we will be discussing is very sensitive and personal, so please be respectful of your own feelings and the feelings of others in participating in this module. If at any point you need to take a break, feel free to quietly leave and return. And if our session raises any issues or questions that you would like to discuss further, please let a facilitator know after our session.

"Please be sure to use respectful language throughout this module. Though we encourage discussion, please make sure that those discussions happen in respectful ways, and that disagreements are expressed in a courteous way. Derogatory language or negative stereotyping do not have a place in this module.

"This session welcomes the presence of those from any and all (or no) faith traditions, and believes in the potential of all participants, regardless of faith tradition or lack thereof, to be good and supportive allies to LGBTQIA+ people struggling with issues of religious identity and affiliation."

IMPORTANT DISCLAIMER: *"Please note that while we as your facilitators have done considerable reading and research into the topics that we will be discussing today, we are not personally members of clergy or theological scholars. In our session today, we will provide you with resources to have productive conversations about religious issues with LGBTQIA+ community members and resources for LGBTQIA+ community members currently struggling with reconciling their LGBTQIA+ and religious identities (including suggested readings and community resources). We intend for this session to be a beginning place for this discussion and engagement, rather than a definitive and all-inclusive course on LGBTQIA+ issues and all religious traditions."*

PROCESS QUESTIONS:
- Are the ground rules for this session clear?
- Do you have any questions or concerns about any of these ground rules?
- Do any of these rules require clarification?

IMPORTANT: Allow people to discreetly leave the session, if needed, during the screen name activity that is next.

NOTECARD ACTIVITY & DISCUSSION—30 MINUTES

A. Goals
- To learn more about module participants' current understandings of and thoughts about religion and members of the LGBTQIA+ community.
- To allow participants to begin discussions of their own personal beliefs and concerns (and the ideas which they have observed in their own or other faith traditions) about the intersections between religious and faith traditions and LGBTQIA+ issues and people.
- To allow participants to begin these discussions in a safer anonymous way, as they will initially be discussing an index card expressing someone else's ideas and experiences, rather than their own ideas and experiences (which can be useful in "warming up" participants to discuss these fraught and difficult issues).

B. Directions
- Distribute index cards and writing instruments to participants.
- Write the questions which groups will be reflecting on the board (or have them available on a PowerPoint).
- Tell participants to anonymously write their thoughts about the intersections between religion and LGBTQIA+ issues, and their own personal experiences and beliefs about the intersection of LGBTQIA+ issues and religion, on their note cards.
- Participants will write about the first question listed below on their first note card (which they will label with a "1" on the back of the card), and write about the second question listed below on their second note card (which they will label with a "2" on the back of the card).
- After giving participants about 5 minutes to write, facilitators will then come around and collect these cards (one facilitator collecting all of the "1" cards, and another facilitator collecting all of the "2" cards).
- Be sure to note to participants that if they are not comfortable passing in their card, they do not need to do so. Facilitators will then shuffle and redistribute these cards to participant members, so that each participant receives a "1" card and a "2" card. Give the participants a minute or two to read over the cards they have received. Then break the session into small groups (counting off by four or fives, or a smaller or larger number, depending on the size of the group—the ideal group will have about four or five members), and have them share the ideas and themes that they noticed on their cards with one another. Give them about 5 minutes to have these discussions. Then, bring the group back together as a whole, and ask the group to share their insights.

PROCESS STATEMENT: *"To begin our session, we will be asking you to write on your index cards what your own current views are, about religion and faith-based belief systems regarding the LGBTQIA+ community. You will write about the first question on Card 1, and about the second question on Card 2. You will find these questions at the front of the room on the blackboard (or the PowerPoint). Then, if you are comfortable with doing so, you'll be discussing these ideas with a small group which we'll break you into, and then we'll discuss these issues together as a larger group."*

1. What challenges do you think LGBTQIA+ members of faith traditions continue to face in contemporary society? How do you think faith traditions impact LGBTQIA+ people?
2. If you yourself have been or are a member of a faith or spiritual community, what are your own personal experiences and beliefs about LGBTQIA+ people and issues, and what are the beliefs and values of that community? (If this question does not apply to you just focus on question 1.)

The following are common responses taken from previous sessions:

NOTE: This is not a completely comprehensive list, but rather an outline of the most frequently received responses from previous sessions. We would recommend keeping an ongoing list of common responses and keep those listed here in mind as you facilitate your session. Also please note that for this section, we have combined common answers we have received for Questions 1 and 2, as the content of these responses is often quite similar.

- Challenges in personally reconciling gender identity and/or sexual orientation with teachings of faith tradition
- Struggling with internalized homophobia, biphobia, transphobia, and self-hatred, if raised within a faith tradition which defines being LGBTQIA+ as "wrong" or "against God"
- Challenges of being told by religious leaders, fellow members of religious community, and family and friends that homosexuality is a "sin" or an "abomination"
- Challenges of being taught by religious leaders, fellow members of a religious community, and family and friends that sexual orientation is a "choice" and a faithful person can "choose" not to be LGBTQIA+ (and sometimes facing efforts to "convert" person to heterosexuality)
- Being taught that religious doctrines and scriptures of faith tradition condemn LGBTQIA+ people (that they are going to hell, that God hates them, etc.)
- Being taught that the only way for LGBTQIA+ people to find acceptance within their religious community and/or from God is for them to permanently remain celibate
- Difficulty of rejecting teachings of religious institution and religious family and friends that LGBTQIA+ people cannot be religious, cannot be moral, and cannot find acceptance from their religious community or from God
- Not having full access to all religious rites and rituals within a particular religious community if one is out as LGBTQIA+
- Being denied access to positions of religious leadership and positions working with youth in a religious community (because of fears of LGBTQIA+ people as "corrupting" young people)
- Lack of visibility of LGBTQIA+ people in religious teachings, religious scripture, and religious community (as fellow community members and/or as religious leaders)
- Lack of affirmation for LGBTQIA+ couples and lack of access to marriage equality within religious institution
- Rejection by religious community, and religious family and friends, after coming out as LGBTQIA+
- Struggling with individual people and even entire congregations being accepting of LGBTQIA+ people, but remaining with a broader religious tradition which is not accepting of LGBTQIA+ people
- Struggling to make change in favor of the acceptance of LGBTQIA+ on an institutional, as well as a personal level (i.e., trying to change the policies of a religious institution, rather than simply finding personal affirmation from specific members of that institution)
- Challenge of finding and/or creating a new, affirming religious community and/or spiritual belief system
- Deciding to leave non-affirming religious community for a new, affirming religious community
- Deciding to leave organized religious communities altogether
- For agnostic or atheist allies, working to understand the importance of religious community and/or beliefs for struggling LGBTQIA+ family, friends, and community members

PROCESS QUESTIONS:
- What about your group's insights from the index cards you received did you find particularly striking? Surprising? Significant?
- Are there elements of the intersections between faith traditions and the LGBTQIA+ community which we are missing on our list of the common themes and issues which we have already discussed? If so, what are they?
- What challenges, if any, did you have in writing and thinking about the intersections of faith traditions (your own, or others with which you are familiar) and LGBTQIA+ issues?

Tips for Facilitators
- Please be sure to stress throughout that participants need only share as much as they feel comfortable: if they are not comfortable filling out either or both note cards for this exercise, or turning their note cards in to facilitators, please make it clear that they do not need to do so. The note card activity is entirely anonymous, but it is still possible (especially in smaller groups) that participants might wish to opt out of part of the activity. Facilitators underlining this option throughout can be useful in ensuring participants' comfort level.
- Please also be mindful of the time constraints of this activity, and be aware that this exercise will not be able to "resolve" all discussions about LGBTQIA+ issues and religion which it raises in the limited time allotted. It is very likely that facilitators will not be able to fully delve into all the issues and concerns raised in this introductory exercise during the 30 minutes allotted, which is totally fine. Since facilitators will be making a list of participants' insights on the board, they will be able to return to and expand on these points, concerns, and issues raised by participants throughout the session. (Some of these issues may also need to go into the "Parking Lot" and be addressed by facilitators individually after the session is over.)
- Please also keep in mind that this exercise may raise painful or difficult topics for participants to consider. Since participants are asked to discuss their own personal experiences concerning LGBTQIA+ people and issues in faith communities, some participants will likely bring up painful experiences of discrimination and oppression. As facilitators, please be conscious of the emotional, challenging nature of this exercise and check in with participants to ensure that they are receiving the necessary support and encouragement from facilitators, and that facilitators maintain a supportive, welcoming environment throughout.

FILM CLIP FROM *FOR THE BIBLE TELLS ME SO* & DISCUSSION—15 MINUTES

A. Goals
- Introduce several of the key debates within the Abrahamic faiths about LGBTQIA+ issues.
- Outline and discuss the reasons why having an in-depth scriptural discussion with an LGBTQIA+ person (or someone challenging the idea that an LGBTQIA+ person can reconcile their involvement with an Abrahamic faith tradition with their sexual orientation and/or gender identity) is not a productive approach for allies.
- Provide resources and an introduction to discussions about specific Bible passages which have been interpreted in an anti-LGBTQIA+ way, and learn about the existence and nature of different affirming reinterpretations of these passages.

B. Directions
- Have the film clip queued up at the beginning of the session, watch the clip, and discuss.
- The film clip "What Does the Bible Say" on the interpretation of Bible verses runs from 18 minutes and 45 seconds to 24 minutes and 30 seconds.
- Watch the brief film clip from *For the Bible Tells Me So*, and then discuss the ideas and issues raised in the clip.

PROCESS QUESTION (Before the clip):
- Could we see a show of hands, who would be comfortable having a biblical scripture debate with another person that believes homosexuality is a sin?

NOTE: It will vary session by session as to how many participants will raise their hands. In some sessions, the majority of participants will believe that they can—and should—engage in such scriptural debates, and in some sessions, few or no participants will.

C. Group Discussion

PROCESS STATEMENT: *"Engaging in debate about scripture is often counterproductive, as it can devolve into arguments which are more confrontational than useful. (And depending, may demand that you have knowledge about particular sacred texts, which you do not have.) However, LGBTQIA+ students in need of this information may want to engage in a discussion of sacred texts, and learn more about how and where to gain information about affirming interpretations of scripture. In this part of our session, we want to draw your attention to some of the resources in your packet, and some of our recommended readings, which will be useful for LGBTQIA+ community members seeking such information."* (Point to the Clobber Passages handout.)

VIDEO PROCESS STATEMENT: *"In this section of our session, we will be watching a brief clip from the documentary* For the Bible Tells Me So. *This clip is designed to allow participants to learn more about some of the biblical passages most commonly used against LGBTQIA+ people, and to hear these passages reinterpreted by open and affirming theologians, scholars, and religious leaders. Once we watch the clip, we'll discuss the ideas which the film raises."*

PROCESS STATEMENT FROM CLIP ONE: *"Here in the clip we just viewed, individuals were responding to those who would use scripture to condemn LGBTQIA+ people. Yet, they did not directly address other interpretations of the six or so passages commonly used. In your Clobber Passages handout, you can find these as well as affirming same-gender couples: Jonathan and David, and Ruth and Naomi. We do not have time to address every passage here today and our intent is not to arm you for debate on these passages but to know that LGBTQIA+ and allied people of faith interpret these passages from a liberation theology point of view. An example of this is the story of Lot found in the Koran and the Bible."*

PROCESS STATEMENT: *"One of the most cited as anti-gay is the story of Lot and the sin of Sodom and Gomorrah, which is in reality not about homosexuality at all but, rather, is about the sin of inhospitality. Thousands of years ago, humans in the Middle East lived in an agrarian culture. Herding of animals was common. It was considered sinful to not offer shelter or a place to bed for the night to a fellow herder.*

This hospitality was commonplace and an important facet of the culture that is the crux of the story. Lot was providing shelter to strangers but the townspeople wished to hurt them by raping them. Rather than turning over his guests to the mob, Lot offered his daughters to be raped by them instead. This story is therefore clearly not about consensual same-gender-loving relationships. The sin of Sodom is not about homosexuality, but rather the sins of inhospitality and rape. This sexuality-sensitive interpretation is how LGBTQIA+ people of the Christian, Jewish, and Muslim faiths can reconcile this story with their own gender and/or sexual identities."

PROCESS POINTS:
- Mention Islam and homosexuality. Similar stories in the Koran (Liberating Qur'an: Islamic Scripture Kugle Handout).
- Mention same-gender relationships in the Bible: Jonathan and David, Ruth and Naomi (Clobber Passages Handout).

PROCESS QUESTIONS:
- Was the information contained in the clip surprising to you? Did it give you any new perspectives on how the Bible has been (and is) used against LGBTQIA+ people? About how the Bible might be used in an open and affirming way?
- How can we as allies use the information contained in this clip in positive ways when working with students struggling with multiple identities as people of faith and LGBTQIA+?

Tips for Facilitators
- Choose your own example if the story of Lot is not suitable.
- Do not let this example turn into a debate about scripture and scriptural interpretation in the room. This particular section is not designed to encourage debate about scripture, but rather to provide examples for LGBTQIA+ people and their allies of how specific scriptural passages can and have been reinterpreted by scholars to be affirming.

- Point to the Clobber Passages handout and emphasize that as allies, it is Safe Zone members' responsibility to give LGBTQIA+ community members (who desire them) resources about affirming interpretations of scripture, rather than personally engaging in debate about those scriptures.

THE GRACE MODEL—30 MINUTES

A. Goals
- Practice speaking with someone working to reconcile faith with sexuality/gender.
- Use the GRACE model by Bozard and Sanders (2011) as a framework for discussion.

B. Directions
- Split participants into small groups.
- Hand out one scenario per small group.
- Play video: go.uis.edu/GRACEmodel.
- Play the video through 5:00 minute mark at the end of the "Goals" slides.
- At this point, hand out various student "scenarios" (which are provided later in this chapter).
- Have the groups think about how they would address "Goals" with their particular student. Give them 10 minutes at most to read and discuss.
- Have each group share their scenario and their thoughts on "Goals" with the rest of the attendees (15 minutes).
- Spend 5 minutes wrapping up the GRACE model and offer the video and materials for further self-instruction to review the other steps.
  ◦ If offering a longer session, play the video through "Renewal of Hope" and stop when Brady starts his demonstration with Maureen.
- Have each of the groups think about how they would address "Renewal of Hope" with their particular student.
- Have each group share their scenario and their thoughts on "Renewal of Hope" with the rest of the attendees.
- Play the video through "Action" and stop when Brady starts his demonstration with Maureen.
- Have each of the groups think about how they would address "Action" with their particular student.
- Have each group share their scenario and their thoughts on "Action" with the rest of the attendees.
- Play the video through "Connection" and stop when Brady starts his demonstration with Maureen.
- Have each of the groups think about how they would address "Connection" with their particular student.
- Have each group share their scenario and their thoughts on "Connection" with the rest of the attendees.
- Play the rest of the GRACE model presentation.
- Answer any questions or comments.

C. GRACE Model Scenarios

1. Emilio is a freshman first-generation college student. He is struggling to maintain his grades and is also taking care of his family. He has several younger siblings that are dependent on him and his mother for support. Emilio comes into your office and his appearance is haggard. His personal hygiene is lacking and there are large bags under his eyes.

   After brief small talk Emilio reluctantly discloses some details about his personal life. He states that he would like to talk about options available for someone who is Catholic and gay. Emilio has a boyfriend and is ashamed to be seen in public with him because of his family's beliefs and religious values. He knows that his shame is affecting his relationship. He is upset because he does not believe that he can balance his relationship and his family's expectations for him.

   When questioned further, Emilio states that he has never felt a strong connection to the Catholic tradition. However, Emilio becomes agitated when you bring up the idea of possibly converting to another religion.

2. Katrina is a sophomore studying political science who hopes to get an internship at the capitol. Her grades are excellent and she is involved in volleyball and is also an active member in the APO (Alpha Phi Omega) service fraternity. She states that most of her friend group comes from her fraternity and that they have been an incredible support system for her. She presents as bright and clean with good personal hygiene.

   During the initial small talk she discusses her love for Pomeranians. She defines her relationship with her family as "good." She mentions that her family tolerates her dating other women, but that they do not want "that nonsense" coming home from school with her. When she attempts to push the issue with her family they state that her grandmother has a weak heart and would not be able to handle the fact that she is bisexual. They have told her that she needs to stop being so selfish. You can see the blood rush to her face and her shoulders tense as she retells this story.

At one point she scans your offices and her eyes rest on a flag that has the word "Acceptance" written across it. Each letter in the word "acceptance" is a symbol from a different religion (i.e., the "T" is a cross). Katrina scoffs and mumbles something about religion being a bunch of "hocus-pocus" believed in by "wack-a-doos." She then launches into a discussion about safe dating in relationships between two women. She also asks you if you are aware of any literature on how to help others come to terms with one's sexual orientation.

3. Jack presents as very timid. He does not make eye contact and mumbles frequently. You saw him pacing outside of your office for approximately 5–10 minutes before you went outside and asked him if he needed something. He appeared startled but also relieved that you invited him into your office. You notice that he winces as he sits down. You ask him if he is okay and he quickly says that he is fine.

    After you ask him how you can help, he states that he is struggling with his sense of spirituality. You have a steady conversation for a few minutes about his background in a Jewish family and his decision to transition to Paganism. He states that it was difficult for his family to accept at first, but they eventually came around. He is even able to joke about it at family holidays. He expresses a strong interest in finding a Pagan community as well as how to create a Pagan student group at the university.

    Jack appears to be warming up when he adjusts his shirtsleeve and you see a series of bruises. You ask Jack about the bruises and he immediately becomes defensive. There is a moment of silence and you ask Jack if there is anything else he would like to discuss. He mumbles something about his sexuality. When asked to clarify he states, "Look, things like this happen all the time when you're gay. . . . I shouldn't have been so stupid. It won't happen again." He mumbles something about walking across campus late at night. When you attempt to question him further he shuts down.

4. Allison is a graduate student and is working on her MBA. She stated that she had seen the Safe Zone logo on your door and had finally worked up the courage to come in and talk to you. She says that she is struggling in her current relationship with another woman. She has grown up in the Baptist tradition and she still feels a strong connection to it. Her family is also very accepting of her identity as a lesbian. However, she has been relegated to self-study with her Bible because she has yet to find a congregation that is okay with her being open about her sexuality.

    To complicate matters her partner is against organized religion. They have had frequent arguments about Allison's desire to go to church. Allison says her partner has told her to "give up on it. Those religious idiots don't care about you, why should you care about them or their God?" Allison appears to be hopeless and frustrated. She states that she cannot stay for much longer because she has a class in a few minutes. When you question her further about the arguments with her partner and what Allison wants she states: "I am sorry I bothered you with this. It's stupid that I am even trying to do this. I am never going to feel 100 percent comfortable with my church, relationship, or sexuality. I just need to learn to accept that."

Tips for Facilitators

- This portion of the session will need at least 30 minutes to work through to "Goals" of the GRACE model. Consider offering a longer session to cover more steps in the model.
- Offer a separate session to review the GRACE model in its entirety.
- If at any point time starts to run out you can simply play the rest of the presentation and have them discuss it all at the end.
- It is not necessary to have them discuss each letter of the GRACE model. Determine which letters lend to the best discussion and utilize those letters.
- You may also summarize a particular letter of the GRACE model instead of having the video play. This could be used as a method to save time.
- If you decide to refer students to a particular place of worship as described in the "Action" stage, make sure you research and vet the places you refer students to.
- Attempt to use real-life examples, such as an experience you had calling a church to confirm they are accepting, to clarify points in the presentation, as this will make the material more relatable for participants.

EVALUATION AND TAKEAWAY CLOSING ACTIVITY—15 MINUTES

A. Goals
- Provide a brief overview of the contents of the session by allowing participants to voice their personal experience.
- Close the session on a high point.
- Allow for evaluation and feedback.

B. Directions

- Pass out the Evaluation Sheet and allow a few minutes to complete.
- Closing Activity: *"We'd like to conclude our session today by distributing a list of resources which you can draw on in your work as an ally at our institution. The list contains a variety of different resources about books, films, and websites about a variety of different religions and LGBTQIA+ issues, and local religious communities and ministers which/who are open and affirming to the LGBTQIA+ community. We hope that these resources will be useful for you in working with LGBTQIA+ students who might find additional resources, and learning more about open and affirming religious communities of value.*

   To conclude our session, we would also like to explore what are "you leaving here and what are you taking with you? Perhaps it's a myth or new piece of information or a story you heard. Think about this while completing your evaluation. Does anyone want to go first?"

Tips for Facilitators

- Please stress to participants that the list of resources provided is not intended to be fully comprehensive or exhaustive or to represent the full breadth of scholarship on the issues discussed, but rather to provide introductions and overviews to key facets of the session. Also, be sure to note that facilitators welcome suggestions from participants about potential resources to add, particularly when it comes to potentially affirming religious communities in the local area.
- Please emphasize how important participant feedback is to facilitators, how seriously they take it, and how useful it is for them in crafting future sessions. Strongly encourage participants to leave specific, written feedback about what they thought worked especially well during the session, and what they felt needed improvement. (It can sometimes be a challenge to get participants to leave this extensive feedback, as the evaluation portion comes at the end of the session, and participants can sometimes feel rushed for time. So be sure to allot sufficient time for participants to share their thoughts. Start evaluations before you begin with the closing activity.)
- Please note to participants that facilitators are always available if participants have more questions or concerns they want to discuss after the session is over, and that the end of the session does not need to mean the end of the discussions which the session raised.

CHAPTER 7

Gender & Transgender Workshop

KERRY JOHN POYNTER

"Instead of saying that all gender is this or all gender is that, let's recognize that the word gender *has scores of meaning built into it. It's an amalgamation of bodies, identities, and life experiences, subconscious urges, sensations, and behaviors, some of which develop organically, and others which are shaped by language and culture. Instead of saying that gender is any one single thing, let's start describing it as a holistic experience."*

—*Kate Bornstein*

This chapter references handouts (available as a single PDF formatted for easy and clear printing on 8.5" × 11") that supplement the curriculum and assessment pieces of this book. Please email resourcematerial@rowman.com to request the PDF, providing both the title and editor of this book along with proof of purchase (receipt).

DESCRIPTION

Transgender people continue to be an invisible, often forgotten part of the LGBTQIA+ community. This session helps participants develop self-awareness and compassion, and develop the tools to think critically about their own assumptions and previously held understanding as related to gender. Participants will learn about the gender binary, learn accurate terms, explore potential gender transition processes, and consider common topics and challenges in higher education. This session is recommended for any person wanting to learn how to become a better ally to this population.

CONTEXTUALIZATION

Western culture continues to support a gender binary that relies on individual characteristics and actions to define male or female, masculine and feminine. When discussions of transgender people occur they often deal with specific and limiting discussions centered solely on sex confirmation surgeries and access to health care. This leaves out other broader considerations about gender and the spectrum of gender non-conforming people's identities.

Although medical access can be important for some trans individuals, it is but one of the topics any aspiring cisgender ally to trans people should learn. An effective trans ally will understand gender and biological sex, how the gender binary operates in society, how one may consciously or unconsciously reinforce this binary, gender as a continuum of multiple gender identities, and common themes for trans, transgender, gender non-conforming, as well as intersex individuals.

The abbreviation "trans" is often used to refer to a non-binary person or community of people that are between a binary of male or female who cross boundaries intended to contain a limiting view of gender. This term also allows a person to state a gender variant identity (such as transsexual/transgender) without having to disclose possible hormonal or surgical status/intentions. Gay, lesbian, and bisexual people can be gender non-conforming as well, but their sexual orientation should not be assumed because of their gender expression.

Terminology used to describe a continuum of gender, beyond the binary of male and female, is ever evolving and thus should be carefully considered when interacting with trans individuals. Popular culture and media in the Western world often use the word "transgender" when referring to a person that is transsexual (MTF: male to female; FTM: female to male). However, other terms and identities exist under the trans umbrella such as genderqueer, cross-dresser, gender-bender, female or male impersonators (drag performers), and intersex, to name a few. These terms are but only a few of the myriad in use by trans and cisgender allies.

A cisgender (sounds like sisgender) or cis person matches with the gender identity and gender expression expectations that were assigned to them based on their physical sex and are *universally considered valid*. Just as definitions of masculine and feminine change with culture, location, and time, these trans terms can change as well. Studying them is appropriate but solely attempting to recite them by memory does not make a strong trans ally!

Confusion about trans terminology and the difference between sex and gender can be centered on intersex versus transsexual identities. These are two distinct categories that may experience some similar transition processes but the similarity ends there. An intersex person is born with sex chromosomes, external genitalia, or an internal reproductive system that is not considered "standard" for either male or female (preferred term to the obsolete "hermaphrodite").

It is estimated, based on a survey of medical literature, that 2 percent (some estimates are as high as 4 percent) of live births are intersex (Blackless, Charuvastra, Derryck, Fausto-Sterling, Lauzanne, & Lee, 2000). Many of these births receive "corrective" genital surgery. Medical consensus has not adequately determined accurate courses of action to modify intersex bodies yet we should remain critical of attempts to surgically intervene (mutilate?) infants, when no medical reason exists, due to a cultural insistence on a binary of gender linked solely to genitals.

Allowing intersex individuals to claim their own gender identity later in life may precipitate transition processes similar to transgender individuals. Intersex individuals are not typically considered transgender but may experience gender transition processes similar to a transsexual or trans person, particularly if their genitals have been altered at birth and/or they were assigned an incorrect gender.

Medical transition for transsexuals includes a myriad of options including hormones, nongenital surgeries, and sex confirmation surgeries (Brown & Rounsley, 2003). Not all transgender people choose or need to go through these medical options to legally change their sex. Surgeries for female to male (FTM) transsexuals typically include three surgeries while male to female (MTF) may only include one.

Gender confirmation surgeries are prohibitively expensive. "In the United States today, (gender) confirmation surgeries can cost from $10,000 to $45,000 for MTF's and from $25,000 to $100,000 for FTM's who have a phalloplasty, hysterectomy, vaginoctomy, and mastectomy" (Brown & Rounsley, 2003, p. 209). Non-genital surgeries can include a tracheal shave, baldness correction, and voice surgery. Unfortunately, most insurance companies do not cover these procedures, but as understanding and advocacy continues, adopting these procedures as part of health insurance will become industry standard (Human Rights Campaign, 2014). These surgeries are a part of a larger transitioning process that also includes the social and cultural transition among the community, work, and family.

Visibility

It may seem that transgender visibility is a recent phenomenon. The history and existence of trans people in the United States can be traced to the early days of the women's movement and the beginnings of the modern-day lesbian, gay, bi, trans, queer (LGBTQ) rights movement (Stryker, 2008). However, trans people can be found throughout history in numerous cultures (Feinberg, 1996; Jacobs, Thomas, & Lang, 1997; Nanda, 1999; Roscoe, 1997).

Indeed, there is now a growing critical discourse in academia on the existence of multiple genders and sexes (Herdt, 1997). These multiple distinct identities, built on one's own gender identity, provide visibility to those that locate themselves within a continuum of gender and expression. This gender continuum includes women, genderqueer people, and men (gender identity); and feminine, gender non-conforming/androgynous, and masculine (gender expression) (Killerman, 2013). Everyone, trans and cisgender, falls within this continuum dependent on their identity and how they choose to express it based on location, community, and culture.

Visibility has been a contributor to a generational shift among those coming out as transgender in their youth. During the early twenty-first century more youth have come out as transgender while transgender adults in their forties and fifties have come out later in life (Beemyn & Rankin, 2011). This has occurred in part due to access to readily available information such as the Internet, awareness in popular culture, and being able to meet other transgender people. Older transgender individuals often have repressed their feelings due to opposition from society and family.

With visibility comes another set of challenges for trans people. The gender binary is enforced in part by violence against gender non-conforming people. This gender-based violence targets victims because of their real or perceived gender, gender identity, or gender expression (Nibley, 2009; Wilchins & Taylor, 2006). Additionally, trans youth are targeted or bullied, regardless of sexual orientation, in primary/elementary education as well as higher education (Rankin, Weber, Blumenfeld, & Frazer, 2010).

"Research shows that hostility toward gender non-conformity starts early and is commonplace. In one recent study, 54% of youth reported that their school was unsafe for guys who aren't as masculine as other guys, while one-quarter (27%) complained of being bullied themselves for not being masculine or feminine enough. In another, 61% of students reported seeing gender non-conforming classmates verbally attacked, and more than one-fifth (21%) reported seeing them physically assaulted" (Wilchins & Taylor, 2006).

A lack of safety then extends to employment. Workplace discrimination is pervasive, especially for trans people of color. Additionally, transgender people are four times more likely to have a household income under $10,000 per year compared to the general U.S. population (Grant, Mottet, & Tanis, 2011). Consequences of this violence, discrimination, and bullying include a suicide rate of 41 percent, compared to 1.6 percent of the general population, as well as mental health concerns including gender dysphoria (Grant, Mottet, & Tanis, 2011).

It should not be surprising that transgender people can experience gender dysphoria, in a society that does not understand, in a culture that values strict male or female specific identities. The American Psychological Association and the *Diagnostic and Statistical Manual of Mental Disorders* now describe gender dysphoria as distress and not as a psychological disorder (APA, 2014). Not all transgender people should be diagnosed with gender dysphoria.

Even among the LGBQA (sexual minority) community there has been criticism and confusion about the inclusion of, and need for, the "T" (Aravosis, 2007; Stryker, 2007). This ambivalence leads to trans advocacy being left out of organizing and support functions of mainstream gay and lesbian organizations.

LGBQA+ cisgender people also need education on trans identities. Although the case has been made that gender identity is not the same as sexual orientation, it should not be forgotten that GLB folk also have to reexamine gender norms when in same-sex relationships. Perhaps the most salient reason cisgender GLB people should be concerned about trans people is that harassment, bias, and hate crimes are often perpetrated against people that are perceived to be LGBTQIA+ based solely on their gender identity/expression (Ahmed & Jindasurat, 2014).

As youth and young adults develop their gender identity and sexual orientation, many experiment with gender expression, and build more nuanced and complex relationships to gender and sexuality regardless of their sexual orientation. This can be in conflict with a Western society and culture that is organized around a gender binary. Due to this strict binary, it can be difficult to facilitate dialogues about gender identity and expression on a continuum. Facilitation and education should be centered around encouraging the participants to consider how they create and express their own gender as well as how they may reinforce a binary in their everyday lives. This curriculum is an attempt to address this need.

READINGS FOR FACILITATORS
The following annotated readings are intended as starting points for new learners on gender and transgender topics. They support the learning goals of the curriculum explained in this section. Facilitators should use them as means of self-education and reference for those participants inquiring for additional information. They will also be beneficial to group discussion among co-facilitators before presenting and especially in facilitating the activities contained in this curriculum.

- Brown, M. L., & Rounsley, C. A. (2003). The transexual dilemma. In *True selves: Understanding transsexualism—For families, friends, coworkers, and helping professionals* (pp. 5–29). San Francisco: Jossey-Bass.

The authors explain transexuality in a clear, concise fashion for the novice learner. Topics covered include gender dysphoria, prevalence of transsexuals, a brief review of surgeries, common terms that may be confusing, sex versus gender, biological and socialization theories of causation, and a brief history of transgender people. New learners and facilitators should begin their education with this chapter.

- Brown, M. L., & Rounsley, C. A. (2003). Medical and surgical options. In *True selves: Understanding transsexualism— For families, friends, coworkers, and helping professionals* (pp. 196–211). San Francisco: Jossey-Bass.
  The authors explain the many possible medical and surgical options available to transsexual people. Hormones are explained in detail with the affects on a female-to-male (MTF) or a male-to-female (FTM) person. Surgical options include non-genital options that are most common as well as explanations of sex reassignment surgery (often called sex confirmation surgery) for MTF and FTM individuals and the associated costs. The chapter concludes by explaining surgeries as a personal choice that not every transsexual person undergoes and the possible psychological results. Facilitators will benefit by having an overview of possible medical and surgical options as questions on this topic will arise.

- Nibley, L. (Director). (2009). *Two spirits* [Motion picture on DVD & Study Guide]. United States: Cinema Guild.
  This documentary educates on Two-Spirit Native Americans through the story of Fred Martinez who was murdered for being gender non-conforming or "Two-Spirit." The film includes an introductory review of Two-Spirit (previously labeled Berdache by colonizing Europeans) people and how Europeans policed the multiple genders of Native Americans. Viewers are left wondering how we are still policing gender in contemporary society. Facilitators will gain helpful historical information on Two-Spirit people that will help in explaining gender beyond male and female in non-European cultures and how bias, harassment, and hate crimes manifest in society toward gender non-conforming people. Please see the additional suggested readings contained in this chapter for more information on Two-Spirit Native Americans and other cultures from around the world.

- Stryker, S. (2008). Transgender terms and concepts. In *Transgender history* (pp. 1–29), Berkeley, CA: Seal Press.
  Historian Susan Stryker provides a history of transgender people in the last century. The first chapter is an overview of terms and concepts including a brief introduction to a biological basis to gender identity, a brief look at religion, and gender identity disorder (now called dysphoria). This chapter pairs nicely with "The Transexual Dilemma" by Brown and Rounsley (2006) and will help new facilitators with introductory knowledge on terms and transgender concepts.

- Thomas, A. (Director). (2006). *Middle sexes: Redefining he and she* [Motion picture on DVD]. United States: Home Box Office.
  Middle Sexes provides insight into gender as a continuum of identities by interviewing people from around the world in various cultures that are transsexual, intersex, and gender non-conforming such as the "ladieboys" in Thailand. Science is also included and the section on biology of transsexual and intersex individuals proves useful when explaining the differences between the two (also used in this curriculum). Facilitators will find this useful in further understanding how gender versus sexual orientation manifests in people from various backgrounds and how different societies respond.

- Wilchins, W., & Taylor, T. (2006). *50 under 30: Masculinity and the war on America's youth*. Gender Public Advocacy Coalition. Retrieved July 27, 2012, from http://iambecauseweare.files.wordpress.com/2007/05/50u30.pdf.
  GenderPAC released a report in 2006 that advocated for an expansion of hate crimes reporting to include gender-based violence. This report describes how gender non-conforming youth are specifically targeted by males with murderous aggression that are enforcing standards of masculinity. Victims are most often people of color, poor, not transfeminine, and largely ignored by the media. This report is a good follow-up to the *Two-Spirits* film (2009) when explaining how gender-based violence continues to be used to police gender expression of LGBTQ people.

REFERENCES

Adams, M., Bell, L., & Griffin, P. (Eds.). (2007). *Teaching for diversity and social justice: A sourcebook* (2nd ed.). New York: Routledge.

Ahmed, O., & Jindasurat, C. (2014). *Lesbian, gay, bisexual, transgender, queer and HIV-affected hate violence in 2013* (pp. 1–138, Rep. No. 2014 Release Edition). New York, NY: National Coalition of Anti-Violence Programs.

American Psychological Association (2014). Gender dysphoria. In *Diagnostic and statistical manual of mental disorders*. Accessed July 21, 2014, from http://www.dsm5.org.

Aravosis, J. (2010). How did the T get in LGBT? In D. T. Meem, M. Gibson, & J. Alexander (Eds.), *Finding out: An introduction to LGBT studies* (pp. 172–74). Los Angeles: Sage.

Beemyn, G., & Rankin, S. (2011). *The lives of transgender people*. New York, NY: Columbia University Press.

Bornstein, K., & Bergman, S. B. (2010). *Gender outlaws: The next generation*. Berkeley, CA: Seal Press.

Blackless, M., Charuvastra, A., Derryck, A., Fausto-Sterling, A., Lauzanne, K., & Lee, E. (2000). How sexually dimorphic are we? Review and synthesis. *American Journal of Human Biology, 12*(2), 151–66. doi:10.1002/(SICI)1520-6300(200003/04)12:23.0.CO;2-F.

Brown, M. L., & Rounsley, C. A. (2003). The transsexual dilemma. In *True selves: Understanding transsexualism—For families, friends, coworkers, and helping professionals*. San Francisco: Jossey-Bass.

Davies, S. G. (2007). *Challenging gender norms: Five genders among Bugis in Indonesia*. Belmont, CA: Thomson Wadsworth.

Feinberg, L. (1996). *Transgender warriors: Making history from Joan of Arc to Dennis Rodman*. Boston, MA: Beacon Press.

Grant, J. M., Mottet, L. A., & Tanis, J. (2011). *Injustice at every turn: A report of the national transgender discrimination survey* (pp. 1–221). Washington, DC: National Gay and Lesbian Task Force.

Herdt, G. (1997). Third genders, third sexes. In D. Duberman (Ed.), *A queer world* (pp. 65–81). New York, NY: New York University Press.

Human Rights Campaign. (2014). Finding insurance for transgender-related healthcare. Washington, DC. Accesssed July 21, 2014, from http://www.hrc.org/resources/entry/finding-insurance-for-transgender-related-healthcare.

Jacobs, S., Thomas, W., & Lang, S. (1997). *Two-spirit people: Native American gender identity, sexuality, and spirituality*. Chicago & Urbana, IL: University of Illinois Press.

Killerman, S. (2013) *The social justice advocate's handbook: A guide to gender*. Austin, TX: Impetus Books.

Nanda, S. (1999). *The hijras of India*. Belmont, CA: Wadsworth, Cengage Learning.

Nanda, S. (2000). *Gender diversity: Crosscultural variations*. Prospect Heights, IL: Waveland Press.

Nakamura, K. (1998). Transitioning on campus: A case studies approach. In R. Sanlo (Ed.), *Working with lesbian, gay, bisexual, transgender college students: A handbook for faculty and administrators* (pp. 179–86). Westport, CT: Greenwood Press.

Rankin, A., Weber, G., Blumenfeld, W. & Frazer S. (2010). *2010 state of higher education for lesbian, gay, bisexual & transgender people*. Charlotte, NC: Campus Pride.

Roscoe, W. (1997). Gender diversity in native North America: Notes toward a unified analysis. In D. Duberman (Ed.), *A queer world* (pp. 65–81). New York, NY: New York University Press.

Schilt, K. (2010). *Just one of the guys? Transgender men and the persistence of gender inequality*. Chicago: University of Chicago, 2010. Print.

Stryker, S. (2010). Why the T in LGBT is here to stay. In D. T. Meem, M. Gibson, & J. Alexander (Eds.), In *Finding out: An introduction to LGBT studies* (pp. 174–76). Los Angeles: Sage.

Simmons, J. (Director). (2005). *Trans generation: Four college students switching more than their majors* [Motion picture on DVD]. United States: Sundance Channel.

TIPS FOR FACILITATORS

- Use the Readings for Facilitators to familiarize yourself with the topic of transgender people before learning how to facilitate the session.
- Take time to discuss the point of each reading with your co-facilitators. Seek out faculty or staff with expertise in gender studies and/or sexuality studies to help lead discussions.
- Assign roles for each facilitator in the session.
- Arrange a practice session with knowledgeable and interested members of the community. Ask for feedback.
- Use the facilitator and session evaluation forms (chapter 5) to receive feedback from the practice session. Incorporate feedback into next session.
- Example process statements and questions are provided below to help provide context to that particular section of the curriculum. Use these as examples to learn from and not exactly to read verbatim. Use your own words and ways of communicating the same concepts.
- This curriculum provides only a cursory overview of intersex people and issues. Be prepared to explain that being intersex is not necessarily transgender. If extended questions arise on intersex issues then consider a separate session on this topic.

CURRICULUM—2–3 HOURS

Curriculum Outline
- (Before Session Begins) Trans/Intersex Ally Quiz—15 minutes
- Welcome, Intro, PGPs, What Is Safe Zone?, Ground Rules, Learning Outcomes—10 minutes
- Gender Binary—Gender the Stick Figures—20 minutes
- Gender Bread Person & Sex Definitions Visual Map—5 minutes
- Gender Continuum Activity—25 minutes
- A Cisgender Privilege Checklist (briefly mention)
- Middle Sexes Video: Transgender and Intersex—15 minutes
- Gender-Neutral Pronouns Handout—5 minutes
- (Briefly Mention) Action Tips for Allies of Trans People
- Scenarios—Concerns and Challenges—25 minutes
- Evaluation and Takeaway Closing Activity—10 minutes

Learning Outcomes
- Understand the gender binary.
- Comprehend how we all are affected by strict definitions of masculine or feminine.
- Share knowledge of accurate definitions and terms.
- Explore potential gender transition processes and identities.
- Common concerns and challenges in higher education.

Handouts
- Trans/Intersex Ally Quiz
- A Cisgender Privilege Checklist
- Gender Bread Person
- Gender Neutral Pronouns Usage Table
- Action Tips for Allies of Trans People
- Campus Pride Index Score and Suggested Steps for Trans Inclusivity

Trans/Intersex Ally Quiz—How Much Do You Know?—15 minutes
Created by Erica Peterson and Eli Green. Used with permission.

Pass out copies as participants enter the room. Ask them to fill out and score themselves so [as] to assess their knowledge in preparation for the session to begin. Answer key is on the last page.

Please keep in mind that some of these questions and their respective answers may be debated within the gender variant and intersex communities. In no way do we mean to enforce that our answers are the only correct answers. Rather, these questions are meant to start a dialogue and raise awareness about gender variant and intersex issues.

INTRODUCTIONS, DISCLAIMERS, AND GROUND RULES—10 MINUTES
Use the introductions section explained in chapter 4 Fundamentals on page 28. Include introductions, PGPs, Ground Rules, Parking Lot, and review of the Safe Zone program.

THE GENDER BINARY—GENDER THE STICK FIGURES ACTIVITY—20 MINUTES
Created by Jessica Pettitt, Kerry Poynter, and students from the Inqueery peer education program at the University of Illinois Springfield.

Learning Goals
- Show how the gender binary operates in our culture.
- Understand how gender is different than the categories of sex or sexual orientation.
- Gender can be expressed differently by culture, geographic region, ethnic identity, and history.

Supplies
- Various color dry erase markers or chalk
- Gender Bread Person visual
- Scrap paper for anonymous questions

Handouts
- Genderbread Person (Figure 7.1)
- Evaluation

Outline
- Introduction, PGP's, directions
- Draw the stick figures
- Process the activity:
  - How did we gender these stick figures?
  - Sex vs. gender (Genderbread Person)
  - What race, ethnicity, class did you assume?
  - Explain gender as a spectrum of expressions. Not everyone fits the binary.

Directions
- Draw two stick figures on the board. Make sure there is room around them to draw/write their traits.
- Name one Tina and one Steven.
- Assign a facilitator to draw the items for Steven and another to draw for Tina. Assign a third facilitator to read the questions. A fourth facilitator can be used to take turns asking the questions.
- In the interest of time, while one facilitator is drawing, the next question should be asked. Do not wait around for the drawing to be finished before moving on to the next question.

Introduction: Introduce yourselves along with your preferred gender pronouns (PGPs). Facilitator that is going to read the questions during the activity begins by explaining that the activity is to get them to learn about gender and the gender binary. Read definition of gender binary from the common terms sheet. Go over general Safe Zone guidelines (confidentiality, step up/step back, etc.) if not already done. Then introduce the activity.

Tips for Facilitators
- This activity could be taught to student facilitators as peer-to-peer educators. Having students lead activities or discussions is a useful way to create an interesting learning session as their voices or stories add personal depth to the content.
- Some audiences will like to have fun with the activity and deliberately play with the binary of gender by gendering the stick figures with items that create gender non-conforming stick figures. Usually this is accompanied by laughter, giggles, and smiles. If this happens, make sure to point out the problem with laughing at gender non-conforming or trans people and the real possibility of people on your campus.
- We recognize that using a ginger bread person or a stick figure has been a staple of social justice work for a few decades. We wish to honor those educators, trans folk, and feminists that have come along before the writing of this activity. Some educators prefer to use the Gender Unicorn at http://www.transstudent.org/gender. A ginger "cookie" activity in the shape of a person was first published in *Teaching for Diversity & Social Justice* (Adams, Bell, & Griffin, 2007).

INTRODUCTORY PROCESS STATEMENT: *"Hello! My name is* [insert name, PGPs, let other facilitators introduce themselves]. *Today we are talking about gender. The best way I know how to do this is to first get everyone involved. So here you see that I have two stick figures. What I would like for you to do is to help me gender these figures in a typical if not stereotypical way. We are keeping to the binary for those advanced folks out there so you don't need to get too creative—stick to the basics. So how this will work is we will go around the room and ask all of you questions that will add traits, clothing, and personality characteristics to the stick figures and we will draw it. We are not artists, but will try our best."*

Make sure that everyone understands the rules; then begin the activity: *"Gender is the socially constructed traits, characteristics, and behaviors that are assigned and expected from men and women based on an individual's clearly delineated sex organs. That being said, Are you ready to start?"*

Further Directions for Facilitators

Facilitator asks the first section of questions while the other two presenters draw the traits onto the stick figures. Halfway through, the first facilitator can switch with one of the people drawing and ask the remaining questions.

Second facilitator states that we are shifting to the identities and personalities of the stick figures.

Discussion (watch time): After all the questions have been asked, shift to the debriefing. Choose a facilitator to introduce this but the process questions will alternate with presenters, until all the questions are asked and debriefed. Make sure to thank the audience for the great participation at the end.

COMMON TERMS

Use these definitions to jog your memory when questions ultimately arise during the processing of the activity.

Asexual—Person who is not sexually attracted to anyone or does not have a sexual orientation.

Cisgender—describes someone who feels comfortable with the gender identity and gender expression expectations assigned to them based on their physical sex and is universally considered valid.

Gender—the socially constructed roles, behaviors, activities, identity, expression, perception, and attributes that a given society considers appropriate for men and women.

Sex—A medical term designating a certain combination of gonads, chromosomes, internal and external gender organs, secondary sex characteristics, and hormonal balances. Because usually subdivided into "male" and "female," this category does not recognize the existence of intersexed bodies.

Preferred Gender Pronouns—English has two common pronouns when addressing people, he/his for males and she/her for females. Individuals are gendered by these pronouns. There are some individuals who do not wish to be gendered as such, and they prefer neutral pronouns (see Ze/Hir). Preferred Gender Pronouns are the pronouns an individual would like to be called and recognized by.

Gender Binary—The idea that there are only two genders—male/female (sex) or man/woman (gender) and that a person must be strictly gendered as either/or.

Gender Identity—A person's sense of being masculine, feminine, or agender (gender neutral).

Sex Identity—How a person identifies physically: female, male, intersex, or neither.

Transgender—A person who lives as a member of a gender other than that expected based on anatomical sex at birth. Sexual orientation varies and is not dependent on gender identity.

Gay—1. Term used in some cultural settings to represent males who are attracted to males in a romantic, erotic, and/or emotional sense. Not all men who engage in "homosexual behavior" identify as gay, and as such this label should be used with caution. 2. Term used to refer to the LGBTQI community as a whole, or as an individual identity label for anyone who does not identify as heterosexual.

Lesbian—Term used to describe female-identified people attracted romantically, erotically, and/or emotionally to other female-identified people.

Bisexual—A person emotionally, physically, and/or sexually attracted to cis males/men and cis females/women. This attraction does not have to be equally split between genders and there may be a preference for one gender over others. Pansexual and Omnisexual are terms to define those emotionally, physically, and/or sexually attracted to multiple gender expressions and identities.

Queer—1. An umbrella term which embraces a matrix of sexual preferences, orientations, and habits of the not exclusively heterosexual and monogamous majority. Queer includes lesbians, gay men, bisexuals, trans people, intersex persons, the radical sex communities, and many other sexually transgressive (underworld) explorers. 2. This term is sometimes used as a sexual orientation label instead of "bisexual" as a way of acknowledging that there are more than two genders to be attracted to, or as a way of stating a non-heterosexual orientation without having to state who they are attracted to. 3. A reclaimed word that was formerly used solely as a slur but that has been semantically overturned by members of the maligned group, who use it as a term of defiant pride.

Ze/Hir—Alternate pronouns that are gender neutral and preferred by some gender-variant persons. Pronounced /zee/ and /here/ they replace "he"/"she" and "his"/"hers," respectively. Others prefer sie/hir or they/them.

IMPORTANT: When an audience member uses a gender pronoun, then write it down next to Tina or Steven and identify that it has happened. Use gender-neutral pronouns such as they or them if you need to up to the point of an audience participant using a gendered pronoun such as he or her.

First Facilitator Drawing Questions:
1. What type of shirt is the Tina stick figure wearing?
2. What type of shirt is the Steven stick figure wearing?
3. What type of bottoms (pants, shorts, skirt) is the Tina stick figure wearing? (If she is in a dress, suggest leggings, tights, or socks.)
4. What type of bottoms (pants, shorts, skirt) is the Steven stick figure wearing?
5. What type of shoes is the Tina stick figure wearing?
6. What type of shoes is the Steven stick figure wearing?
7. What type of hairstyle does the Tina stick figure have?
8. What type of hairstyle does the Steven stick figure have?
9. What is the genitalia of the Tina stick figure?
10. What is the genitalia of the Steven stick figure?
11. Does the Tina stick figure have any facial hair or makeup?
12. Does the Steven stick figure have any facial hair or makeup?
13. What type of jewelry (watch, necklace, bracelet, earrings) is the Tina stick figure wearing?
14. What type of jewelry (watch, necklace, bracelet, earrings) is the Steven stick figure wearing?
15. What type of bag does the Tina stick figure have?
16. What type of bag does the Steven stick figure have?
17. What type of hat does the Tina stick figure have?
18. What type of hat does the Steven stick figure have?
19. What is another accessory the Tina stick figure has?
20. What is another accessory the Steven stick figure has?

PROCESS STATEMENT: *"Now we are going to shift to the identities and personalities of the figures."*

Second Facilitator Drawing Questions:
21. What is the Tina stick figure's occupation?
22. What is the Steven stick figure's occupation?
23. What is the Tina stick figure's hobby?
24. What is the Steven stick figure's hobby?
25. What is the Tina stick figure's gender identity?
26. What is the Steven stick figure's gender identity?
27. What is the Tina stick figure's sexual orientation?

28. What is the Steven stick figure's sexual orientation?
29. What would Tina eat on a date?
30. What would Steven eat on a date?
31. If Tina and Steven were to go on a date, which would pay for dinner?

PROCESSING THE ACTIVITY—15 MINUTES

A. Goals
- Understand sex versus gender.
- Gender is socially constructed and many of us attempt to fit into a binary of gender and gender expression that is masculine or feminine.
- Gender is a spectrum. We all fit somewhere on the spectrum determined by our culture, family, circumstance, location, or space.

B. Supplies
- Gender Bread Person on the screen or refer to handout

C. Directions
- Facilitate discussion of the stick figure activity using the process questions and points below.
- Allow for participants to reflect on how they do or do not exactly fit within a binary of gender.
- Briefly use the Gender Bread Person to explain the differences between gender, gender expression, sex, and sexual orientation.

PROCESS STATEMENT: *"We just had some fun figuring out the gender of Tina and Steven. Let's talk about how we did that and what we were thinking during the activity that created our decisions."*

PROCESS QUESTION:
- What is gender?
- How did you determine the gender of these two stick figures?
- How did the story of our figures evolve?

PROCESS POINTS:
- There are gender indicators such as clothes, hair, jewelry, hobbies, and occupation.
- These indicators attempt to place people in two categories, but there are others such as trans, agender (gender neutral), genderqueer.
- Was there anything beyond the names that made solidifying the figures as one gender or the other easy and reasonable? (Examples could be sexual organs, pronouns that were used, items of clothing, etc.)

Extra: Laughing During the Drawing
If the group had fun or laughed with the characters' gender, that is, played with the binary, during the drawing of the activity then make sure to point this out and use it as a learning moment. Cite examples from the drawing activity.

- There was an altering of the traditional gender binary during the activity.
- We were laughing at some traits and characteristics.
- Realize the reality of this: These can be real identities, real people facing giggles and hushed conversations about their gender.

PROCESS POINTS:
- We place individuals into categories (two categories with secret complicated others).
- If we can't understand something, we fear it, make fun of it, ostracize it, "other it."
- This is how the gender binary works: it categorizes and wants us to stay in those limiting categories.
- Transcendence of the gender categories is not categorical in the existing gender system in our general society.

- Individuals are ostracized, held to standards, made fun of because of the gender binary and their inability to conform to these two limiting options.
- It is important to emphasize that those that are not trans in the audience, as well as facilitators that aren't trans, are cisgender and have cisgender privilege.
- Recognizing cisgender privilege is the first step in placing one's self on these continuums and once inside of the model it is significantly harder to "other" gender non-conforming and/or trans people.
- We all have a gender identity, do specific gendered roles, and express our gender in different ways. Our gender is perceived by others and we perceive the gender of others.

PROCESS QUESTION: What is gender versus sex versus sexual orientation?

PROCESS STATEMENT: *"Gender in our society is viewed as coming from sex organs, but it is from the societal constructs we have created around the sex organs and not the biology itself. The human body of any sex can look very much the same when undressed. It is the social construction of gender that attempts to create the difference."*

PROCESS QUESTIONS:
- What sex did we give Tina and why?
- What sex did we give Steven and why?
- What sexual orientation did we give Tina and why?
- What sexual orientation did we give Steven and why?

PROCESS POINTS:
- Gender makes us assume physical characteristics of individuals.
- Assumed sex organs cause society to gender individuals.
- Gender is a presentation of socially constructed ideas, expressions, etc.
- Gender in our society is viewed as coming from sex organs, but it is from the societal constructs we have created around the sex organs and not the biology itself.
- The role of an ally is to validate the gender expression of others regardless of their perceptions.
- Gender expression does not pertain to sexual orientation.

PROCESS QUESTIONS BY CULTURE, RACE, CLASS, AND HISTORICALLY:
- What race/culture were you thinking about or assuming these stick figures were?
- Were you aware that you had done this, or is it just coming to your attention?
- How might gender be expressed differently if we changed the race, culture, or geographic location of the stick figures?
- If Tina and Steven practice a religion, what did you assume it was? What if it was Muslim? Or Buddhist?
- What if Tina and Steven were alive a century ago? Would their gender identity be different? How would it be expressed?

PROCESS STATEMENT: *"If switched from the White imagination of picturing all dominant identities (unless you pick yourself as a reference point and you aren't coming from dominant or privileged identities), we would typically then make figure adjustments based on stereotypes of marginalized communities. Nothing has to change about Tina's or Steven's clothes or bodies to shift other identities."*

Some Historical Examples
- Native American gender expressions historically included more than three genders.
- Some cultures have viewed the color pink as a masculine color. Until World War I, blue was always for girls (like the Virgin Mary) until navy uniforms were visible, then pink became girls.
- Gender norms evolve over time—pants change over time for men (knickers to bell-bottoms) like skirt lengths change for women. When women began to wear pants they changed too (hot pants to culottes). Men really only got the kilt in the other direction or historically in Ireland.

FACILITATOR STORIES: HOW I DO NOT FIT A BINARY OF GENDER—5 MINUTES

Directions
- Each facilitator shares a story or experience when they have not easily fit within a binary of gender/expression.
- Ask participants to do the same by voluntarily sharing their own stories. Split them into pairs if no initial responses.
- Repeat learning outcomes and share any resources.

PROCESS QUESTIONS:
- Do any of you feel that you fit perfectly into the gender binary, normative expressions for men and women, all the time? Can we get some examples?
- If so, how and why? How did that affect you?
- Do any of you shift your gender expression based on context? Work? School? Class? Friend's house? Grandmothers? Region of the country or world?
- If no responses, split everyone into pairs: "Share with each other a brief story or situation when you learned you were not meeting expectations for your gender in your culture, family, school, classroom, place of worship, or other location." Then get some examples from a few groups. This strategy will enable more responses.

Process the Stories
- Notice any differences in reactions between genders in this room.
- Maybe the women agree they don't fit, where the majority of men didn't say anything, stiffened up, or were very quiet.
- In our Western society, okay to be the privileged masculine, women can claim masculine traits, but men cannot claim feminine traits as their very identity as men would be questioned.
- This is how the gender binary, as a social construction, can be limiting to all of us.

Outro

PROCESS STATEMENT: *"Gender is the way in which an individual expresses themselves. It is not related to their sexual identity, or even their genitalia. It is a form of expression that we have learned depending on our culture, ethnicity, geographic location, and historically. It is socially constructed."*

Points to touch on:
- The gender binary exists and affects everyone as we attempt to fit in either extreme.
- Gender in our society is a continuum that includes masculine, gender neutral, and feminine qualities.
- We often incorrectly base these gender traits on our genitalia from birth when assigned a sex.
- Gender is not clear cut; it is fluid and evolves over time for each individual.
- Gender is a social construct—we are taught gender and teach it to each other.
- Not everyone fits into the binary completely—remember this when interacting with individuals in the future.
- "If there are further questions, please feel free to ask or come to the [insert resources on campus such as a Gender & Sexuality Resource Center]. Thanks for allowing us to present and for the great discussion."

Tips for Facilitators
- Participants may initially use the names of "Tina" and "Steven" as their only answers to how they gendered the stick figures. Make sure to follow up their responses with questions that make the binary more visibly aware such as "How did Tina become gendered as opposed to Steven?"
- Be prepared to point out how the "other" categories of gender (such as trans, genderqueer, agender) fit on a spectrum by using the Gender Bread Person (Figure 7.1) and a Common Terms handout.
- Assign a section for each facilitator, particularly the three processing sections, before beginning the activity. Not every example question needs to be asked depending on the responses from the participants. In the interest of time, move on if a participant makes your point during the discussion.
- Always connect questions and comments back to the original drawings of Tina and Steven in order to make your points visual.

The Genderbread Person v3.3

by it's pronounced METROsexual .com

Gender is one of those things everyone thinks they understand, but most people don't. Like *Inception*. Gender isn't binary. It's not either/or. In many cases it's both/and. A bit of this, a dash of that. This tasty little guide is meant to be an appetizer for gender understanding. It's okay if you're hungry for more. In fact, that's the idea.

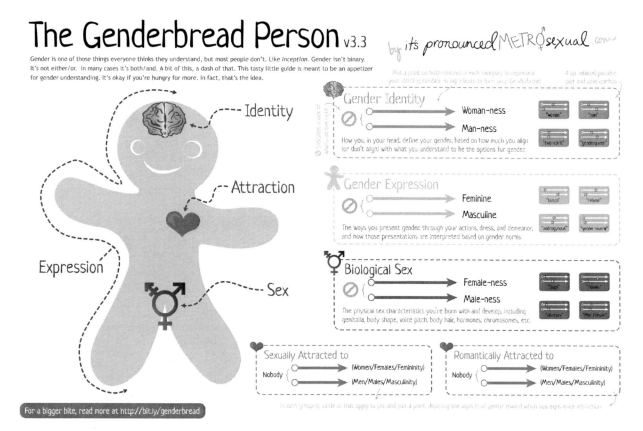

For a bigger bite, read more at http://bit.ly/genderbread

Figure 7.1. GenderBread Person.

GENDER CONTINUUM ACTIVITY—25 MINUTES

By Evangeline Weiss and Kerry Poynter. Used with permission.

NOTE: In order to facilitate this activity, attain the full version titled *Femininity and Masculinity: An Exploration of the Relative Elements of Gender Identity* in Murphy and Ribarsky's (2013) *Activities for Teaching Gender & Sexuality in the University Classroom* by Rowman & Littlefield Publishers.

A. Goals
- Further understanding of the gender binary and how it affects everyone.
- Create a situation to feel what it is like to have your gender scrutinized by others and somewhat like a trans person.

B. Materials
- Two signs: "Most Masculine" & "Most Feminine" or on chalk/dry erase board on opposite ends of the room.

C. Directions
- Explain that "we are about to engage each other in an activity that asks you to decide who is the most feminine and most masculine and then line up accordingly."
- Explain: "Please introduce yourself to the people next to you and then make a decision on who is more masculine and change places with them."
- Explain: "Please also make a decision if you are more feminine and if needed, change places with a person next to you."
- Allow participants to struggle and attempt to move along the continuum.
- Make sure to remind which end of the room is masculine and which is feminine.
- Approach individual sets of people and ask how they are making decisions.
- Spend about 10 minutes.

PROCESS QUESTIONS DURING ACTIVITY:
- How are you making your changes on the continuum?
- What made you decide to move?
- Anyone else making similar decisions?
- What characteristics are you using to place others on the continuum?
- How did it feel to do this activity?

PROCESS POINTS AFTER ACTIVITY:
- Appearance, activities, hobbies, and interests influence ideas of masculine or feminine.

PROCESS STATEMENT: *"Sounds like some things that influence our ideas about masculinity and femininity are the way we appear (clothes, hair, makeup, jewelry), the types of activities we engage in (mowing the lawn, fixing the plumbing, cooking, taking out the trash, vacuuming, etc.) and some of the hobbies we engage in."*

- Transgender people feel scrutinized when we ask personal questions.

PROCESS STATEMENT: *"Asking and answering personal questions about our gender performance/gender identity seems like it was uncomfortable for us. We feel scrutinized—as if we wonder/hope the listener agrees with us. This may be similar to the type of scrutiny that transgender people feel when they interact with us."*

- How close you are to someone can determine the kind of questions.

PROCESS STATEMENT: *"Being curious about other people's gender is a healthy way to get curious about your own. There were probably some questions you had that you did not ask. It's interesting to think about where the lines are between healthy curiosity and what might seem invasive. Sometimes, trans people get asked deeply personal questions that are offensive. We need to think about how close we are to people before we ask them certain questions."*

- Gender is situational.

PROCESS STATEMENT: *"Gender also appears to be relative to other people—it's situational. If we did this spectrum in your classroom or church or family, you might end up in a different place on the continuum. If someone else had not been here today, it might have impacted your place in the spectrum. When we talk about gender being relative—that's what we mean. You are feminine/masculine compared to someone else."*

- Spaces are gendered.

PROCESS STATEMENT: *"Spaces are gendered, too. What if we did this at a sporting event? Or at the theatre? Different spaces invite us to perform gender differently. And, we may choose to 'do' gender differently when we go specific places—we may choose some spaces just because of how they invite us to perform gender."*

A CISGENDER PRIVILEGE CHECKLIST—5–10 MINUTES

By Ezekiel Reis Burgin. Used with permission.

A. Goal
- Highlight privileges for cisgender people.

B. Directions
- Split participants into small groups. Assign each group a particular section of the checklist to review, pick an item to discuss, then prepare to share.

PROCESS STATEMENT: *"This checklist provides those of us that are cisgender a better understanding of things we take for granted because our gender is socially accepted. Please take a moment and review the items in your group. Although we do not have time to review every item today, we will touch on a few of them after group discussion."*

- Briefly mention sex confirmation surgery, transition processes, and the costs associated with them. This is described in the contextualization section.

C. Terminology

Ze/hir

"Ze," "hir," and "hirself" (pronounced like "here") are one of the more common English language gender-ambiguous/neutral pronoun sets. (Example: *Ze went to the corner store to buy hirself some ice cream. Hir friend accompanied hir.*) This pronoun set is used in this document not only about people who actively prefer those pronouns to be used, but for anyone whose gender is not specified, including hypothetical cisgender individuals. This is to help allies practice parsing pronoun sets they may not have been comfortable with, to be more inclusive of people who identify outside the gender binary, and because other options (such as "he/she" or "they") are either incomplete or have problematic history regarding their use when referring to transgender individuals.

Cisgender

When reading this list, please keep in mind the following definition of ***cisgender***: *A person who was raised as, and historically and currently is perceived by others as the same gender ze perceives hirself to be.*

It is in contrast to ***transgender***, *a person whose gender is different from what it was assumed to be at birth, or who was raised under the expectation that hir gender was different than it was or is.* Unlike transgender people, cisgender people's determinations of their sex and gender are universally considered valid.

MIDDLE SEXES VIDEO: TRANSGENDER AND INTERSEX—15 MINUTES

A. Goals
- Understand the difference between Intersex and Transgender
- Introduction to the biological science of Intersex and Transgender

B. Directions
- *Middle Sexes*—Max Beck Video—15 minutes in length—about chromosomes and intersex, explanation of genetics/biology transexuals, 12:00–27:00.

Tips for Facilitators
- Consider providing a separate Intersex session.
- Make sure to point out numbers of intersex people and that intersex is biological sex while transgender is gender identity.

GENDER-NEUTRAL PRONOUN USAGE TABLE—15 MINUTES (if time permits)

A. Goals
- What is a gender-neutral pronoun?
- How to use gender-neutral pronoun

B. Directions
- Explain the table and pronouns.
- Groups of two, create a brief story about someone, then practice telling the story using gender-neutral pronouns.
- Helpful information about pronoun usage can be found on the Gender Neutral Pronoun Blog: https://genderneutralpronoun.wordpress.com.

	Subject	Object	Possessive Adjective	Possessive Pronoun	Reflexive
Female	She	Her	Her	Hers	Herself
Male	He	Him	His	His	Himself
Gender Neutral	Ze	Hir	Hir	Hirs	Hirself
Spivak	E	Em	Eir	Eirs	Emself
Singular They	They laughed	I called them	Their eyes gleam	That is theirs	They like themselves

How to pronounce gender neutral pronouns:

Ze	Hir	Hirs	Hirself	E	Em	Eir
/zee/	/here/	/heres/	/hereself/	/ee/	/em/	/air/

Figure 7.2. Gender-Neutral Pronouns Usage Table.
Source: Created by Eli Green; used with permission.

ACTION TIPS FOR ALLIES OF TRANS PEOPLE HANDOUT—5 MINUTES

By Samuel Lurie, Eli Green, and Erica M. Cornelius. Used with permission of LGBTQ Services at the Massachusetts Institute of Technology.

A. Goal
- Introduction to action oriented activities and ways to be an ally

B. Directions
- Split into groups of two.
- Ask each group to share something new they learned from the tips.
- This is a brief review, ask a couple of the groups to share.

The following are several actions tips that can be used as you move toward becoming a better trans ally. Of course, this list is not exhaustive and cannot include all the "right" things to do or say—because often there is no single, easy, or "right" answer to every situation a person might encounter! Hopefully this list will provide you with food for thought and a starting place as you learn more about trans people, gender identities/presentations, and gender difference.

- Don't assume you can tell if someone is transgender.
- Transgender and transsexual people don't all look a certain way or come from the same background, and many may not appear "visibly trans." Indeed, many trans people live most of their lives with very few people knowing their trans status.
- Don't make assumptions about a trans person's sexual orientation.
- Gender identity is different than sexual orientation. Sexual orientation is about who we're attracted to. Gender identity is about how we know our own gender. Trans people can identify as gay, straight, bisexual, pansexual, or asexual.
- Be careful about confidentiality, disclosure, and "outing."
- Some trans people feel comfortable disclosing their trans status to others, and some do not. Knowing a trans person's status is personal information and it is up to them to share it with others. Do not casually share this information, or "gossip" about a person you know or think is trans. Not only is this an invasion of privacy, it also can have negative

consequences in a world that is very intolerant of gender difference—trans people can lose jobs, housing, friends, and sadly have even been killed upon revelation of their trans status.

- Understand the differences between "coming out" as lesbian, gay, or bisexual (LGB) and "coming out" as trans.
- Unlike "coming out" in an LGB context, where the act of disclosing one's sexuality reveals a "truth" about that person's sexual orientation, disclosing one's trans status often has the opposite effect. That is, when a person "comes out" as trans, the listener often assumes the "truth" about the trans person is that they are somehow more fundamentally a member of their birth sex, rather than the gender/sex they have chosen to live in. In other words, sometimes "coming out" makes it more difficult for a trans person to be fully recognized as the sex/gender they are living in.
- Do not tolerate anti-trans remarks or humor in public spaces.
- Consider strategies to best confront anti-trans remarks or jokes in your classroom, lab, office, living group, or organization. Seek out other allies who will support you in this effort.
- If you don't know what pronouns to use, ask.
- Be polite and respectful when you ask a person which pronoun they prefer. Then use that pronoun and encourage others to do so.
- Be patient with a person who is questioning their gender identity.
- A person who is questioning their gender identity might shift back and forth as they find out what identity and/or gender presentation is best for them. They might, for example, choose a new name or pronoun, and then decide at a later time to change the name or pronoun again. Do your best to be respectful and use the name and/or pronoun requested.
- Don't try to tell a person what "category" or "identity" they fit into.
- Do not apply labels or identities to a person that they have not chosen for themselves. If a person is not sure of which identity or path fits them best, give them the time and space to decide for themselves.
- Don't assume what path a trans person is on regarding surgery or hormones, and don't privilege one path over another.
- Affirm the many ways all of us can and do transcend gender boundaries, including the choices some of us make to use medical technology to change our bodies. Some trans people wish to be recognized as their gender of choice without surgery or hormones; some need support and advocacy to get respectful medical care, hormones, and/or surgery.
- Don't ask a trans person what their "real name" is.
- For some trans people, being associated with their birth name is a tremendous source of anxiety, or it is simply a part of their life they wish to leave behind. Respect the name a trans person is currently using.
- Don't ask about a trans person's genitals or surgical status.
- Think about it—it wouldn't be considered appropriate to ask a non-trans person about the appearance or status of their genitalia, so it isn't appropriate to ask a trans person that question either. Likewise, don't ask if a trans person has had "the surgery." If a trans person wants to talk to you about such matters, let them bring it up.
- Don't ask a trans person how they have sex.
- Similar to the questions above about genitalia and surgery—it wouldn't be considered appropriate to ask a non-trans person about how they have sex, so the same courtesy should be extended to trans people.
- Don't police public restrooms.
- Recognize that gender variant people may not match the little signs on the restroom door—or your expectations! Encourage schools, businesses, and agencies to have unisex bathroom options, and offer to accompany a trans person to the bathroom, in a "buddy system," so they are less vulnerable.
- Don't just add the "T" without doing work.
- "LGBT" is now a commonplace acronym that joins lesbian, gay, bisexual, gay, and transgender under the same umbrella. To be an ally to trans people, lesbians, gays, and bisexuals need to examine their own gender stereotypes, their own prejudices and fears about trans people, and be willing to defend and celebrate trans lives.
- Know your own limits as an ally.
- Don't be afraid to admit you don't know everything! When speaking with a trans person who may have sought you out for support or guidance, be sure to point that person to appropriate resources when you've reached the limit of your knowledge or ability to handle the situation. It is better to admit you don't know something than to provide information that may be incorrect or hurtful.
- Listen to trans voices.
- The best way to be an ally is to listen with an open mind to trans people themselves. They are the experts on their own lives! Talk to trans people in your community. Consult the reading and film lists of this Allies Toolkit to find out where to learn more about trans lives.

SCENARIOS: CONCERNS AND CHALLENGES—15 MINUTES

Goal
- Highlight some common challenges for transgender students using potential scenarios.

Advance Preparation
An important facet of becoming a better trans ally is to also understand how policies, services, and procedures on campus can be trans inclusive. Make sure to complete the Campus Pride Index (http://www.campusprideindex. org/) in advance so as to share results and actionable steps your campus can take. Additionally, use the *Suggested Best Practices for Supporting Trans Students* available from the Consortium of Higher Education LGBT Resource Professionals (https://lgbtcampus.memberclicks.net/assets/consortium%20suggested%20trans%20policy%20recommendations-compressed.pdf) as a handout. Ask and expect your members to address these best practices within their departments and organizations.

PROCESS STATEMENT: *"We are going to spend some time discussing a few case studies to give an example of a few concerns that a transgender person may experience on campus or in daily life."*

Case Study One (Video): "Alexander Smith"
- Download video to your computer or cue up the video from Vimeo at http://vimeo.com/38324333.
- Test in advance to make sure equipment is properly hooked up and works.

Directions
- Explain that we are going to watch a video of a trans person by the name of Alexander Smith.
- Play video and discuss the topics covered.

Group Discussion

PROCESS QUESTIONS:

- What were some of the topics expressed by Alexander?
- How does Alexander identify? (FTM, "man," and heterosexual)
- What were some of the ways that Alexander transitioned? (hormones, "voice deepened," mastectomy/top surgery)
- What were some of his concerns? (people wanting to know his genitalia, questioning his sexual orientation) Relate these to the Cisgender Privilege Checklist.

PROCESS STATEMENT: *"Alexander shares some personal experience with us in this short video, but there are multiple ways we can create an inclusive campus by not just how we interact but the policies and services we provide to transgender people. We have provided you a list of best practices and our rating from the Campus Pride Index. The following scenarios reflect some of these policies and common challenges."*

Materials
- Pass out Campus Pride Index rating results and *Suggested Best Practices for Supporting Trans Students*.
- Pass out case studies or project them on a screen.

PROCESS STATEMENT: *"This is designed for students, faculty, staff, and administrators involved with a transgender student who is transitioning on campus. These are based on actual incidents at university campuses, followed by analysis and discussion."*

- *"Transitioning is the process of moving from one gender to another—male to female (MTF), female to male (FTM), something in between or neither—and is the stage at which transgender and transsexual students need the most support and advocacy. By definition, transitioning is a public event, and as a supportive administrator, faculty, or staff member, you will deal with various critical moments in your student's transitioning process. Be assured that most of these are temporary road bumps and that with your help and guidance students can successfully transition while on campus"* (Nakamura, 1998, p. 179).

Case Study Two—Peer Problems: Restrooms

Case studies two and three were originally authored by Karen Nakamura (1998), used with permission of Karen Nakamura and Ronni Sanlo, adapted by Kerry Poynter.

- "As manager of the student radio station, Christine's transition was very public. The administrator of campus affairs heard over the grapevine that some female students objected to a man in their bathrooms. The administrator talked with Christine and she agreed to use the only gender-neutral restroom on campus—the faculty bathroom in the administrative building. Unfortunately, a key was required to access this bathroom, and it was not available during non-business hours" (Nakamura, p. 180).

PROCESS QUESTIONS:
- What are the concerns in this scenario?
- Are there any problematic issues?

PROCESS POINTS:
- "The targets of restroom policing are usually male-to-female (MtF) transgender people, although many butch lesbians or other masculine-appearing women also complain of being harassed in the women's restroom, despite being biological women" (Nakamura, p. 180).
- "For many (cisgender) women, the women's bathroom provides a psychological refuge from sexism and male harassment in the workplace. They may see the introduction of an MtF trans or masculine woman as an unwanted intrusion of 'male presence' into their 'last safe haven'" (Nakamura, p. 180). There is no evidence that transwomen are the cause or perpetrators of sexual assaults or harassment of cisgender women in women's restrooms.
- Title IX and the Occupational Safety and Health Administration (OSHA) in the United States, require that trans students and employees have equal access to the use of facilities and restrooms that are consistent with their gender identity.
- Requiring Christine to only use the gender-neutral restroom across campus or in the building, locked or not, or one across campus is likely to put the university in legal jeopardy. Be careful about relying on unverified rumors or complaints as the basis of your actions. Talk to all of the parties involved and decide on a mutually agreeable solution that upholds Title IX and OSHA requirements. If nobody is being threatened then this is not the fault of Christine but rather the complainers.

Case Study Three—Administrative Issues: Health Care

- "The student health plan at Becky's university specifically rejects transgender healthcare. In reality, the doctors at the (university health center) have been helping her with her hormone regimen, and the pharmacy has been covering these costs as well. She doubts that the university will cover her sex reassignment surgery (if she gets it before graduation), but upon hearing that other (transgender people) have been able to get coverage, she has thought about hiring a lawyer to help her push her case" (Nakamura, p. 185).

PROCESS POINTS:
- A small minority of the states in the United States have outlawed transgender healthcare exclusion while a few provide healthcare to state employees. Some states provide coverage through Medicare and a growing list of insurance providers. Figure out if your state and or provider is one of these. The Human Rights Campaign keeps a running list of states and insurance providers.
- Campus health providers should update forms to include check boxes for "transgender," "Other _____," and preferred name and gender pronouns. If you are unsure how to address someone, it is always polite to ask.
- Keep comments directed to care and not about questions out of curiosity or in an attempt to train yourself and others. Do the training outside of your patient visits!
- Do not ask about genitals if it is unrelated to the care you are providing and never disclose transgender identity to someone that does not need the information for care.
- Sex confirmation surgeries are "an expensive and dramatically life changing process, it is usually accompanied by irreversible sterility. Like any major step, it should be aided by good counsel and careful thought. The best advice

for (transgender) students is to take their transitioning slowly and to not feel rushed or pressured from any source. The university can greatly aid in this process by making the real-life test of living as the new gender as comfortable as possible. You and the university have an important responsibility to provide a student with a safe and supportive environment during transitioning" (Nakamura, p. 186).

Case Study Four—Faculty Inclusion: Preparing for Class

- It is a couple days before the semester begins. You are a member of the faculty preparing for the first week of classes. You receive an email from Dean Smart who informs you that a student has contacted him for help. The student in question wishes to remain anonymous at this point, identifies as a transgender male, but his former name will appear on the class roster. The dean is sharing this information by request of the student. Dean Smart is not sure why this would be an issue, relays the message, and wishes you a great first week of classes. You consider the information and begin to wonder why this is important to the student. Furthermore, you are unsure which class the student is in. What are the issues and how do you prepare?

PROCESS POINTS:
- There are a myriad of reasons for the class roster to not show the new name or preferred name: campus policy doesn't allow, legal name change process is still underway, or financial reasons.
- Outing the student is not an option.
- Prepare in advance for EACH class that first week.
- Consider introductions that allow for students to name themselves.
- Ask for preferred gender pronouns (PGP's) during introductions.
- Do not call out names from the class roster and instead use a sign in sheet that is passed around class. A simple gesture such as this sends an important signal of inclusion.
- Transgender "students are often disappointed after their transition when people still refer to them with their old name and pronoun. What they do not realize is that this is due more often to ignorance than malice. Many non-transsexual people simply lack information that could balance their fears and concerns. Faculty should recognize the visibility and authority of their position. If other students hear the professor using the inappropriate gender and pronoun toward the student, they may start to refer to the student this way as well.
- "Unintentionally 'outing' a transgender student in front of an entire class may lead to harassment or violence at a later date. It is important to clarify with the student what name and pronoun (they) would like to use. This may change during the transition process. For example, one student originally named 'Chris' first changed her pronoun designation from 'him' to 'her' and then at a later date changed her name to a less gender-ambiguous one. Administrators play an especially vital role in keeping everyone informed of these changes as they occur. Because most of these problems are due to ignorance or misunderstanding and not malice, having the student talk to the individuals involved is often the best solution" (Nakamura, p. 183).

Possible Letter of Authorization for Transgender Students
"To Whom It May Concern:
Jane Doe (student id #123-456) has formally requested a change of name and gender, which the University has accepted. From now on, he is to be referred to as John Doe. All of his student records should be changed to reflect his new name and gender. Mr. Doe is to be accorded all rights and privileges accorded to other male students. I thank you in advance for your cooperation" (Nakamura, p. 181).
Dean Smart

Tips for Facilitators
- Use the following online resources to assess your school and to provide a list of actionable institutional practices and policies for your session participants:
  - Suggested Best Practices for Supporting Trans Students (Consortium of Higher Education LGBT Resource Professionals): www.lgbtcampus.org/policy-practice-recommendations
  - Campus Pride Trans Policy Clearinghouse: www.campuspride.org/tpc
  - LGBT-Friendly Campus Pride Index: www.campusprideindex.org
  - Lambda10—Fraternity and Sorority Transgender Resource Guide: http://www.campuspride.org/lambda10

- Title IX in the United States of America requires access to facilities and services consistent with the gender identity of a student. This applies to restrooms, gendered programs, athletics, etc. Make sure to point this out during discussions of the reasons for addressing transgender inclusion.

EVALUATION AND TAKEAWAY CLOSING ACTIVITY—10 MINUTES

A. Goals
- Provide a brief overview of the contents of the session by allowing participants to voice their personal experience.
- Close the session on a high point.
- Allow for evaluation and feedback.

B. Directions
- Pass out Evaluation Sheet and allow a few minutes to complete.
- Closing Activity: *"What are you leaving here and what are you taking with you? Perhaps it's a myth or new piece of information or a story you heard. Think about this while completing your evaluation. Does anyone want to go first?"*
- Have each person briefly share their answers to the question above.
- Thank them for participating in the session. Sign the Safe Zone pledge if this is their third session (second advanced session).

Tips for Facilitators
- Please emphasize how important participant feedback is to facilitators, how seriously they take it, and how useful it is for them in crafting future sessions. Strongly encourage participants to leave specific, written feedback about what they thought worked especially well during the session, and what they felt needed improvement. (It can sometimes be a challenge to get participants to leave this extensive feedback, as the evaluation portion comes at the end of the session, and participants can sometimes feel rushed for time. So be sure to allot sufficient time for participants to share their thoughts. Start evaluations before you begin with the closing activity.)
- Please note to participants that facilitators are always available if participants have more questions or concerns they want to discuss after the session is over, and that the end of the session does not need to mean the end of the discussions which the session raised.

CHAPTER 8

Safe Dating, Sex, & Relationships Workshop

MICHAEL STEPHENS AND KERRY JOHN POYNTER

"In today's highly digital, immediacy-driven culture . . . [and for] lesbian, gay, bisexual, transgender, and queer (LGBTQ) individuals, the internet might be even more important, as there are unique barriers to meeting partners in a non-virtual context (e.g. physical safety or determining others' sexual orientation) that LGBTQ people encounter, [that] heterosexuals do not as often face."

—Miller, 2005, p. 476

This chapter references handouts (available as a single PDF formatted for easy and clear printing on 8.5" × 11") that supplement the curriculum and assessment pieces of this book. Please email resourcematerial@rowman.com to request the PDF, providing both the title and editor of this book along with proof of purchase (receipt).

DESCRIPTION

This session covers LGBTQIA+ dating and relationships with such topics as hooking up online and safe sex, dating scripts, sex and sexuality, HIV and STD disclosure, and an overview of intimate partner violence. This session is recommended for those who interact with students who are beginning to date and/or engage in sex.

CONTEXTUALIZATION

A myriad of reasons exists as to why healthy relationships between people of the same sex are not part of the vernacular in the public and private sphere. Sexual intimacy between people of the same sex is rarely, if ever, covered during sexual education courses in high schools. In fact, some states (Texas, Alabama, and South Carolina) in the United States have laws that only allow for negative opinions about LGBTQIA+ relationships to be discussed in health education courses (Guttmacher Institute).

A culture in the United States that refuses to provide comprehensive sex education for heterosexual people means that LGBTQIA+ youth are also not being provided information relevant to them. Parents that may attempt to discuss healthy same sex relationships and sexual activities do not always have the knowledge to impart to their offspring or mentees. The LGBTQIA+ community has a history—beginning in the 1980s—of creating their own educational services in response to the HIV/AIDS epidemic. However, this is often overshadowed in the contemporary focus on marriage equality and outlawing discrimination on the basis of sexual orientation and gender identity. In order to appropriately support LGBTQIA+ youth, services and programs need to have a sex-positive focus that addresses healthy sex and relationships.

There are obstacles that LGBTQIA+ people have to overcome that are not present in heterosexual dating. Examples of these obstacles these individuals face are invisibility—being in rural areas where there is a small pool of potential partners, women's socialization to not initiate relationships, misinformation and fear of HIV/AIDS or sexually transmitted diseases (STDs), and little access to other LGBT individuals. The LGBTQIA+ community is increasingly going digital to overcome some of these obstacles when meeting potential dates (Miller, 2005).

The Internet provides 24/7 access to others in the LGBTQ community. Typically gay men appear to meet people online more than lesbians do (Miller, 2005). In a study by Liau, Millett, and Marks they found that 40 percent of gay men have used the Internet to find sexual partners (Miller, 2005). If people don't meet online they are left to explore meeting people in gathering places such as bars or nightclubs.

Ultimately, it is a fact that in certain geographic locations, there are no LGBTQIA+ bars, bookstores, or businesses, leaving a person to use their intuition or "gaydar" for possible romantic or sexual connections or find another medium than in-person contact—enter: mobile-based social media (Miller, 2005). For those who are not comfortable in disclosing their identities this serves as a safer opportunity for interacting with other queer people. This all boils down to a wider availability for the LGBTQIA+ community whereas they may otherwise have been excluded.

The modern-day "highly digital, immediacy-driven culture" and the use of technology in gay dating has changed this process over the years for sexual minorities. This may even serve as an important role to combat the many unique barriers they face in meeting partners where their heterosexual counterparts may not face (Miller, 2005). Dating is not only web-based, it's mobile device or application-based (such as Grindr)—to the point that even web-based social networks have now gone mobile (e.g., Adam4Adam). Beyond dating being mobile, this also provides immediacy to finding a mate that was not existent in previous times.

A major gratification for going on mobile sites or apps is the anonymity, which allows for a queer sense of belonging whether or not you are outward with your identity (Miller, 2005). Summarizing the research, the Internet and mobile-based applications provide an immediate and unlimited outlet for LGBTQ individuals to seek a connection where previously they were left to their own devices. It should be noted that many of these apps were designed for men seeking men (MSM), leaving those that are not cisgender male out of these services; however, this is changing. The use of MSM-specific social networking expands the sense of queer community that is "no less real and no less queer, but more diverse, more focused on individual agency, and far more ubiquitous" (Miller, 2005, p. 482).

Safety Issues

The online world brings a host of safety issues that both sexual minority and heterosexual youth should keep in mind. Some items to consider are (Poynter & Bickers Bock, 2007):

- Choosing a screen name that conveys your interests.
- Removing profile info that strangers do not need. Set limits to personal info.
- Picking a site or app that caters to those you want to meet.
- Using a non-work or school email to remain anonymous.
- Pick a public place to meet that is easy to depart from and decide if anyone accompanies you.
- Let someone know where you are going and provide an emergency contact.
- Leave contact info of the person you are meeting with someone you trust.
- Set boundaries for physical contact. Choose less risky activities; always use a condom for anal/vaginal penetration or latex dam for oral stimulation of the anus or vagina.

When searching for a partner (either online or offline), men typically prefer men who are physically masculine and have traditional masculine traits—and who are HIV negative (Hunter, 2012). Lesbians tend to prefer women who are feminine; however, research shows that this is not as strong of a bias as it is for gay men. Forty-eight percent of the men reported having sex on their first date. Lesbians more often negotiated first-date activities—12 percent of women reported having sex on their first date and those with previous heterosexual dating experiences rejected physical intimacy more often than those with little experience (Hunter, 2012). Data like this shows that sex education should include how to have a conversation about sexual activity prior to or during a first date.

Discussions of sexual activity between people of the same sex in the public sphere, if it happens, tend to be one of derision, viewed as icky, or referred to as "sinful" by arbiters of patriarchal religions. However, sexual acts that are viewed as the exclusive domain of people of the same gender are practiced by everyone (National Survey of Sexual Health and Behavior, 2010).

Instead of passing judgment on sexual activities, educational efforts need to focus on the myriad types of sexual activities and the risk of transmitting HIV or another sexually transmittable infection (STI) such as syphilis, gonorrhea, chlamydia, genital herpes, or the human papillomavirus (HPV). Anal and vaginal penetration are the most risky. Anilingus (rimming), fellatio (oral), and cunnilingus are less risky. The use of adult toys, mutual masturbation, frottage (rubbing), and solitary masturbation have little or no risk at all.

An emphasis on a sex-positive discussion that allows for reviewing potential activities, the risk for each, and how to have a conversation with a partner(s) will give LGBTQIA+ young adults the tools to make informed decisions, not to mention the consent on what activities will make them feel safe but also stay safe.

There is often a stigma for dating or intimacy with people that are HIV positive. For people (regardless of their sexual orientation) who do not have HIV but are in a high-risk group (e.g., MSM), there is a one-pill-a-day regime in order to prevent HIV infection. The brand name for this pill is Truvada, which contains two medicines—tenofovir and emtricitabine—which are utilized in the treatment for those who have HIV. To obtain this medication you must talk to your healthcare provider. After this point there is a requirement of a general physical, and HIV with other STD tests, and kidney and liver tests to ensure there are no ailments in these areas. There are also a number of assistance programs for those who do not have insurance or cannot afford the medication. Meeting someone with HIV should not be a barrier to dating or a healthy sex life with them if they use pre-exposure prophylaxis (PrEP) and/or engage in less risky activities.

PrEP has been shown to reduce one's risk of HIV infection who are at high risk by up to 92 percent as long as the medication is taken consistently (CDC, 2015). One important factor is that the medication is meant to be combined with condoms and other forms of prevention to provide 100 percent optimal protection. Truvada does not protect against other sexually transmitted diseases.

Research has shown strong evidence that PrEP reduces the risk of HIV transmission in clinical trials as a prevention method for high-risk populations (CDC, 2015). None of the studies found any significant safety concerns with use of the daily oral PrEP other than side effects of an upset stomach or loss of appetite but these were mild and usually resolved in the first month of administration.

Gender Role Dating Differences

Although humans are engaging in many of the same sexual activities, there are some differences in dating practices between people of the same sex when compared to heterosexual dating. Strengths exist as a result of the freedom from societal parameters or rules of dating "scripts" for same-sex relationships versus heterosexual relationships. Some of these strengths are a sense of freedom from gender roles and heightened intimacy such as lesbian relationships that showed more egalitarian roles than heterosexual dating.

Traditionally, lesbians were found to reject traditional gender roles by either mutually negotiating their interactions or even switching roles depending on the specific interaction. In spite of these strengths, the flip side is that sometimes the friction between freedom and a tendency to fall back into gendered roles leads to stress and problems (Hunter, 2012).

Hunter (2012) discusses an ambiguity when a relationship shifts from friendship to romance—it can be difficult to tell if a friend has a sexual interest in you. LGBTQIA+ people have claimed they do not know how to date in spite of some societal rules such as: monogamy starts when couples begin dating, having sex for pure physical pleasure or having a relationship primarily for sex were viewed as stereotypically male, the expectation for women to prioritize the romantic or emotional connection over sexual activity, and that no partner should not be more sexually dominant than the other partner or receive more sexual attention than the other partner. Hunter (2012) describes the major differences of dating experiences that LGBTQIA+ individuals face that their heterosexual counterparts may not. She also highlights the privilege that exists in not having to rewrite the heterosexual "script" of dating.

Courtship and marriage historically have been very different for heterosexual versus homosexual couples. Even in recent times with the Supreme Court ruling of 2015 for marriage equality, there are still hurdles that married same-sex couples have to face such as a lack of support for their relationship. Commitment for these individuals could mean different things for different couples. Commitment for one same-sex couple could mean living together, another might be sexually exclusive, whereas another commitment could mean being sexually nonexclusive or an open relationship (Hunter, 2012). Notions of same-sex couples copying traditional heterosexual couples (i.e., husband and wife) are often obsolete and rely on patriarchy.

Intimate Partner Violence

Another safe-dating issue that can be present in all forms of intimate relationships is domestic violence or intimate partner violence (IPV). IPV "is the willful intimidation, physical assault, battery, sexual assault, and/or other abusive behavior perpetrated by one intimate partner against another. It includes physical violence, sexual violence, threats, and emotional abuse" (National Coalition Against Domestic Violence [NCADV], 2014b, p. 1). The term IPV is often used when referring to LGBTQIA+ people because "domestic violence" connotes normative ideas of coupling or families that LGBTQIA+ people have historically not been afforded, included, or welcomed (Kray, 2015).

It is heterosexism, the idea that only heterosexual relationships are normative, that in part drives the conversation about IPV into the closet. A fear that same-sex relationships will "look bad" if the issue is addressed (Kray, 2015). Additionally, some educators, a few Second Wave feminists, and service providers have irrational fears that including LGBTQIA+ IPV issues is an attempt to disrupt heterosexual cisgender women's services. "Highlighting IPV in the LGBT community is not intended to distract from the pressing public health problem of violence against heterosexual women" (Ard & Makadon, 2011, p. 632) but rather to add to and inform provider practices.

LGBTQIA+ populations experience intimate partner violence at least as frequently as heterosexual women—21.5 percent of men and 35.4 percent of women have reported a history of cohabitation with a same-sex partner and IPV experiences as compared to opposite-sex cohabitation, 7.1 percent and 20.4 percent (NCADV, 2014b; Ard & Makadon, 2011). Examples of IPV in LGBTQIA+ relationships include the threat of outing to parents, friends, place of worship; gender-based insults ("You are too gay" or "You are too butch to be a real woman"); identity theft; withholding medication (for a person who is transitioning or has HIV); and threatening to take away children that are not able to be legally adopted or placing custody at risk by outing (Berastain, 2013).

Individuals that are transgender may suffer even a greater burden according to Ard and Makadon (2011), where their reports of physical abuse were 34.6 percent versus 14 percent of gay and lesbians in a survey study of 1,600 people in Massachusetts. Examples of transgender IPV include "using offensive pronouns such as 'it' to refer to the transgender partner; ridiculing the transgender partner's body and/or appearance; telling the transgender partner that he or she is not a real man or woman; ridiculing the transgender partner's identity as bisexual, trans, femme, butch, gender queer, etc.; denying the transgender partner's access to medical treatment or hormones or coercing him or her to not pursue medical treatment" (NCADV, 2015).

Many of these individuals have experienced prior violence and discrimination, as well as a failure of the LGBTQIA+ community to appropriately respond to these situations, which has made LGBTQIA+ victims less likely to seek help with experiences of IPV (Ard & Makadon, 2011). It is also those LGBTQIA+ people with multiple oppressions that face the biggest threat, including people of color, the differently abled, and undocumented (who may fear being reported) (Kanuha, 2007; Kray, 2015).

Those LGBTQIA+ individuals who do seek IPV assistance are faced with severely limited options. LGBTQIA+ shelter or housing services are rare to nonexistent in most regions (Ard & Makadon, 2011; Berastain, 2013). In shelters that currently do exist, men may not be admitted to shelters, regardless of their experiences of victimization, or transgender women—individuals born male may not gain access to women's shelters. These individuals are left to fend for themselves, go back to their abusers, or faced with finding other means of support, which may require outing themselves.

There are many issues covered in this curriculum including a liberation in a new dating world with a sex-positive point of view. This curriculum also covers the elimination of patriarchal ways of dating to addressing the urgent needs of safety in sexual and romantic relationships. These are not always the fun, simplistic topics of romantic love that are the caricature of LGBTQIA+ political movements, but nonetheless need to be a part of a comprehensive safe-dating/sex conversation.

READINGS FOR FACILITATORS

The following annotated readings are intended as starting points for new learners on the topic of safe dating and healthy relationships. They support the learning goals of the curriculum explained in this section. Facilitators should use them as a means of self-learning and reference for those participants inquiring for additional information. They will also be beneficial to group discussion among co-facilitators before practicing and especially in facilitating the activities contained in this curriculum.

- Ard, K. L., & Makadon, H. J. (2011). Addressing intimate partner violence in lesbian, gay, bisexual, and transgender patients. *Journal of General Internal Medicine, 26*(8), 930–33.
  Ard and Makadon attempt to bridge the institutional neglect for the LGBTQIA+ population in the medical community and efforts for IPV victim support and prevention. Useful to learning how LGBTQA+ individuals, especially transgender, experience IPV at least as frequently as heterosexual women, yet there are fewer services to accommodate and help, and how it can manifest differently in same-gender relationships.

- Berastain, P. (2013). Domestic violence in LGBT communities. Huffington Post Gay Voices. Accessed April 22, 2013, at http://www.huffingtonpost.com/pierre-r-berastain/intimate-partner-abuse-in_b_2765797.html.
  Pierre Berastain uses descriptive examples to describe how IPV manifests in same-sex relationships and the barriers that exist for LGBTQIA+ people reporting experiences of IPV. Barriers to accessing services include a lack of inclusive screening, a lack of resources beyond female-bodied shelter services, and homophobia/transphobia among social workers/judges/law enforcement. This article, which can be used as a handout in this curriculum, is an excellent addition to the handouts by NCADV, Kray (2015), and Ard and Makadon (2011).

- Centers for Disease Control and Prevention. (2015). PrEP. Retrieved on August 25, 2015, from http://www.cdc.gov/hiv/basics/prep.html.
  The Centers for Disease Control and Prevention (CDC) details on their web page general knowledge and frequently asked questions about pre-exposure prophylaxis—also known as PrEP. PrEP is marketed with the product name of Truvada. The article provides straightforward answers to how it works and how well, who should take it, how safe it is, how to speak to a doctor about it, how often to use it, why to not stop using condoms, and concludes with downloadable graphics that easily explain its use. Facilitators of this session will find this explanation of PrEP relatively easy to understand as they prepare for the HIV disclosure scenario.

- Hunter, S. (2012). Meeting others. In *Lesbian and gay couples: Lives, issues, and practice* (pp. 3–15). Chicago, IL: Lyceum Books, Inc.
  Hunter's article breaks down key differences in homosexual and heterosexual dating as well as the obstacles an LGBTQ individual can face in these experiences. A lot of dating has shifted to utilizing the Internet, which provides individuals 24/7 access to the LGBTQ community, where otherwise they were left to explore meeting people in gathering places such as bars or nightclubs or publications such as gay yellow pages. Hunter punctuates the notion of asking LGBTQIA+ persons to define their relationship versus using socialized preconceived notions, wherein the notions of same-sex couples copying traditional heterosexual couples (i.e., husband and wife) is obsolete and considered patriarchal.

- Hunter, S. (2012). Micro-level issues and practice with lesbian and gay couples. In *Lesbian and gay couples: Lives, issues, and practice* (pp. 77–96). Chicago, IL: Lyceum Books, Inc.
  The author delves into a number of "micro-level" issues that can occur in same-sex relationships due to the negative effects of gender socialization and sexual violence. Essentially, people in same-sex relationships must create their own agreed upon standards instead of relying on traditional male-female models that rely on heterosexist and patriarchal modes of operation. New learners will find this useful when facilitating the dating scripts section of the curriculum.

- Kanuha, V. K. (2007). Compounding the triple jeopardy: Battering in lesbian of color relationships. In N. J. Sokoloff & C. Pratt, (Eds.), *Domestic violence at the margins: Readings on race, class, gender, and culture* (pp. 71–82). New Brunswick, NJ: Rutgers University Press.
  This chapter from the book *Domestic Violence at the Margins* provides a needed lens into how IPV among lesbians of color in same-sex relationships can be drastically different from heterosexual relationships. This difference is due to not only what role homophobia plays but also between racism and homophobia. The author provides an in-depth analysis of these multiple oppressions by explaining how lesbians of color take enormous risks when deciding which community(ies) to seek help from. New learners of the curriculum in this chapter should compare and contrast this information with the introductory readings by Berastain (2013), Kray (2015), and Ard and Makadon (2011).

- Kray, K. (2015). "Don't make us look bad": The invisibility of LGBTQIA+ intimate partner violence. Retrieved August 24, 2015, from http://everydayfeminism.com/2015/02/invisibility-lgbtqia-intimate-partner-violence.
  Kel Kray provides an overview of the prevalence and scope of IPV in the United States, while explaining how heterosexism and cissexism leads to the invisibility of this issue and that people of color, undocumented, and other marginalized people face the greatest threat. The author also explains that survivors have difficulty reporting IPV due to negative responses

from law enforcement; policy, staff, and residents of shelters designed solely for gender-normative female bodies; and family members. The article concludes with concrete steps to take to provide support to survivors of IPV, serving as a concise introduction to this topic, and will pair well with further readings.

- Miller, B. (2015). "They're the modern day gay bar": Exploring the uses and gratifications of social networks for men who have sex with men. *Computers in Human Behavior, 51,* 477–82.
  This article reviews modern-day "highly digital, immediacy-driven culture" in the context of gay dating and how technology has changed this process over the years. MSM-specific social networking expands the sense of queer community that is "no less real and no less queer, but more diverse, more focused on individual agency, and far more ubiquitous." For sexual minorities this medium can serve as a way to combat barriers to meeting others especially for those locations without LGBTQIA+-specific businesses, provide needed anonymity for those who are not outward with their identity, provide a sense of safety for these individuals, and save individuals from the sting of rejection they may face to in-person contact.

- National Coalition Against Domestic Violence. (2014a). *Domestic violence and lesbian, gay, bisexual, and transgender relationships.* Retrieved on August 13, 2015, from http://www.calegaladvocates.org/library/item.512380-NCADV_LGBT_Fact_Sheet.
  The NCADV provides this handout online to explain domestic violence (IPV) in same-gender relationships and explains types of abuse, transgender abuse, HIV/AIDS abuse, and barriers to seeking services. The Power and Control Wheel, often used to explain domestic violence in heterosexual relationships, is adapted here to explain how homophobia, heterosexism, biphobia, and transphobia affect domestic violence in same-gender relationships. New learners to this topic will find the abundance of statistics and the types of abuse helpful when attempting to explain how domestic violence manifests in same-sex relationships.

- National Coalition Against Domestic Violence. (2014b). *LGBTQ victims of sexual violence.* Retrieved on August 13, 2015, from http://www.ncadv.org/images/LGBTQ_Victims.pdf.
  The NCADV provides an easy to digest overview of IPV. This two-page document cites recent published statistics (2012–2014) that show equal, or in some cases higher, reports to that of the heterosexual community. It attempts to give LGBTQIA+-specific aspects of IPV (although not exhaustive), transgender-specific aspects which are often not included in IPV trainings, and barriers to seeking services. Learners of the curriculum will find the recent stats and trans-specific aspects useful as they are unique in the literature on this topic.

- Poynter, K., & Bickers Bock, L. (2007). Online dating safety checklist. Retrieved on September 6, 2015, from http://www.uis.edu/lgbtq/wp-content/uploads/sites/83/2013/12/Online-Dating-Safety-Checklist.doc.
  Poynter and Bickers Bock (2007) list some precautions and safety tips when considering online dating. These writers cover in a simple, one-page format topics of things to consider before chatting with someone, planning your meeting, preparing to go out and meeting someone, and safe-sex tips. This document attempts to prepare and ensure its readers safety when involving themselves in online chatting and/or dating. Specific to this curriculum, facilitators can provide their learners with this checklist as a takeaway to utilize in their own lives or provide to others.

SUGGESTED READINGS

- Island, D., & Latellier, P. (1991). *Men who beat the men who love them: Battered gay men and domestic violence.* Bingham, NY: Haworth Press, Inc.
- *Journal of Sexual Medicine.* (2010). Findings from the National Survey of Sexual Health and Behavior (NSSHB), Center for Sexual Health Promotion, Indiana University, Volume 7, Issue Supplement s5, pages 243–373.
- *Aaron's dictionary of gay terms.* (n.d.). Retrieved August 13, 2015, from http://www.aaronsgayinfo.com/Fterms.html.
- *Robert Scott's gay slang dictionary.* (n.d.). Retrieved August 13, 2015, from http://www.odps.org/glossword/index.php?a=index&d=8.

Tips for Facilitators
- Use the readings to familiarize yourself with the topics included in this session before learning how to facilitate the session.
- Take time to discuss the point of each reading with your co-facilitators. Seek out faculty, staff, or community leaders with expertise in sexuality studies, health education, and intimate partner violence for additional discussion and clarification of any points about which you have questions.

- Assign roles for each facilitator in the session.
- Arrange a practice session with knowledgeable and interested members of the community.
- Use the facilitator and session evaluation forms (chapter 10 of this volume) to receive feedback from the practice session. Incorporate feedback into next session.
- Example process statements and questions are provided below to help provide context to that particular section of the curriculum. Use these as examples to learn from and not exactly to be read from verbatim. Use your own words and ways of communicating the same concepts.
- Be aware that this topic is often a distinctly fraught and challenging one for participants and they will likely come into the session with strong feelings about the subject matter.
- Due to potentiality for this topic to be triggering for individuals who have or know someone who has faced the harmful effects of these topics, especially the section about intimate partner violence (IPV), facilitators should have a disclaimer at the beginning of the session stating these topics are covered in this session. The option should be available to leave the session without consequence or fear of being shamed, if an individual is feeling triggered or emotional from this discussion. A follow-up measure with this participant and alternative for receiving credit should also be set for these instances.
- It is important to emphasize the need for respectful language and the importance of including a diverse assortment of perspectives at the beginning of the session as well as throughout the session.
- It is also incredibly helpful to research and create a resource list of campuses, local agencies, and shelters that are affirming and provide education and support services for sexual assault and domestic violence survivors. It is also vital to contact these organizations in order to understand if these services are intended exclusively for cisgender women or how inclusive they are of transwomen, transmen, and cisgender men.

CURRICULUM—2 HOURS

Curriculum Outline
- Introductions, Disclaimer: Penis! Vagina! Oh my!, and Ground Rules—10 minutes
- Screen Name Activity Icebreaker—10 minutes
- Dating Scripts and Meeting Others—15 minutes
- Hooking Up and Online Dating: Keeping It Safe—20 minutes
- Sex and Sexuality—20 minutes
- HIV and STD Disclosure Scenario and Discussion—15 minutes
- Intimate Partner Violence (IPV)—20 minutes
- Evaluation and Takeaway Closing Activity—10 minutes

Learning Outcomes
- Educate participants about sex and dating between people of the same sex.
- Inform participants on concepts of dating safely when using the Internet.
- Introduce STD/STI disclosure as part of a healthy conversation with partners.
- Assist participants on how to identify intimate partner violence (IPV) in same-sex relationships.

Materials
- Markers
- Large newsprint or sticky back-paper
- Scrap paper
- Video: "Domestic Abuse—Gay Male Victim"
- Vignette document (projected): "HIV Scenario Disclosure"
- Process questions document (projected) for the HIV and STI disclosure activity

Handouts
- Online Dating Safety Checklist (available as part of the downloadable PDF at https://rowman.com/ISBN/9781475825268)
- Online Dating Sites and Apps
- The Unhealthy Relationship Quiz (available as part of the downloadable PDF at https://rowman.com/ISBN/9781475825268)
- Intimate Partner Violence in LGBTQ Communities
- NCADV LGBT Fact Sheet (two sided)
- NCADV LGBTQ Victims (two sided)
- Reporting Sexual Assault (edit for your use)
- Campus & Local Resources (create your own)

INTRODUCTIONS, DISCLAIMER, & GROUND RULES—10 MINUTES
Use the introductions section explained in chapter 4 Fundamentals on page 28. Include introductions, PGPs, Ground Rules, Parking Lot, and review of the Safe Zone program.

DISCLAIMER SECTION
Directions: After introducing the session topic, incorporate words that may be utilized in the session and have participants say these words in tandem to reduce the tension that may be in the room.

PROCESS STATEMENT: *"In this module, we will be discussing safe sex and relationships among LGBTQIA+ individuals. We cannot have a discussion of sex without key terms. We are all mature adults in this room, but we want to eliminate any discomfort you may feel about stating such terms. So, let's all say a few of these together to hopefully make you all feel more comfortable about hearing such terms and using them maturely. Repeat after me: Penis, vagina, anal, oral. . . ."*

- After all the snickering and joking subsides, introduce a more serious disclaimer about this session.

PROCESS STATEMENT: "*While we've started out with a bit of fun and loosening up, we do need to realize that during this session, we will be addressing topics and discussing information that can be very personal and sensitive to individuals in this room. We will be addressing issues like sexual assault and domestic violence. It is very likely that many individuals in this room have personally experienced such victimization either themselves or among people they know and care about. It is thus very important that you realize that this information will be discussed and it is vital to be mature and respectful in our handling of these issues. This is important because we do not know who has been affected through such experiences.*

"*It's also very important to acknowledge the impact that such information can have on you, based on your personal experiences, in order to help you avoid any further traumatization from these discussions. If at any time you feel that you cannot continue in this training, please feel free to leave and enroll in a different session in the future to satisfy your Safe Zone training requirements. Thank you all, in advance, for your mature and respectful handling of the information that will be presented today.*"

IMPORTANT: Allow people to discreetly leave the session during the screen name activity that is next.

SCREEN NAME ACTIVITY ICEBREAKER—10 MINUTES

A. Goals
- Introduce meanings that online users may be expressing in their screen names.
- Begin the discussion of sexual identity and their online representation.
- Begin to assist the audience in thinking of safety and other considerations with online dating.

B. Directions
- Split participants into groups of two.
- Pass out two to three names or acronyms to each group.
- Introduce the activity and explain the objectives.

PROCESS STATEMENT: "*When using the Internet or dating apps, it is common to create a screen name or username. This username, usually consisting of an acronym or shortened version of a word, can communicate sexual interests and identities or who I am to potential partners. These are self-chosen and important to whom someone is trying to convey something upon first glance.*

"*For this activity we are going to break you up into pairs to utilize the different words provided to make a screen name. In your group you will discuss what someone might be trying to communicate to someone that sees it online. Combine the words provided and be creative! You may also add your own words to personalize this screen name. Take the next 5 minutes to create your screen name and discuss them in your group.*"

- Process the activity, gleaning their self-definitions or creative descriptions of the names.
- Tie this to identified learning points of identity and self-identification.

The following are examples of acronyms and words that participants can use to make their screen names (you will want to update these terms over time as trends change frequently!):

BDSM, ISO, LDR, MBA, MSM, WSM, MtF, FtM, A/S/L, Globetrotter, 4:20, 411, Alist, 429, Abigail, Abuse, AB, '10,' AC-DC, 44, Active, 69, Top, Dom, Bottom, Vers, Fem, BB, Bear, Twink, Otter, Daddy, Springfield, 6pac, stud, boy, Girl, Btm, bball, soccer, ripped, cutie, blonde, wantsum, jock, lookin, college, 4tops, hot, str8, bf, mrrd, gf, LTR, need, IL, nice, butch, 81, boyish, lipstick, trans

C. Game Processing

PROCESS QUESTIONS:

- What names did you come up with? Is anyone comfortable sharing?
- What do you think these words may mean? (Self-defined guesses)
- What could the importance of these screen names be? What are their purposes?

PROCESS POINTS:
- Identity—something that is self-described. Parts of identity can exist beyond physical appearance and how it is important to let individuals self-identify or choose these themselves.
- Self-identification (rather than be labeled; example of trans—it could be important to have this information public in order to find a compatible mate or peer).

NOTE: The main idea for this activity is for people to ponder what meanings these names can carry. There are always questions of what these words do commonly mean. A list of terms that can be used as a resource can be found on "aaronsgay.info.com" at http://www.aaronsgayinfo.com/Fterms.html.

Tips for Facilitators
- It might benefit the group process to go around the room and remind the groups of the main points of the directions; that is, make your own screen name, add words in there to personalize, be creative, and discuss with your group what you think the words communicate to others online.
- Encourage participants to share other acronyms or screen names they are familiar with while processing the activity.
- It is not important for participants to know what each of these screen names means, but that screen names are an important part of online dating.
- Do not be surprised if participants of an older generation are new to the concept of online dating and the use of screen names.

DATING SCRIPTS & MEETING OTHERS—15 MINUTES

A. Goals

- Introduce intricate differences for the LGBTQIA+ community versus people who identify as heterosexual.
- Create a dialogue on these difficulties and generate ideas for how one might overcome these obstacles and/or help a student do so.

B. Directions
- Have one facilitator address the group, while another takes notes, shorthand, of their responses to the process questions of this group activity adapted from the reading resource by Ski Hunter (2012), *Lesbian and Gay Couples: Lives, Issues, and Practice.*
- Start the activity with a short group activity in groups of two to three people discussing the following process questions—allow for 4 to 5 minutes for this discussion to happen.

C. Small-Group Discussion
PROCESS QUESTIONS:

- What are ways that you date?
- How do you meet people?
- What are traits you look for in a prospective partner?

D. Larger-Group Discussion
PROCESS QUESTIONS:

1. What obstacles do LGBTQIA+ people experience in meeting each other?

PROCESS POINTS:

- Invisibility—haven't disclosed their sexual identity.
- Geography—rural location; small town.
- Small pool of potential partners, even more limited for racial/ethnic lesbians/gays.
- Socialization—women not socialized to initiate relationships.
- Group identity—those individuals that are not cisgender or male may find that the most popular or well-used apps do not have a diversity of sexualities or gender expressions. Some users of these apps may find that the preferences that are considered normative cater to those of White cisgender males.

2. How do they overcome obstacles and meet?

PROCESS POINTS:

- Get set up by friends and family members.
- Support networks.
- Internet—especially helpful to those who have not publicly disclosed sexual identity or who are limited by geographical location. The Internet has offered an ease of creating this community, thus easing the pain of rejection online versus face-to-face.
- LGBTQIA+ publications have historically been one of few places to find a date until the advent of the Internet.
- LGBTQIA+ bars/clubs (except for those in AA/substance abuse).
- Job/occupation.

3. When lesbians or gay men date, do they do things differently than heterosexuals who date, or is the process a similar one? If similar, what are their behaviors when dating?

PROCESS POINTS:

- Gay men tend to prefer men who are physically masculine, attractive, and have traditionally masculine traits, and who are HIV negative.
- Lesbians tend to prefer women who are feminine; research has shown this is not as strong of a bias as it is for gay men.
- All stages of a first date are the same as those of heterosexual women and men.
  ◦ Discussing plans, dressing up, getting to know one's date, going out, and initiating physical contact.
- Gay men played out more traditional male roles in arranging a date and other activities (48 percent of the men reported having sex on their first date).
- A majority of lesbian respondents rejected traditional gender roles by either mutually negotiating their interactions or switching roles depending on the specific interaction.
- Nearly half of gay men reported having sex on their most recent first date, compared with only 12 percent of lesbians. Sex education should include how to have a conversation about sexual activity prior to or during a first date.

PROCESS QUESTION:
- What are some stereotypes about lesbian and gay couples?

PROCESS POINTS:

- Stereotypes will hinge on gender roles and who is the man or woman in the relationship. Include a few points about gender socialization and how same-sex relationships do not need to follow the same roles taught to people in heterosexual relationships.
- There is no prescribed way to be a same-sex couple, so each couple must develop its own parameters and rules. This can also cause stress and conflict.

Tips for Facilitators
- Participants should realize that dating practices among LGBTQIA+ people are not all that different than heterosexual relationships albeit with some differences in how people meet, overcoming obstacles to meeting, and negotiation of dating scripts not dependent on gender socialization.
- It is important to note, which is hopefully clear from this lesson, that there can and are differences for those experiencing and defining their relationships or sexual interactions with same-sex individuals. Be open to LGBTQIA+ people disagreeing with the dating issues presented here as they tell their own stories. Averages and trends are important to discuss and do not invalidate someone's own experiences, which may be contrary to what is "typical."
- If the number of participants is small (<15) it might be a time-saver to facilitate this section without splitting into smaller groups. Use the small groups only if people are not forthcoming as a means to encourage dialogue.

HOOKING UP & ONLINE DATING: KEEPING IT SAFE—20 MINUTES

A. Goals
- Learn how to date online safely.
- Create a dialogue that de-stigmatizes online dating.
- Understand the process of online dating and hooking up and associated accepted norms.

B. Direction
- Use the Online Dating Safety Checklist to facilitate this section. Pretend that the participants are helping to set up a fictional dating profile on a web page or app of their choice. Use this as a creative way to work through all the points of this section.
- The facilitator will address the group with two process questions to bring back some experiences from the screen name activity icebreaker.

C. Handouts
- Online Dating Safety Checklist
- National Coalition Against Domestic Violence (two)
- Domestic Violence in LGBTQIA+ Communties

PROCESS STATEMENT: *"We are about to engage in a group discussion about how to date and hook up safely online. As we just learned, many queer people are using the Internet as well as engaging in sexual activities on the first date. We will learn more about sex in our next section. For now, we ask that you set aside any personal moral judgments about hooking up so we can have a conversation about these topics that are not always discussed. Please find your Online Dating Safety Checklist and we are going to create a fictional dating profile together."*

D. Screen Name—Large-Group Discussion
PROCESS QUESTIONS:

- What kind of personal information might be disclosed through your screen name?
- How are you conveying what you're looking for online with your screen name?

The facilitator will continue the dialogue with five questions inviting the audience to explore personal information in online disclosures—the "shoulds" and "should nots."

E. Online Personal Information—Large-Group Discussion
PROCESS QUESTIONS:

- What types of information do people share online?
- Where do people post personal information online?
- What type of information are you wanting to share?
- What do people unconsciously disclose?

PROCESS POINT:

- EXAMPLES: Being out online, but not anywhere else, or displaying under-age alcohol use (other examples: pictures may show a child with them or a pet they own).

PROCESS QUESTION:

- What things do you probably want to keep private?

PROCESS POINTS:

- Phone number
- Address
- Where you live, school or home address
- Your full name
- Student/work email (create an anonymous email account for online dating)

The facilitator will continue the dialogue about where you choose to chat or meet individuals online.

PROCESS POINTS:

- Review the different types of people and discussion found at different websites and dating apps (refer to handout).
- Ask participants to suggest other sites or apps they might be familiar with.

EXAMPLES OF DATING APPS OR SITES
GAY:

Grindr (app)	gay.com (site)	chemistry.com (site)
match.com (site)	perfectmatch.com (site)	OkCupid.com (site/app)
spark.com (site)	mennation.com (site)	outpersonals.com (site)
Scruff (app)	iDate gay (app)	adam4adam.com (site/app)
guyhive.com (site)	craigslist.com (site)	gay.date.com (site); Tindr (app)

LESBIAN:

idate gay (app)	Speeddate (app)	Curv (app)
match.com (site)	lesbotronic.com (site)	Tindr (app)
chemistry.com (site)	OkCupid.com (site/app)	Curvepersonals.com (site)
spark.com (site)	craigslist.com (site)	Perfectmatch.com (site)

TRANS:

OkCupid.com (site/app)	Tgpersonals.com (site)	Transgendersearch.com (site)
Findatransgender.com (site)	Transdatingsite.com (site)	Transrelationship.com (site)

The facilitator will continue the dialogue about what web page or app you choose, why, and how you can go about choosing to meet someone you met online.

PROCESS POINTS:

- Ask students, "How can you stay safe?"
- Compare their answers to our checklist.
- Review checklist items that we have already talked about.

Tips for Facilitators
- The experiences of the participants may be varied with online dating. There will be participants that have had experience dating online and have been through the process of creating a profile and there will be others that have not. This could affect the flow of discussion—that is, how specific you have to cover the logistics of profile creating.
- The main idea is safety and the participants can begin to think about how they would go about keeping safe or helping students figure out ways to do this as safely as possible.
- Some participants may not support the practice of hooking up—or one-night stands. This could be an opportunity to explain that this is a sex-positive workshop to prepare participants to assist students on campus. We want students to make informed decisions about sex and dating safety. It is important not to shut down important conversations due to your own personal beliefs or judgments on hooking up.

SEX AND SEXUALITY—20 MINUTES

A. Goals
- Validate sexuality for LGBTQIA+ as well as heterosexual people.
- Help students make educated choices about sexuality based on risk level.
- Define sex beyond penetration.
- (Bring condoms and dams.)

B. Directions

- Provide each participant a scrap piece of paper to write on. Explain that this is an anonymous activity and to not write their name on these sheets. The facilitator will utilize a prompt for the group to answer. He or she will then explain that their scraps of paper will be collected and shuffled to keep the identity of the person anonymous.

PROCESS STATEMENT: "*Write on a scrap piece of paper the answer to this question. What have you heard or know about sexual activities between people of the same gender? Remember, this is anonymous. No name or identifying information.*"

- Another facilitator will gather these and shuffle them as another facilitator writes the question on the board—linking similar items together.

PROCESS POINT:

- Debunk any stereotypes such as scissoring for female couples that do not exist except in heterosexual pornography fantasies.

While the facilitators are gathering the papers and writing them on the board another facilitator will lead a group discussion with four process questions. Connect the items written on the anonymous responses (or written on the board) to the list of sexual activities that everyone participates in.

C. Larger-Group Process Questions
PROCESS QUESTIONS:

- How did you learn about sex? Sex ed/health class in high school? Your parents? Online?
- How do LGB people learn about sex? Very likely not in sex ed/health class and not usually parents. Often through other mature sexual partners or the Internet (pornography), which are not always the best sources.
- Let's look at our responses to our anonymous question. What are some ways that heterosexual people express intimacy? Are they present here?

PROCESS STATEMENTS:

- *"The most common form of sexual expression between people is the same regardless of the gender: oral sex."*
- *"We often think of the genitals as the only sexual organs but what is actually the most commonly used sexual organ of your body? Your brain."*
- *"Forms of sexual activity—regardless of sexuality":*
  - *Vaginal (risky)*
  - *Anal (risky)*
  - *Fellatio/oral (low risk)*
  - *Toys (low risk)*
  - *Frottage/rubbing (no risk)*
  - *Mutual masturbation (no risk)*

The facilitator will then review the "Straight People Have 'Gay Sex'" graphic on the screen using the following statistics.

PROCESS STATEMENTS:

- *"By ages 25–29, eight of every nine women have performed fellatio, and half have done it in the past month."*
- *"By ages 25–29, 88 percent say they've received oral sex from a man, and 72 percent say they've received it in the last year. (Men confirm this: 86 percent say they've given it, 74 percent in the last year.) That's pretty close to the 91 percent of men aged 25–29 who say they've received oral sex from a woman and the 77 percent who say they've received it in the past year."*
- *"20 percent of women aged 18–19 say [they've tried anal sex], and by ages 20–24, the number is 40 percent."*

[From the *Journal of Sexual Medicine*. Findings from the National Survey of Sexual Health and Behavior (NS-SHB), Center for Sexual Health Promotion, Indiana University, October 2010, Volume 7, Issue Supplement 5, pages 243–373.]

Tips for Facilitators
- Just as with the prompt to say the words in the beginning, participants may still snicker and laugh at the sexual words being utilized for this session. It is important to not let that derail the session.
- Make sure to request that everyone respect the process, take it seriously. Do not be afraid to interrupt casual joking and laughing for those that are new to this idea.
- It might be important in order to maximize participation to include a quick reminder that what the participant is writing down will not be linked to its author, but rather it is a confidential way to facilitate this conversation anonymously.

HIV & STD DISCLOSURE SCENARIO AND DISCUSSION—15 MINUTES

A. Goals
- Gain education on methods of safer sex.
- Assessment of individuals' views on STIs/STDs.
- Discuss the current state of protection against HIV.
- Gain awareness of STIs and HIV when dating.
- Learn how to facilitate discussion in these instances.

B. Directions
- The facilitator will display a social story for the group to read.
- *VIGNETTE SCENARIO (PROJECTED IN FRONT OF THE GROUP)*
  - *"Student comes to you and discloses that they just went on a date the previous night. They reported that the date went really well and they really got along with this possible partner. Then when the two were talking on the phone after the date, the student reports that their date informed them that they have a sexually transmitted infection/disease (STI/STD). This troubles the student because they do not know too much about this topic and are starting to think that this person is not going to work for them."*

The facilitator will then direct participants to pair up with their screen name groups to process the scenario.

PROCESS STATEMENT: "*This activity is an opportunity to apply yourself as a potential Safe Zone member. Up on this screen you will see a vignette—or scenario—of a student coming to you with something they need to talk about regarding dating and safety. Read through this scenario and discuss among your screen name activity groups about your initial thoughts and reactions to the vignette.*"

PROCESS QUESTIONS (PROJECTED IN FRONT OF GROUP):

- How would you respond to this student?
- What if the student responds that the STI is HIV? Does this change your perspective or advice?
- What if the student that came to you for your help was the one with the STI/STD—does this change your response or view of the situation? What if the STI/STD is HIV?

After 5 minutes, reconvene in the larger group and process the discussions and the scenario.

ADDITIONAL PROCESS QUESTION:

- With the second question of the STI is now HIV, rather than something that has less social stigma, did that change any of the group's opinions or concerns? How they would handle the situation?"

PROCESS POINTS:

- Educational efforts need to focus on the myriad types of sexual activities and the risk of transmitting HIV or another sexually transmittable infection (STI) such as syphilis, gonorrhea, chlamydia, genital herpes, or the human papillomavirus (HPV). For example, there is a vaccine against HPV as well as hepatitis A and B.
- Condoms when used effectively can help prevent transmission of HIV and other STDs. Dental dams can provide a barrier, so long as there is no fluid exposure, to prevent herpes, HPV, etc.
- Follow the guidelines for engaging in the less risky sexual activities outlined previously. HIV or STIs should not be a barrier to potential partners.
  - A medication called Truvada is now available that will prevent transmission—when used effectively, particularly with a condom, it dramatically reduces (up to 92 percent) your chances of becoming infected. There is a trend of people using Truvada "PrEP," or pre-exposure prophylaxis, as an option for prevention that are at high risk of getting HIV. The brand name for this pill is Truvada, which contains two medicines—tenofovir and emtricitabine. To utilize this medication effectively it should be taken consistently every day and should be used with other prevention options such as condoms (cdc.gov) Truvada is 92 percent effective as long as the medication is taken consistently. One important factor is that the medication is meant to be combined with condoms and other forms of prevention to provide 100 percent optimal protection. Truvada does not protect against other sexually transmitted diseases. For more information: http://www.cdc.gov/hiv/basics/prep.html.
  - There is also the option of "PEP," or post-exposure prophylaxis. This involves the taking of antiviral drugs after a single high-risk event to stop HIV from making copies of itself and spreading through your body. It must be taken as soon as possible in order to be effective—and always within three days of a possible exposure (cdc.gov). For more information: http://www.cdc.gov/hiv/basics/pep.html.

Tips for Facilitators
- Popular dating sites and apps change on a regular basis. Make sure to update the list provided here.
- Some participants will exhibit an HIV phobia that does not allow for dating people that are HIV positive. Use these as educable moments to de-stigmatize HIV and STIs. It is possible to have an intimate relationship thanks to PrEP and by following the less risky sexual activities outlined in this curriculum. (Generally there is an opinion shift from an STI, which is curable by an antibiotic, to someone with HIV, which explains why there is a delay in identifying the STI as HIV until after the group has begun processing.)
- Consider interchanging HIV with HPV, syphilis, or other STIs. Be prepared to respond to questions about these STIs and how to protect from them and/or cure them.

INTIMATE PARTNER VIOLENCE (IPV)—20 MINUTES

A. Goals
- Gain an understanding of intimate partner violence (IPV) and unhealthy relationships.

NOTE FOR A PROCESS STATEMENT: *"This isn't the experience of all same-sex relationships. Because such violence can happen in any relationship regardless of sex or gender."*

- View a video—vignette account of an IPV experience.
- Gain an understanding of the power and control wheel.
- Process and discuss obstacles LGBTQIA+ individuals may face with IPV.

B. Directions
- Complete the Unhealthy Relationships Quiz to introduce the topic.

PROCESS STATEMENT: *"The following behaviors are some warning signs that the relationship you're in may not be healthy. You're the best judge of the health of your relationship! If one or more of the listed behaviors are happening in your relationship and you're feeling like your life is becoming smaller, more filled with fear, or less happy because of them, it might be time to reach out for help."*

- The facilitator will go into a brief overview of the definition of intimate partner violence.

C. Intimate Partner Violence (IPV) Video
- Facilitators will ask the participants to divide themselves into groups of two or three people before showing the video.
- Facilitator will start the video vignette "Domestic Abuse—Gay Male Victim" http://www.youtube.com/watch?v=I3PeZ4m7mng.
- During the video, one of the facilitator(s) will hand out to each group a large sheet of Post-it paper.
- The facilitators will then give the group 5 minutes for discussion and to write their group answers on the Post-it paper.

PROCESS STATEMENT/PROMPT: *"Please number your sheet from 1 to 3 and then answer this question: What do you see as problematic in the relationship? List three things."*

PROCESS QUESTION:

- How are any of these issues unique to a same-sex relationship?

PROCESS POINTS:

- Threat of outing.
- Gender-based insults.
- HIV disclosure.
- Threats/violence.
- Additional examples of IPV not found in the video are: identity theft, withholding medication, using offensive pronouns such as "it," ridiculing partner's body/appearance, questioning their partner's ability to be a "real man or woman," threatening to take away children not legally adopted or placing custody at risk by outing.
- The Transgender community experiences a greater burden of IPV when compared to gays and lesbians (34.6 percent versus 14 percent) (Ard and Makadon, 2011).
- Transgender people, people of color, and the undocumented can face the biggest threat to reporting due to a lack of inclusive services or fear of being deported.
- Sexual assault can also be a form of IPV. It is defined as sexual penetration without consent, by use of physical force, coercion, or threat. This can also include unwanted touching. Sex crimes can be prosecuted even if the victim knew

the attacker, the victim did not fight back, the victim had sex with the attacker before being raped, or the victim was drunk or unconscious.

D. Unhealthy Relationships and the Power and Control Wheel
PROCESS POINTS:

- Refer to Domestic Violence in LGBT Communities handout and process issues from the video and others not mentioned.
- Some issues are found in same-sex relationships and some are universal.

The Power and Control Wheel

PROCESS STATEMENT: *"The farthest outer rim of the Control Wheel are the factors at the structural societal levels that contribute to LGBT intimate partner violence. Basically, the different types of discrimination and bias. The next inner circle shows the actual methods of violence, which can be physical or sexual. The internal sections highlight the actual methods of control and abuse. We saw some of these in our video."*

PROCESS QUESTIONS:

- What are some things that you can keep an eye out for that show someone may be experiencing IPV/domestic violence?
- What are some obstacles that you would see for a victim to report IPV to you or others? What if they are LGBTQ?

PROCESS POINTS:

- Lack of resources (shelters, support groups)
- LGBT phobia
- Lack of awareness of IPV in same-sex relationships
- Lack of training for service providers about LGBT IPV
- Fear that airing these problems will take away from progress/equality in the public sphere

Tips for Facilitators
- Some participants will think that all same-sex relationships exhibit IPV due to this section. Make sure to occasionally reiterate the research on how prevalence is similar to heterosexual relationships.
- Sexual assault is not covered in any detail in the IPV section. Consider sharing how your school or institution is providing this educational service through other means and encourage attendance. Make sure these efforts are inclusive of same-sex dating as well as transgender people or develop an additional curricula on this topic. A handout on reporting sexual assault is included with this session.

EVALUATION & TAKEAWAY CLOSING ACTIVITY—10 MINUTES

A. Goals
- Provide a brief overview of the contents of the session by allowing participants to voice their personal experience.
- Close the session on a high point.
- Allow for evaluation and feedback.

B. Directions
- Pass out Evaluation Sheet and allow a few minutes to complete.
- Closing Activity: *"What are you leaving here and what are you taking with you? Perhaps it's a myth or new piece of information or a story you heard. Think about this while completing your evaluation. Does anyone want to go first?"*
- Have each person briefly share their answers to the questions above.
- Thank them for participating in the session and to sign the Safe Zone pledge if this is their third session (second advanced session).

REFERENCES

Aaron's dictionary of gay terms. (n.d.). Retrieved August 13, 2015, from http://www.aaronsgayinfo.com/Fterms.html.

Ard, K. L., & Makadon, H. J. (2011). Addressing intimate partner violence in lesbian, gay, bisexual, and transgender patients. *Journal of General Internal Medicine, 26*(8), 930–33.

Berastain, P. (2013). Domestic violence in LGBT communities. Huffington Post Gay Voices. Accessed April 22, 2013 at http://www.huffingtonpost.com/pierre-r-berastain/intimate-partner-abuse-in_b_2765797.html.

Centers for Disease Control and Prevention. (2015). PrEP (pre-exposure prophylaxis). Retrieved August 25, 2015, from http://www.cdc.gov/hiv/basics/prep.html.

Hunter, S. (2012). Meeting others. In *Lesbian and gay couples: Lives, issues, and practice* (pp. 3–15). Chicago, IL: Lyceum Books, Inc.

Hunter, S. (2012). Micro-level issues and practice with lesbian and gay couples. In *Lesbian and gay couples: Lives, issues, and practice* (pp. 77–96). Chicago, IL: Lyceum Books, Inc.

Island, D. & Latellier, P. (1991). *Men who beat the men who love them: Battered gay men and domestic violence.* Bingham, NY: Haworth Press, Inc.

Journal of Sexual Medicine. (2010). Findings from the National Survey of Sexual Health Behavior (NSSHB), Center for Sexual Health Promotion, Indiana University, Volume 7, Issue Supplement 5, pages 243–373.

Kanuha, V. K. (2007). Compounding the triple jeopardy: Battering in lesbian of color relationships. In N. J. Sokoloff & C. Pratt (Eds.), *Domestic violence at the margins: Readings on race, class, gender, and culture* (pp. 71–82). New Brunswick, NJ: Rutgers University Press.

Kray, K. (2015). "Don't make us look bad": The invisibility of LGBTQIA+ intimate partner violence. Retrieved August 24, 2015 from http://everydayfeminism.com/2015/02/invisibility-lgbtqia-intimate-partner-violence.

Miller, B. (2015). "They're the modern day gay bar": Exploring the uses and gratifications of social networks for men who have sex with men. *Computers in Human Behavior, 51*, p. 477–82.

National Coalition Against Domestic Violence. (2014a). Domestic violence and lesbian, gay, bisexual, and transgender relationships. Retrieved August 13, 2015 from http://www.calegaladvocates.org/library/item.512380-NCADV_LGBT_Fact_Sheet.

National Coalition Against Domestic Violence. (2014b). LGBTQ victims of sexual violence. Retrieved August 13, 2015 from http://www.ncadv.org/images/LGBTQ_Victims.pdf.

Poynter, K., & Bickers Bock, L. (2007). Online dating safety checklist. Retrieved September 6, 2015, from http://www.uis.edu/lgbtq/wp-content/uploads/sites/83/2013/12/Online-Dating-Safety-Checklist.doc.

Renzetti, C. M., & Miley, C. H. (1996). *Violence in gay and lesbian domestic partnerships.* New York, NY: Haworth Press, Inc.

Robert Scott's gay slang dictionary. (n.d.). Retrieved August 13, 2015, from http://www.odps.org/glossword/index.php?a=index&d=8.

CHAPTER 9

Multiple Identities Workshop

KERRY JOHN POYNTER AND PAMELA SALELA

"Nature does not create discrete categories of human traits or identities. People create these categories to simplify the complexity of multiple identities and multiple realities."

—*Reynolds & Pope, 1991, p. 175*

This chapter references handouts (available as a single PDF formatted for easy and clear printing on 8.5" × 11") that supplement the curriculum and assessment pieces of this book. Please email resourcematerial@rowman.com to request the PDF, providing both the title and editor of this book along with proof of purchase (receipt).

DESCRIPTION

This basic cross-cultural introductory workshop allows for participants to share their own multiple identities; explores the intersections between race, culture, sexual orientation, and gender; and helps to illuminate the challenges of LGBTQ students with multiple identities. An emphasis is made on how different cultures and communities in the United States and abroad understand and define sexuality and gender minorities. Participants will leave with a personal action plan and resources to use and reflect on in their daily life.

CONTEXTUALIZATION

All too often the conversations and workshop sessions about LGBTQIA communities do not consider other intersecting identities. An inherent assumption is White (Poynter & Washington, 2005) or cisgender. The LGBTQIA community has the capacity to teach us about interacting with people of multiple communities, due to its complex diversity spanning class, race, and international borders, but this capacity is often squandered. This session is an attempt to put theory (Abes, Jones, & McEwen, 2007; Reynolds & Pope, 1991) into practice and give participants an introduction to intersectionality, multiple identity resolution, the concept of creating an inclusive community, and an introduction to gender and sexual minorities in cultures from around the world.

We all have multiple identities that comprise our complete selves such as sexual orientation, race, faith, ethnicity, differently abled, gender, socioeconomic status, among others. Some identities are privileged over others that are oppressed. "Oppression is a system that allows access to the services, rewards, benefits, and privileges of society based on membership in a particular group" (Reynolds & Pope, 1991, p. 70). We navigate how we cope with the oppression associated with these identities based on our environment, people we know, and the places we work or socialize. "For individuals . . . marginalized for racial, ethnic, religious, or economic reasons, the discovery that they are (LGBTQIA) compounds their marginalization and produces particular problems of identity integration and community building" (Rust, 1996, p. 54).

Reynolds and Pope (1991) theorized the Multidimensional Identity Model (MIM) to explain how people with multiple oppressions navigate their identities. *"Possible outcomes include identifying with multiple groups and integrating these identities (such as viewing oneself as both African American and lesbian), identifying with one group exclusively to the detriment of others (for example, a woman portrays herself as Native-American culturally and spiritually yet ignores a public LGBT identity due to fear of reprisal in a dominant Christian environment), or identifying with one group at a given time (for example, a Latino male identifies himself as gay in a predominantly White LGBTQIA community yet does not do so among Latino friends and family)"* (Poynter & Washington, 2005, p. 45).

Abes, Jones, and McEwen (2007) built on the work of Reynolds and Pope (1991) with the more complex Model of Multiple Dimensions of Identity. In their model, context also shapes how one views and experiences identities within the realm of family, sociocultural conditions, and the world around them. This concept is used in simplicity during this session when facilitating the Venn diagram activity.

More specifically, we should be endeavoring to create a community at our institutions that allows for LGBTQIA individuals to integrate all of their identities whether in the classroom, a student organization, residence hall, athletics team, or eating establishment. Barbara Smith (1999) explains, *"Perhaps the most maddening question anyone can ask me is, 'Which do you put first: being Black or being a woman, being Black or being Gay? The underlying assumption is that I should prioritize one of my identities because one of them is actually more important than the rest or that I must arbitrarily choose one of them over the others for the sake of acceptance in one particular community"* (p. 15).

Allies to LGBTQIA people need to learn to be intersectional in our work. The concept of intersectionality supports the full identities of each LGBTQIA student or employee. "**Intersectionality** is a framework meant to describe a person or a social problem holistically. Originating from the experiences of women of color who were often pigeonholed by race or gender, or as experiencing racism or sexism, but never both, intersectionality is directed at the gaps in academic literature, law, research, and activism. In short, intersectionality provides fuller and more complex understandings of people's multiple identities and of experiences with racism, sexism, classism, heterosexism, and other forms of discrimination" (Falcon, 2009). When we are intersectional in our work we come to realize that other identities are also marginalized and thus our ally work for LGBTQIA people becomes a gateway to understanding oppression of other identities.

Similarly, engaging in the oppression Olympics that attempts to name one identity as more oppressed is a lost cause that does more harm than good. Audre Lorde (2009) eloquently shared that "within the lesbian community I am Black, and within the Black community I am a lesbian. Any attack against Black people is a lesbian and gay issue, because I and thousands of other Black women are part of the lesbian community. Any attack against lesbians and gays is a Black issue, because thousands of lesbians and gay men are Black. There is no hierarchy of oppression" (p. 70).

Learning to be intersectional in our work means learning how other cultures understand or grapple with gender and sexual minorities. Ethnic minority cultures may not use the same identity labels (such as LGBTQIA) that are common among White European and North American countries. "Individuals from ethnic 'minority' cultures should not be expected to form sexual (and gender) identities based on Euro-American sexual concepts" (Rust, 1996, p. 56).

Contemporary North American subcultures exist, such as the ball culture and down low subcultures, that have been refuges or ways to explore non-normative sexualities and gender expressions. The ball room subculture, centered around house music and competing in dance, fashion, and a style of dance called vogueing, allowed for predominantly gay/bi/queer people of color in urban areas to find community and a support system. This support came from Houses, groups of performers that pledged alliance and that also served as a sort of surrogate family not quite like a gang. These performers competed for trophies and awards at events that were called balls. Jennie Livingston's documentary about the ball culture, *Paris is Burning* (2005), is perhaps the best known work on this subculture.

The down low subculture is a transgressive form of a heterosexual identity among men of color that also happen to be erotically attracted to or have sexual relations with other men. A heterosexual identity allows for them to not be viewed as containing a spoiled masculinity as a gay male that may be negatively viewed as less masculine among some communities of color.

However, down low can be defined differently depending on who uses the term. "Some DL (down low) men identify as straight and have wives or girlfriends but secretly have sex with other men. Others are younger men who are still questioning or exploring their sexuality. Some are closeted gay (or bisexual) men. And then there are African-American (and Latino) brothers who openly have relationships with other men but reject the label gay or bisexual because they equate those terms with white men" (Boykin, 2005, p. 15).

Contemporary Euro-American cultures often ascribe the terms "lesbian," "gay," "bisexual," "transgender," "queer," "pansexual," "intersex," and "asexual" to describe sexual and gender minorities. This has historically not been the same for cultures around the world but this is changing for some with the advent of the Internet and globalization. Cultures in India, Native Americans in North America and the Global South, Africa, Asia, and Polynesia, for example, have historically understood sexual and gender minorities in various ways.

The greatest support for and acceptance of gender variance in native North American cultures existed from 1860 to 1930. It is with the advent of European cultures that false cultural interpretations were projected. The term "Berdache" was imposed on peoples who partly or completely took on aspects of the culturally defined role of the other sex. But the term itself is derogatory, derived from the Arabic word for male prostitution, and superimposes a false meaning. The importance of sacred power was widely associated with sex/gender diversity in native North America. Hence, the term "two-spirit" has been suggested to replace "berdache" to convey the spiritual nature of gender variance.

American Indian cultures included three to four genders: men, women, male variants, and female variants (biological males or females who by engaging in activities associated with the opposite gender were reclassified accordingly). Bisexual orientation of some gender-variant persons may have been a culturally accepted expression of the gender variance. In a multiple-gender system, the partners would be of the same sex but different genders. "Homogender" (within gender), rather than homosexual practices, bore the brunt of negative cultural sanctions. The sexual partners of gender variants were never considered gender variants themselves.

As a result of Euro-American repression and the growing assimilation of Euro-American sex/gender ideologies, both female and male gender-variant roles among American Indians largely disappeared by the 1930s, as the reservation system was well under way.

Numerous other cultures, besides those in North America, have included their own references to sexual and gender minorities: Southeast Asian cultures such as tomboi (Blackwood, 2009), as well as the Hijra and Sahin in India; Bichas, Viado, and Travestis in Brazil; Mahu in Polynesia (Hawaii, Tahiti); Kathoey in Thailand; Bayot, Bantut, Bakla in the Philippines (Nanda, 2000). Although some individuals will adopt a Western mode of labeling, still others wish to honor their cultural history.

Moving along to the continent of Africa, anthropologists and others had long considered "primitive man" pure of homosexuality. Historically (nineteenth to twentieth century) there was a reluctance to report and record homosexuality or give such behaviors acknowledgment, stating they only existed when females were absent, as in the age-stratified homosexuality existent among males (a practice among Dahomey youth). However, closer observations of records shows that many of these pairings actually last for a lifetime. Other theories have circulated among scholars that African homosexualities are a result of exposure to European neuroses. Extensive observation, however, makes it clear that colonialists did not create African homosexualities, though they likely did create the stigma surrounding it to the extent that systems of surveillance and regulation for suppressing it have evolved over time.

In some African "traditional" cultures, gendered systems are not associated with the markers of sexual identity or biology. The female husbands of the Nandi (Kenya) are based on status and frequently associated with wealth. Gender is a role, as opposed to being based on biology. The female husband takes on the social role of a man. However, she is not expected to have a sexual relationship with her wife (female). Her wife, on the other hand, is frequently expected to have sex with a biological male or males for the purposes of procreation and to provide her female husband with a child heir.

One way that a woman may choose to become a female husband can be seen in an example from Nigeria. A woman who had always felt she was meant to be a man and had once been married to a man, divorces without ever having produced any children. She chooses to become a female husband and takes on two wives who produce children for her through their sexual relations with males. Among the Nandi, the purpose of this arrangement is to produce a male heir, since property rights are tied to males.

Although sexual relations are not assumed, many surmise that in many cases, sexual relations are occurring. There may be many motivations outside the institutionalized one for these arrangements including the higher bride price paid by female husbands, female companionship, sexual autonomy, and less male violence within the household, thus providing a more peaceable existence (Roscoe & Murray, 2001, pp. 258–61).

Many of the readings used as background for this workshop have made note of the fact that a preponderance of case studies has focused on male gender diversity. The reasons for this may be complex and not necessarily indicative of a lack of female gender diversity. Indeed, anecdotal evidence points to the wide existence of female gender diversity. Perhaps the relative lack of case studies is due to the nature of sexism and the relatively recent advent of women as scholars and historians of note. After all, s/he who holds the pen can determine the perspective of analysis, and surely the scholarship in this area will grow as diversity within the halls of academia grows.

The concepts in the previous section relate to the readings for facilitators and are directly connected to the goals of the session and will be referenced in the curriculum provided. Facilitators of this session should, however, consider the critical observation regarding male and female gender diversity as they develop their own workshops.

READINGS FOR FACILITATORS

The following annotated readings are intended as starting points on multiple identities for new learners. They support the learning goals of the curriculum explained in this section. Facilitators should use them as a means of self-learning. They also will be beneficial to group discussion among co-facilitators before practicing and ultimately facilitating the activities contained in this curriculum.

- Blackwood, E. (2009). Trans identities and contingent masculinities: Being Tombois in everyday practice. *Feminist Studies, 35*(3), 454–80.

Evelyn Blackwood provides a thorough overview of the culturally identified and sanctioned Tombois of West Sumatra, Indonesia. Tombois are biologically female but gender identified as male. This gender manifestation is not a simple application of Western understandings of lesbian and gay identity, and provides an excellent example of intersectionality within a specific geocultural context.

- Jones, S. R., & McEwen, M. K. (2000). A conceptual model of multiple dimensions of identity. *Journal of College Student Development, 41*(4), 405–14.

The authors explain a model of multiple identities developed from a qualitative study of college women. The model contains intersecting circles of identity, including race, sexual orientation, class, religion, gender, and culture, that alone do not adequately describe a person. Dots on the circles represent the salience of that identity at a particular instance of time. Inner dots by the core are most salient. This article pairs nicely with the Reynolds and Pope (1991) article on multiple oppressions. Facilitators in this session will find this reading useful as they prepare for the Venn Diagram and Valuing Identity activities.

- Lorde, A. (1983). There is no hierarchy of oppressions. *Bulletin: Homophobia and Education, 14*(3/4), 9.

Famed poet Audre Lorde's now classic essay posits the futility of disconnecting one's various identities. She states that to assert any *one* of her identities as her one true or dominant identity would leave her bifurcated and ultimately lead to false dichotomies of multiple oppressions. This brief but powerful personal expose demonstrates the absurdity of being forced to choose from just one of one's oppressed identities, leaving the roots of oppressive ideology untouched within other realms.

- Nanda, S. (2000). *Gender diversity: Crosscultural variations.* Prospect Heights, IL: Waveland Press.

Nanda provides an extensive summative expose of gender diversity within seven distinct cultures through the use of ethnographic data. Geo-cultural areas covered include Native cultures in North America, India, Brazil, Polynesia, Thailand, and the Philippines and historical Euro-American cultures (selective). The examples provided point to the fact that gender variance is a transglobal reality that occurs across cultures. This is a useful source for identifying specific examples when speaking with workshop participants with varying cultural backgrounds.

- Poynter, K., & Washington, J. (2005). Multiple identities: Creating community on campus for LGBT students. In *Gender identity and sexual orientation: Research, policy, and personal perspectives* (pp. 41–47), San Francisco: Jossey-Bass, CA.

This chapter argues for creating a college campus community that is inclusive of LGBTQIA+ people by recognizing their multiple identities. Particular attention is given to race, faith, and sexual orientation. Written for student services personnel, the authors use theory, personal accounts, and offer implications for practice, to argue for wider attention to these topics. This chapter will pair well with the Reynolds and Pope (1991) navigating identity conflict article and was a basis for the creation of the Multiple Identities Safe Zone session.

- Reynolds, A., & Pope, R. (1991). The complexities of diversity: Exploring multiple oppressions. *Journal of Counseling & Development, 70,* 174–80.

The authors critique identity development models as one dimensional and not expansive enough to encompass multiple identities. A Multidimensional Identity Model (MID) with four options is explained that shows how people with multiple oppressions navigate their identities. Movement by individuals between these four options is determined by personal needs, reference group, and environment. Facilitators of this session will find this reading useful when explaining how LGBTQIA+ young adults of multiple identities will navigate the campus environment. Part of this article is quoted in the session. The full integration of identities is the basis of the core in the Venn Diagram activity in this session.

- Roscoe, W., & Murray, S. O. (2001). *Boy-wives and female husbands: Studies of African homosexualities.* New York: St. Martin's Press.

Roscoe and Murray provide detailed case studies of gender variation from across the continent of Africa with scholarly examination coming from sociologists, historians, and linguists. Extensive tables highlight gender and its variations among language families, inheritance systems, subsistence agriculture, postpartum sexual taboos, male genital mutilation, socioeconomic stratification, and more. This work adds to the literature on homosexual behaviors in a global context, broadening the available examples to include the African continent.

- Rust, P. (1996). Managing multiple identities: Diversity among bisexual women and men. In B. A. Firestein (Ed.), *Bisexuality: The psychology and politics of an invisible minority.* Thousand Oaks, CA: Sage Publications.

Paula Rust explains how bisexuals, or any marginalized sexual identity, attempt to integrate with other group memberships, especially other marginalized ethnic, racial, religious, and socioeconomic identities. The author explains the type of cultural differences that exist and that not all people from ethnic minority cultures should be expected to have sexual identities similar to Euro-American labels of LGBTQIA+. The norms of the culture of origin can be different than the Western ideals of individual autonomy and less reliance on family. She explains how people with multiple marginalizations will navigate these identities in a much similar fashion as explained by Reynolds and Pope (1990).

- Sigle-Rushton, W., & Lindstrom, E. (2013). Intersectionality. In M. Evans and C. Williams (Eds.), *Gender: The key concepts (pp. 129–34)* New York: Routledge.

Feminists have been at the forefront of bringing to social awareness the complexities and critical importance of applying an understanding of intersectionality to real-world analysis. This entry touches on the critical body of scholarship of feminist scholars Patricia Hill Collins and Leslie McCall for approaches to this paradoxical dilemma. Those seeking a more nuanced understanding of intersectionality will find this article useful for diving deeper into sociopolitical and theoretical considerations of multiple identities.

- Smith, B. (1999). Blacks & gays: Healing the great divide. In E. Brandt (Ed.) *Dangerous liaisons: Blacks, gays, and the struggle for equality* (pp. 15–24). New York: New Press.

Barbara Smith shares her struggles as an activist within the African American as well as the gay community. These two communities expect her to prioritize one identity over the other due to racism in the LGBTQIA community and homophobia in the Black community. Smith uses examples and quotes to illustrate her points.

Although the examples seem dated (early 1990s) they are still credible examples today. This chapter is an excellent example of the complexity of multiple oppressions detailed in Reynolds and Pope (1991) and is quoted in this session.

Suggested Films

- Livingston, J., Gibson, P., & Oppenheim, J. (Eds.). (2005). *Paris is burning.* Burbank, CA: Miramax Home Entertainment.
- Nibley, L., & Martin, R. (Eds.). (2010). *Two spirits.* Los Angeles, CA: Riding the Tiger Productions.
- Richen, Y. (2013). *The new black.* San Francisco, CA: California Newsreel.
- Schermerhorn, C., & Cram, B. (Eds.). (1997). *You don't know dick: Courageous hearts of transsexual men.* Boston: Northern Light Productions.
- Thomas, A., & Hsu, C. L. (Eds.). (2006). *Middle sexes: Redefining he and she.* United States: Home Box Office.

Tips for Facilitators

- Use the readings to familiarize yourself with the topic of multiple identities before learning how to facilitate the session.
- Take time to discuss the point of each reading with your co-facilitators. Seek out faculty or staff with expertise in anthropology and/or sociology to help lead discussions.
- Assign roles for each facilitator in the session.
- Arrange a practice session with knowledgeable and interested members of the community. Ask for feedback.
- Use the facilitator and session evaluation forms (chapter 10) to receive feedback from the practice session. Incorporate feedback into next session.
- Example process statements and questions are provided below to help provide context to that particular section of the curriculum. Use these as examples to learn from and not exactly to read verbatim. Use your own words and ways of communicating the same concepts.
- Selectively use examples from the readings on different cultures and subcultures to demonstrate the proliferation of multiple identities within the context of sexual and gender minorities.

CURRICULUM—2 HOURS

Curriculum Outline

- Intros, Ground Rules, PGPs, Parking Lot, Sensitive Topics Disclaimer (Race, Sexuality, and Culture), and Learning Objectives—10 minutes
- Introduce the Handouts and Terms—1 minute
- Venn Diagram Activity—5 minutes
- Identity Conflict & Resolution (Reynolds and Pope)—5 minutes
- Valuing Identity (The Color Sticker Activity)—30 minutes
- Prezi: Global Tour of Gender & Sexual Diversity (Countries, Cultures in History, & Contemporary Terminology)—5 minutes
- Student Video: A Conversation with LGBTQIA+ Students of Color—30 minutes
- Personal Action Plan—20 minutes
- Closing Activity and Evaluation—15 minutes

Learning Outcomes

- A basic understanding that sexual and gender minorities are diverse in race, gender, religion, etc.
- An overview of terms and words used in various cultures that describe sexual and gender minorities.
- An understanding of multiple identities and how people can and cannot resolve them in our culture.

Handouts/Materials

- Venn Diagram Multiple Identities
- LGBTQIA+ Multiple Identities Personal Action Plan
- Stickers
- Sticker Color Code Key (one for each table)
- Evaluation Sheet

Use the introductions section explained in chapter 4 Fundamentals on page 28. Include introductions, PGPs, Ground Rules, Parking Lot, and review of the Safe Zone program.

INTRODUCE THE HANDOUTS, TERMS, & VENN DIAGRAM ACTIVITY—5 MINUTES

A. Goals
- Give participants an introduction and basic understanding of the terms used in this session.
- Utilize an activity to assist participants to begin to consider identities as being multidimensional.

B. Directions
- Disseminate the session handouts.

PROCESS STATEMENT: *"The following are a few of the terms associated with this session. Some of them are in use in cultures around the world."*

Identities: The set of innate behavioral or personal characteristics by which an individual is recognizable as a member of a group. A social group status that determines privilege or power.

Berdache: A generic term used to refer to a third-gender person (woman-living-man). The term "berdache" is generally rejected as inappropriate and offensive by Native Peoples because it is a term that was assigned by European settlers to differently gendered Native Peoples. Appropriate terms vary by tribe and include "one-spirit," "two-spirit," and "wintke."

Down low: Commonly associated with hypermasculinized Black and Latino men that do not connect with a White and stereotypical feminized gay identity. Popular media has unfortunately made down low individuals the scapegoat for HIV transmission.

Gender: The social construction of masculinity and femininity in a specific culture. It involves gender assignment (the gender designation of someone at birth), gender roles (the expectations imposed on someone based on their gender), gender perception (how others interpret someone's gender), and gender identity (how someone defines their own gender).

Identities: The set of innate behavioral or personal characteristics by which an individual is recognizable as a member of a group. A social group status that determines privilege or power.

Intersectionality: A framework meant to describe a person or a social problem holistically. Originating from the experiences of women of color who were often pigeonholed by race or gender, or as experiencing racism or sexism, but never both, intersectionality is directed at the gaps in academic literature, law, research, and activism. In short, intersectionality provides fuller and more complex understandings of people's multiple identities and of experiences with racism, sexism, classism, heterosexism, and other forms of discrimination (Falcon, 2009).

Oppression: "A system that allows access to the services, rewards, benefits, and privileges of society based on membership in a particular group" (Reynolds & Pope, 1990, p. 70).

Same-gender loving: A term sometimes used by members of the African American/Black community to express an alternative sexual orientation without relying on terms and symbols of European descent. The term emerged in the early 1990s with the intention of offering Black women who love women and Black men who love men a voice, a way of identifying and being that resonated with the uniqueness of Black culture in life (sometimes abbreviated as "SGL").

Stud: An African American and/or Latina masculine lesbian. Also known as "butch" or "aggressive."

Transgender: Most commonly used as an umbrella term for someone whose self-identification or expression challenges traditional notions of "male" and "female." This collective of people includes transsexuals, crossdressers, drag queens and kings, genderqueers, and others who cross traditional gender categories. "Trans" is often used inclusively as well as a stand-alone identity.

Two-Spirited: Native persons who have attributes of both genders, have distinct gender and social roles in their tribes, and are often involved with mystical rituals (shamans). Their dress is usually a mixture of male and female articles and they are seen as a separate or third gender. The term "two-spirit" is usually considered too specific to the Zuni tribe. Similar identity labels vary by tribe and include "one-spirit" and "wintke."

Venn Diagram—5 minutes
- Draw Venn diagram on board or newsprint paper.
- Facilitators share and explain their own Venn diagram to provide example. Make sure to explain the middle section as the ideal integrated complete self.
- Pass out Venn Diagram Handout.

Figure 9.1. Venn Diagram Multiple Identities.
Source: Created by Kerry Poynter

Poynter, 2010

PROCESS STATEMENT: *"Take a couple minutes to list three identities you see as most important. Share in your group for 5 minutes to compare and understand the identities important to those around you."*

PROCESS POINT:

- *"Not all LGBTQ people are White, Atheist, easily fit into the gender binary, or identify with common labels in the LGBTQIA community. Additionally, we all are not just one identity. For example, Barbara Smith in her essay "Blacks and Gays Healing the Great Divide,' wrote, 'Perhaps the most maddening question anyone can ask me is, Which do you put first: being Black or being a woman, being Black or being Gay?' The underlying assumption is that I should prioritize one of my identities because one of them is actually more important than the rest or that I must arbitrarily choose one of them over the others for the sake of acceptance in one particular community"* (Smith, 1999 p. 15).

PROCESS STATEMENT: *"We would like to share with you our own personal diagrams before you begin. Please take a couple minutes and fill out the Venn diagram sheet. As you finish please share with everyone at your table."*

Tips for Facilitators
- Allow for participants to choose identities that are more relevant to themselves, but we recommend keeping sexual identity and/or gender identity.
- Provide other possible identities to use by pointing to the identities posted on the wall for the Valuing Identity Color Sticker activity.

PROCESS STATEMENT: *"We would like to share with you our own personal diagrams before you begin. Please take a couple minutes and fill out the Venn Diagram sheet. As you finish please share with everyone at your table."*

IDENTITY CONFLICT & RESOLUTION—5 MINUTES
PROCESS STATEMENT: *"We all navigate these identities based on our environment, people we know, and the places we work or socialize." "Possible outcomes include identifying with multiple groups and integrating these identities (such as viewing oneself as both African American and lesbian), identifying with one group exclusively to*

the detriment of others (for example, a woman portrays herself as Native-American culturally and spiritually yet ignores a public LGBT identity due to fear of reprisal in a dominant Christian environment), or identifying with one group at a given time (for example, a Latino male identifies himself as gay in a predominantly White LGBTQIA community yet does not do so among Latino friends and family)" (Reynolds & Pope, 1991; Poynter & Washington, 2005, p. 45).

- **Cultural Norms:** *"Another item to consider when working with LGBTQIA+ or sexual and gender minorities is the cultural norms of their ethnic background"* (Rust, 1996, p. 57).
- **Western Norms:** *"Contemporary Western (European/U.S.) norms 'place less importance on family, especially extended family. The emphasis on individual autonomy and personal growth mediates against a strong sense of family responsibility. Fulfillment is conceptualized in terms of individual fulfillment, not fulfillment of family obligations'"* (Rust, 1996, pp. 57–58).
- **Non-Western Norms:** *"Among these . . . are an emphasis on the importance of the family, respect for elders, the distinction between the private and the public spheres, the availability of concepts for organizing and identifying sexuality, and gender roles"* (Rust, 1996, p. 57).

VALUING IDENTITY (THE COLOR STICKER ACTIVITY)—30 MINUTES

A. Goals
- Help participants identify which identities are valued over others.
- Create a basic understanding of which identities hold power and privilege.
- Inform how participants have not been able to resolve their own identity integration.

B. Materials
- Six color stickers (one for each identity question)
- Large-print paper with the 10 identities written on them posted around the room
- Sticker Color Code Key explaining the six sticker colors associated with each identity question for each table and on screen

C. Directions
- Hang posters around the room that have the following identities written on them: *Socioeconomic Status; Religion/ Faith Beliefs; Disability or Ability; Age; Education; Ethnicity; Race; Gender; Sexual Orientation; Citizenship Status.*
- Facilitate a brief dialogue that has the participants define these identities in their own words.
- Ask participants to move around the room and place their color stickers on the poster of their choosing based on the statements made by the facilitator:
  ○ This is my identity I am most comfortable discussing—Red.
  ○ This is my identity I am least comfortable discussing or I question the most—Orange.
  ○ I have experienced the most joy around this identity—Yellow.
  ○ I have experienced the most pain around this identity—Green.
  ○ This identity is the most invisible to others—Blue.
  ○ This is my identity that I have to defend the most—Purple.

D. Large-Group Discussion
PROCESS STATEMENT: *"We have highlighted some of the ways that people with multiple identities and oppression cope with navigating identity conflict in hopes of resolution. Based on your previous small-group discussion, you have some idea of the multiple identities present in the room. We are now going to participate in an exercise that will allow you to reflect on how you navigate your multiple identities in your daily life. We call this the Valuing Identity Color Sticker Activity."*

PROCESS QUESTIONS:

- Which identity did people indicate they would be most comfortable discussing? What about experiencing joy? Why? Can we have a few people share why they chose these?
- Which identities did they feel the least comfortable discussing? Are these similar to experiencing pain, invisibility, or having to defend them?
- Why do you think people indicated these adverse reactions?

E. Small-Group Discussion

PROCESS STATEMENT: *"Let's spend a few minutes in your small groups (tables). Please create a list of at least five possible emotional or behavioral experiences that contributed to these adverse reactions. Give examples if you can."*

"Now that we have listed some experiences. Let's turn that around. These are examples of what we should avoid re-creating in our daily interactions. They will form the basis of your personal action plan later in the session."

Tips for Facilitators

Project the color code key on a screen and have it printed for participants' ease of use.

- This activity can take a lot of time in your session. Consider using four of the colors instead of six if your time is limited. We recommend red, orange, blue, and purple.
- An identity that is often defended or invisible is the category of religion. If you are able to identify religions that are privileged (our experience is usually Christianity) then utilize this for discussion by emphasizing religions that are truly marginalized within our culture (Muslim, Jewish, Buddhism, Wicca, etc.).
- Be sensitive to the demographic of your institution and aware of the groups that are marginalized and privileged in your environment. Allow your activity to give focus to those identities.

PREZI—GLOBAL TOUR OF GENDER & SEXUAL DIVERSITY—5 MINUTES

A. Goal
- Show how other non-Western cultures have described sexual and gender minorities.

B. Directions
- Set up the Prezi online at GO.UIS.EDU/safezonePrezi or search "SafeZone : A Global Tour of Gender and Sexual Diversity."
- Provide the handout and refer to it.
- Briefly show the Prezi and how it works without spending a lot of time.
- **Alternate version:** Sexual orientation and gender identity throughout history: http://dayagainsthomophobia.org/buzz-worthy/debunking-myth/#.
- Consider an extended use of this Prezi in place of the student video project explained in this curriculum.

C. Group Discussion: The Trouble with Labels

PROCESS STATEMENT: *"We are going to give you some examples of the complexity of diversity within the LGBTQIA community. People of different sexual orientations and gender identities refer to themselves in a variety of ways. For instance, some African Americans use the term 'same-gender loving.' South east Asian cultures have used terms such as 'Tomboi,' Hawaiian cultures use 'Mahu,' Polynesian cultures (Hawaii, Tahiti) use the term 'Mahu,' and Native American tribes now use the term 'Two-Spirit.' This Prezi is available to you to peruse at your own pace. It is a work in progress. If you have any knowledge to add to it then please let us know."*

PROCESS QUESTION:

- How are these cultures similar or different than our current Western understanding of LGBTQ people?

Red Sticker:
This is my identity I am most comfortable discussing.

Orange Sticker:
This is my identity I am least comfortable discussing or I question the most.

Blue Sticker:
This identity is the most invisible to others.

Purple Sticker:
This is my identity that I have to defend the most.

Figure 9.2. Sticker Color Code Key.

Tips for Facilitators
- Assign one or two cultures or regions from the Prezi to a facilitator as time may not permit to review it worldwide.
- The Prezi was designed for self-learning by participants either before or after the session. Consider using it in the session for an extended time in place of the Student Video Conversation explained below.
- If you do have the time, consider using this in smaller groups by providing a laptop/tablet for each group. Assign each group a different culture or region of the world. Explain that each group will provide a brief verbal overview when allotted time is up.

CREATE A STUDENT VIDEO: A CONVERSATION WITH LGBTQIA+ STUDENTS OF COLOR OR GLOBAL TOUR OF GENDER & SEXUAL DIVERSITY PREZI—30 MINUTES

A video of students responding to a set list of guiding questions. Student voices can bring a personal element to the issues occurring on your own campus. Although we cannot share the original video created for this session, contained here are the guiding questions. Students met in advance of the recording and these meetings doubled as a support group. The video was recorded in a professional studio on campus and edited by professional staff. Students signed a waiver that allowed for its use in this session but not for use on the Internet or mass consumption.

A. Guiding Questions

- Introduction: Name, Major, Year, What groups and communities are you involved with? Can you provide one word that explains your experience in student life or in the classroom?
- Do you feel you are able to be your authentic self that integrates all your identities (race, gender, sexuality, culture)?
- Have you ever had to hide your sexuality, gender identity, or racial identity in order to fit in?
- Have you experienced any bias, discrimination, or hate on campus?
- Share your best and worst experience on campus related to your race and sexual/gender identity.
- What suggestions would you have for a Safe Zone ally?

B. Directions

- Bring external containing the video or upload to a cloud-sharing site.
- Check sound and projector in advance.

PROCESS STATEMENT: *"We would like to share with you some student voices from our institution. We spent some time talking about navigating identities. Here we get to listen to how some LGBTQIA people of color have experienced our community."*

AFTER VIDEO PROCESS STATEMENT: *"Let's now consider what we just heard from these students."*

C. Group Discussion

PROCESS QUESTIONS:

- What were some of the positive and negative things you heard?
- How were these people navigating their multiple identities?

Tips for Facilitators

- Consider recording your own videos featuring students, staff, and faculty from your institution.
- Ask prompting questions during your recording that relate to the learning outcomes of this session. Use one or two examples that work best if a larger group is not available or willing.
- Use the Global Tour of Gender & Sexual Diversity Prezi instead of this video section.

PERSONAL ACTION PLAN—20 MINUTES

A. Directions

- Pass out and refer to Action Plan sheet.
- Instruct each person to spend 5 minutes to think about and fill out their sheet.
- Instruct the groups/tables to share some of their ideas with the group.
- Large-group discussion for 5 minutes.

B. Discussion

PROCESS STATEMENT: *"Today we focused on increasing your awareness of our multiple identities and the challenges of navigating them. The next step is to make plans so that you can apply your new knowledge to different aspects of your life. Take a few minutes to think about what action steps can be taken and then complete the following statements."*

Tips for Facilitators

- This activity works best as a small group instead of solo processing.
- Allow adequate time for small groups to share their action plans.
- Collect the action plans and organize the ideas for anonymously sharing with workshop participants via email, blog, social media, or web page. This will create an ongoing record of ideas.

EVALUATION AND TAKEAWAY CLOSING ACTIVITY—10 MINUTES

A. Goals

- Provide a brief overview of the contents of the session by allowing participants to voice their personal experience.
- Close the session on a high point.
- Allow for evaluation and feedback.

B. Directions

- Pass out Evaluation Sheet and allow a few minutes to complete.
- Closing Activity: "*What are you leaving here and what are you taking with you? Perhaps it's a myth or new piece of information or a story you heard. Think about this while completing your evaluation. Does anyone want to go first?*"
- Have each person briefly share their answers to the questions above.
- Thank them for participating in the session. Sign the Safe Zone pledge if this is their third session (second advanced session).

REFERENCES

Abes, E. S., Jones, S. R., & McEwen, M. K. (2007). Reconceptualizing the model of multiple dimensions of identity: The role of meaning-making capacity in the construction of multiple identities. *Journal of College Student Development, 48*(1), 1–22.

Falcon, S.M. (2009) *Intersectionality*. Encyclopedia of Gender and Society. Thousand Oaks: Sage Publications.

Jones, S. R., & McEwen, M. K. (2000). A conceptual model of multiple dimensions of identity. *Journal of College Student Development, 41*(4), 405–14.

Poynter, K., & Washington, J. (2005). Multiple identities: Creating community on campus for LGBT students. In R. Sanlo (Ed.), *New directions in student services: Gender identity and sexual orientation*. San Francisco, CA: Jossey-Bass.

Reynolds, A. L., & Pope, R. L. (1991). The complexities of diversity: Exploring multiple oppressions. *Journal of Counseling & Development, 70*, 174–80.

CHAPTER 10

A Model Assessment

KERRY JOHN POYNTER

This chapter references handouts (available as a single PDF formatted for easy and clear printing on 8.5" × 11") that supplement the curriculum and assessment pieces of this book. Please email resourcematerial@rowman.com to request the PDF, providing both the title and editor of this book along with proof of purchase (receipt).

WHAT IS ASSESSMENT?

An assessment of a program can be done in sometimes the simplest ways: an unplanned conversation with students over lunch that is later documented in writing, including a question in a fun interactive icebreaker before a group event; working with student staff to journal or document their experiences during a support group; or asking a question on a blog or listserv of professionals to receive feedback. The possibilities for assessment are varied.

All too often the need to assess a program or service conjures up fears of having to conduct research, Institutional Review Board proposals, recruiting participants, analyzing results with software, etc. These can occur but assessment is not research! You are assessing if you are meeting the goals and missions and learning objectives of your particular institution or program, not research that guides the creation of theory that is generally applicable to all institutions.

Of course, there are more structured ways to assess and evaluate that are quantitative or qualitative but program coordinators, often of small staffs, do not need to worry about doing research. Do, however, be concerned about how you will assess your Safe Zone allies program from its very inception. "Assessment is any effort to gather, analyze, and interpret evidence which describes institutional, departmental, divisional, or agency effectiveness. . . . [This] ranges all the way from keeping track of who uses our services, programs, and facilities to whether or not such offerings have any impact, or the desired impact, on our clientele. It includes student needs assessments, environmental assessments, comparisons to accepted standards or other institutions, and clientele satisfaction with what we offer" (Upcraft & Schuh, 1996, p. 18).

This chapter provides a brief overview of assessment, a review of published and unpublished Safe Zone assessments from various institutions, and an example seven-step model for a comprehensive Safe Zone assessment program to adopt at onset of creation, implementation, facilitation, and ongoing coordination.

Anecdotal evidence is most often cited as support that these Safe Zone allies programs are meeting their stated goals. However, anecdotal evidence is not going to persuade critics, funding boards, or administrators that may hold decision-making power over the future of these programs. In addition, when attaining possibly scarce resources, an assessment will enable organizers to target resources to areas that are effective, thus creating a quality program (Upcraft & Schuh, 1996). A quality assessment can also help to explain the decisions made.

A few studies have shown that attending Safe Zone workshop sessions, membership in the program, or visibility of the program is positively related to supportive attitudes and an affirming campus climate (Evans, 2002; Finkel, Storaasli, Bandele, & Schaefer, 2003; Worthen, 2011) that provides attitude change, and encourages development of actions that intercede homophobia and transphobia. The most empirically based study on student attitude change (Worthen, 2011) found participation created "enlightened perspectives" that met workshop goals of "increasing awareness" and "cultivating/reinforcing positive attitudes," which are laudable Safe Zone goals (p. 369). Furthermore, students participating, as well as those aware of the program due to its visibility, were significantly related to supportive attitudes when compared with students that were unaware (Worthen, 2011).

Almost no studies have been conducted that report what kind of content learning and learning style is best situated for knowledge acquisition, positive attitude change, and skills training that leads to actions that interrupt homophobia, biphobia, transphobia, and/or inclusive practices. Ryan, Broad, Walsh, and Nutter (2013) found that an ally program and training that emphasized ally development (majority) theory reinforced professional responsibility in staff and faculty yet left out other stated goals of education and positive attitude change.

Woodford, Kolb, Durocher-Radeka, and Javier (2014) examined and explained four types of ally program training models found nationwide and advocated for incremental sessions that allowed time for advocacy-building activities (see chapter 2). Unpublished campus assessments also offer a glimpse into the effectiveness of these programs at individual schools (Bruno, 2005; Dirks, 2011; Poynter & Lewis, 2003).

FORMS OF ASSESSMENT

A quality assessment will have a number of important components. These components include a review of program goals/objectives that support the department or university mission statement, outcomes that specifically describe end results of the program, choosing an evaluation method that enables acquisition of outcomes, implementation including responsibility and schedule, analysis of results, and decisions and recommendations (Bresciani, 2003; Upcraft & Schuh, 1996). Conducting an assessment can be done quantitatively, qualitatively, or by comparison to established programs (benchmarking).

As explained in chapter 2, there exists relatively little published data about the effectiveness of Safe Zone allies programs that exist in North America. Much of it has gone unpublished. A compilation of published and unpublished data does begin to provide a glimpse in how to implement or reinvent these programs that meet learning outcomes, contribute to campus climate improvement, and developmental success for members participating in the program that are learning to be better allies.

A Comprehensive Safe Zone Assessment Model

Items to assess in an LGBTQIA+ Safe Space Ally program include workshop sessions, campus culture change, number and type of conversations as a result of displaying the sign, knowledge and skill acquisition after workshop sessions, awareness of the program in the LGBTQIA+ community, and advocacy for campus inclusion. Evaluation methods can include training exit surveys, online surveys of membership and the LGBTQIA+ community, and advisory board or membership focus group feedback.

A Mixed Methods Safe Zone Assessment Model

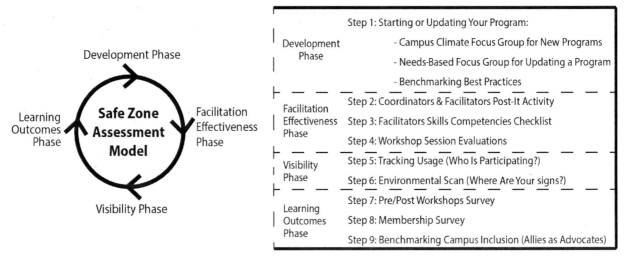

Figure 10.1. Mixed Methods Safe Zone Assessment Model
Source: Created by Kerry Poynter

The assessment model explained here follows the comprehensive assessment model outlined by Upcraft and Schuh (1996, pp. 27–31). It includes tracking usage statistics, needs, satisfaction, session learning outcomes, benchmarking the best, and using national standards. Initial steps are intended for schools that are starting a program while later steps are more beneficial to programs already in existence. A 9-step model may seem cumbersome as the fear of a lack of time is often an impediment to assessment. Many of these steps can be integrated easily into the coordination of the program, do not require more than a few hours of work, are useful at certain steps in the duration of the program over a few years, and are already real-world tested.

DEVELOPMENT PHASE—STEP 1: STARTING OR UPDATING YOUR PROGRAM

Draughn, Elkins, and Roy (2002) offer suggested questions to ask when conducting an informal assessment of the campus environment before creating a Safe Zone allies program. The goal is to come to a better understanding of the needs present at the institution, possible barriers of resistance, and content areas for possible workshop sessions. A focus group of stakeholders should be convened that includes LGBTQIA+-identified students, staff, and faculty as well as their heterosexual allies that have demonstrated their willingness to educate others. Questions to ask your focus group(s):

1. To what extent are topics that affect LGBTQIA+ students visible on campus? How are topics on gender and sexual minorities represented in the curriculum? Student activities?
2. What support systems exist for sexual and gender minorities members of the campus community? Does the institution have, for example, a designated LGBTQIA+ Resource Center or support person? Gender/sexuality or queer studies program? Mentor program?
3. Does the institution have a non-discrimination policy and, if so, is sexual orientation and/or gender identity included in it?
4. How, if at all, is intolerance of homophobia, heterosexism, and transphobia condemned when it occurs? Have incidents of homophobia/transphobia been addressed in the past and in what ways?
5. What aspects of the institutional culture serve as potential barriers to an inclusive, safe environment for LGBTQIA+ students?
6. What members of the LGBTQIA+ community on campus are most visible? Which identities are not visible or receive little attention?
7. Who and what departments are doing the education on LGBTQIA+ topics? What departments are considered the most resistant?

Using these guiding questions, themes can emerge along with areas of demonstrated need. Use these to justify your program and as starting points when creating the nuts and bolts to assemble the sessions as well as where to outreach across campus.

Draughn, Elkins, and Roy (2002) also suggest a list of guiding questions for Safe Zone programs already in existence but in need of reinvention. The University of Illinois Springfield also embarked on an assessment of a program that had been in existence for a number of years. The following is a compilation of those questions from both sources to be used for a series of focus groups:

1. What is the nature of the program? Is it an active, visible presence on campus or a presence in name only?
2. What are the stated goals of the program? Do the goals adequately emphasize both providing support to LGBTQIA+ individuals and working to confront homophobia and heterosexism and transphobia in the campus environment?
3. What are the strengths of the program and how are they meeting the stated goals?
4. Who are the members? Are faculty and administration involved? Students? If not, why?
5. What education do new members receive? What opportunities exist for further education, beyond initial training sessions?
6. What topics are covered? What do the members still need to become better allies? Please provide examples.
7. What have you gained from participating in the program? Explain.
8. What ways can you further contribute to the program?
9. From what campus constituencies and community resources does the program receive support? Financial support? Vocal support?
10. Where do you see the Safe Zone signs more often on campus? Where do you not?

Conducting these focus groups will allow for content-rich data gathering but benchmarking best practices can show you how to use it. If you are developing your program, compare your plans with similar schools in your region and/or size or conference. Do not reinvent the wheel if your colleagues down the road have already answered similar questions you have. Invite facilitators and coordinators from area universities to consult with you as you develop the program. Ask these consultants to experience your new workshop sessions as you practice facilitation so as to provide feedback in preparation for launching the program. Although this volume is intended to provide a best practice model for a Safe Zone program, schools could have different needs based on region, size, and demographics.

FACILITATION EFFECTIVENESS PHASE—STEP 2: COORDINATORS & FACILITATORS POST-IT ACTIVITY
Members that serve on a coordinating committee and/or as facilitators will have a particular base of experiences to assess. Their experiences with the program could yield helpful insights. Use this activity as a way to assess the coordination of the program as well as the work of the facilitators. Consider inviting a moderator that is not part of the committee or facilitation team. This is also an opportunity to build consensus about new goals and future decisions. Give each person a dozen Post-its with directions to keep the activity anonymous. Make sure everyone has the same kind of writing utensil and same color Post-its. Have each person respond to the following questions by writing the question number that corresponds to their written response. Encourage two to three responses to each question:

1. If something about the program could be changed with the intent to improve it, what would it be?
2. What are the strengths of the program?
3. What do I contribute to the program? (Individual strengths, etc.)
4. What do I need in order to improve in my role as a facilitator and coordinator?

Have everyone post their responses on a wall or board with all numbered responses grouped together. Discuss themes as a group and document them. This activity may seem simple but can be an effective vehicle for improvement of a facilitation and/or coordination team. Compile responses into themes and work with committee members to make them a part of stated goals and learning outcomes.

FACILITATION EFFECTIVENESS PHASE—STEP 3: TRAINING SKILLS COMPETENCIES CHECKLIST
Your workshop sessions are only as good as your facilitators. Take the time to discuss strengths and limitations of your sessions and the facilitation of them as you become more familiar with the content. Use the *Training Skills Competencies Checklist* during the initial practice phase to provide feedback to facilitators on their facilitation skill sets.

FACILITATION EFFECTIVENESS PHASE—STEP 4: WORKSHOP SESSION EVALUATIONS
Use the *Workshop Session Evaluations* to continually assess facilitation skills with content learning. Always provide constructive feedback that shares strengths with limitations. Document facilitation skill sets and content areas where improvement is needed and design practice retreats for all facilitators.

VISIBILITY PHASE—STEP 5: TRACKING USAGE (WHO IS PARTICIPATING?)
Consider how numbers registered, attended, and by affiliation (student, staff, faculty) will be collected. An online form or database can be created that collects and stores this information. You will want to know how many people are participating, if employees or students are registering more or not, and which session times work best for which audiences by affiliation.

Each participant should be tracked by which session they have registered and attended. Use this information to target advertisements to those that have either shown interest but did not show up, or that are participating in your program but have not yet attended all your sessions. Although electronic mail and social media are contemporary forms of communication that are useful, a phone call or paper invitation in the mail can go a long way to help you stand out from the rest. Use your database to glean information so as to target those participating in your program. A first academic year of 100 new trained members on a small campus of 5,000 students should be considered a success with room to grow.

VISIBILITY PHASE—STEP 6: ENVIRONMENTAL SCAN (WHERE ARE YOUR SIGNS?)

The hallmark of these programs is the visible placement of signs, stickers, and other materials across the campus on office or residence hall doors. An environmental scan of all hallways and public locations inside all buildings has proven to be an effective assessment of the visibility of the program. You will want to know where the signs are visible and where they are not.

A canvassing of all buildings at Iowa State University (Evans, 2002) employed this technique as part of a larger ethnographic study. This study suggested that the recently formed Safe Zone program increased visibility for LGBTQIA+ people as well as support for them.

Hire student staff to roam all the hallways, lounges, and public places to document on a map where they see the signs or stickers. Give them specific directions, an example of your sign, a campus map, and listing of all members to follow to indicate building, academic/student affairs department, and floor. Color-code your map with areas of high concentration and low concentration. If you keep a list of members by department, compare this list with your map.

Issue new signs to members if needed and remind them of how the program works. If members are not involved anymore, initiate communication to understand why. This mapping of stickers may find that certain academic areas will find support such as design, education, English, counseling, student services offices, and very few in business, mathematics, engineering, and agriculture. Concentrate future outreach to areas of the university with less visibility.

LEARNING OUTCOMES PHASE—STEP 7: PRE-/POST-WORKSHOPS SURVEY

Northwestern University administered a pre- and post-survey with the introductory workshop sessions. This session covered terminology, history, identity development (coming-out process), how to be an ally in a department/office, listening skills, and student stories through a panel format. Other sessions were offered on being a transgender ally, a fluid/pansexuality session, and a broader social justice intersectionality session. Participants received a sticker for each session.

A pre- and post-test were administered to participants attending the introductory session to figure out if participants learned more about the content stated in curricula goals. "The gains made by trainees in knowledge of LGBT history, understanding of LGBT identity development, and understanding of appropriate language to use when discussing (LGBTQIA+) topics (were) significant" (Northwestern, 2011).

Campus Labs was used to administer the survey. "Feedback we got was about how to be an ally, people wanted to know what to do. We developed a section on how to advocate in your student organization, your department . . . here are some concrete things you can do. Things like how to change forms, how to add a question in-

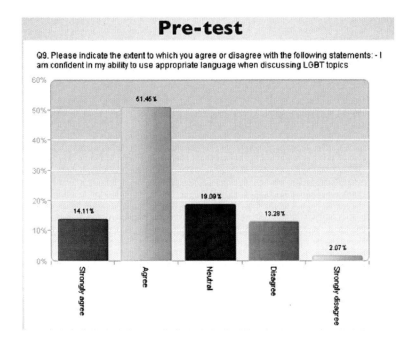

Figure 10.2. Northwestern University—Language Pre-Test Bar Graph.
Source: Created by D. A. Dirks; used with permission.

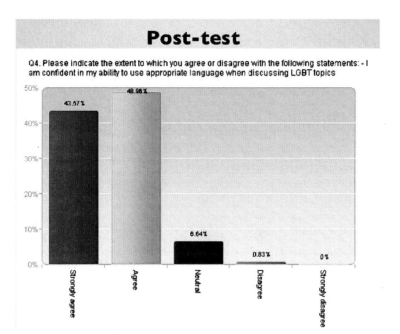

Figure 10.3. Northwestern University—Language Post-Test Bar Graph.
Source: Created by D. A. Dirks; used with permission.

clusive of gender . . . something you can act on instead of 'here's how to be a good ally just be nice' which is not that helpful. People responded well to concrete takeaways" (D. A. Dirks, personal communication). Feedback was used from facilitators as well as participants to improve the trainings. Facilitators were empowered to edit session activities to suit learning styles using an interactive. "To me that was so rewarding also to be able to have facilitators take ownership . . . instead of me asking them to fix something . . . to benefit from the experience of the community building occurring among facilitators" (D. A. Dirks, personal communication).

Pre- and post-assessments should have the same entry points and ending points; basically your questions should remain the same. Administer the pre-test, facilitate the session, then administer the post-test. Reviewing results of pre-tests can be an effective means of gauging levels of content understanding that could be used to adapt curricula, so time is spent wisely, and is a basis of comparison for the post-test. There are disadvantages to this survey design, but many will be mitigated if the surveys are administered directly before and after a 2 to 3-hour session since you will be in control of the time. However, your participants could potentially score high at the pre-test, which will limit improvement in post-test scores, thus indicating that facilitators need to design a more rigorous training.

LEARNING OUTCOMES PHASE—STEP 8: MEMBERSHIP SURVEY

Once your members have completed your workshop session(s), are posting their sign for a period of time, communicating about the program, and working to provide an environment free from homophobia, biphobia, and transphobia, then check in with them by surveying their experiences. Use results to update workshop sessions by stressing further needed learning outcomes or offer brush-up sessions on particular topics.

George Mason University surveyed members of their Safe Zone program. The coordinator wanted to know if the program "increased awareness" of LGBTQIA+ topics, which "aspects of the Safe Zone training workshop equipped" members to be better allies, if there was behavioral and language change due to information from the program, and if members effectively "handled the situation with the person who approached" them (Bruno, 2005, pp. 55–58).

Members had attended a day-long session about homophobia, biphobia, trans identities, and how to put knowledge into action (role plays), with resources. This allowed the university "to get better information down the line because there wasn't any follow-up to understand how they used the material . . . to think about how to adjust the training so it was still salient" (Bruno, personal phone conversation).

"Campus climate questions were also included to help demonstrate why the program was important . . . a fear that resources would be taken away from the program . . . in a state (Virginia) that isn't always great about LGBT issues and (how) the office is contributing [to] the campus climate" (Bruno, personal phone conversation). It was interesting to note that although the program was meeting stated goals for heterosexual allies, the LGBTQIA+ students participating were using the program to understand their own process of identity development.

LEARNING OUTCOMES PHASE—STEP 9: BENCHMARKING CAMPUS INCLUSION (ALLIES AS ADVOCATES)

These aforementioned surveys are good at assessing interpersonal change for members participating in the program but do little to understand institutional change. Safe Zone members must be expected to be advocates for inclusive policies, services, and operating procedures. Future assessment must ask these developing allies how they have impacted institutional change by connecting best practices. For example, use the *Campus Pride Index* (campuspride.org) and the *Suggested Best Practices for Support Trans Students* (lgbtcampus.org) to organize a group of members from departments campus-wide and collectively fill out both documents. Expect members to take an active role in communicating results, then creating a plan for placing those recommendations into practice in each respective office.

CONCLUSION

A well-thought-out assessment strategy will enable successful outcomes. Do not wait until after launching the program, running the program, to implement your assessment. This is a recipe for disaster as your assessment will take longer and not yield useful results. A model Safe Zone program assessment occurs at the onset of decision making, during facilitator skills development learning, at workshop sessions, for the visibility of the program, the development of your members as better allies, and eventually gauging inclusive climate change. Finally, your assessment work need not solely benefit your institution. Your colleagues at other schools desperately need to learn about your successes and tribulations. Consider sharing it at professional conferences and/or in publications.

APPENDICES

The following appendices are made available for adaptation. Please credit the original authors.

- Session Evaluations
- Training Skills Competencies Checklist
- Northwestern University Pre-/Post-Workshop Survey
- Membership Survey—George Mason University Questions

REFERENCES

Ballard, S. L., Bartle, E., & Masequesmay, G. (2008). *Finding queer allies: The impact of ally training and safe zone stickers on campus climate*. Retrieved November 4, 2015, from http://files.eric.ed.gov/fulltext/ED517219.pdf.

Bresciani, M. J. (September 2003). *The relationship between outcomes, measurement and decisions for continuous improvement*. National Association for Student Personnel Administrators, Inc. NetResults E-Zine. http://www.naspa.org/netresults/index.cfm.

Bruno, M. (2005). *The impact of the George Mason University Safe Zone program on the lesbian, gay, bisexual, transgender, and questioning community and the Safe Zone allies* (Unpublished master's thesis). George Mason University, Fairfax, VA.

Dirks, D. A. (2011). *Safe space survey report.* Northwestern University, Evanston, IL.

Draughn, T., Elkins, B., & Roy, R. (2002). Allies in the struggle: Eradicating homophobia and heterosexism on campus. In E. P. Cramer (Ed.), *Addressing homophobia and heterosexism on college campuses* (pp. 9–20) Binghamton, NY: Harrington Park Press.

Evans, N. (2002). The impact of an LGBT Safe Zone Project on campus climate. *Journal of College Student Development, 43*, 522–39.

Finkel, M., Storaasli, R., Bandele, A., & Schaefer, V. (2003). Diversity training in graduate school: An exploratory evaluation of the Safe Zone project. *Professional Psychology: Research and Practice, 34*(5), 555–61.

Poynter, K., & Lewis, E. (2003). *SAFE on campus assessment report.* Durham, NC: Duke University, Center for LGBT Life.

Ryan, M., Broad, K. L., Walsh, C. F., & Nutter, K. L. (2013). Professional allies: The storying of allies to LGBTQ students on a college campus. *Journal of Homosexuality, 10*(1), 83–104.

Upcraft, M.L,, & Schuh, J.H. (1996) *Assessment in student affairs: A guide for practitioners.* San Francisco, CA: Jossey-Bass.

Woodford, M. R., Kolb, C. L., Durocher-Radeka, G., & Javier, G. (2014). Lesbian, gay, bisexual, and transgender ally training programs on campus: Current variations and future directions. *Journal of College Student Development, 55*(3), 317–22.

Worthen, M. G. (2011). College student experiences with an LGBTQ ally training program: A mixed methods study at a university in the southern United States. *Journal of LGBT Youth, 8*(4), 332–77.

About the Editor

Kerry John Poynter has over 20 years of experience working with college students at a number of institutions including Duke University, Columbia University, and New York University. However, he began his career in the Midwest at Western Michigan University in 1997, where he coordinated the then titled "LGB Office," one of only a dozen at the time, as a graduate student and received his M.A. in Administration of College Student Affairs in the Department of Counselor Education & Counseling Psychology. He currently is the Executive Director of the Diversity Center and oversees the LGBTQA Resource Office at the University of Illinois Springfield.

Among his experiences he has managed a 2,500 sq. ft. LGBTQIA+ student center; coordinated LGBTQIA+ Safe Zone allies programs at five different universities; written and awarded a number of grants; conducted numerous trainings on LGBTQIA+ topics with faculty, staff, and students; assessed campus climates and services in fraternity/sorority life, residence life, health services, and human resources, among others; empowered students through peer-to-peer education; and has led advocacy efforts for more inclusive policies for transgender students, among others.

His research and writing interests include the development of heterosexual allies of LGBTQIA+ people, the use of technology in multicultural education, and sexual and gender minorities with multiple cultural identities. A free DVD called *SAFE on Campus*, chronicling his Safe Space Ally program training (out of print), was funded in part by the American College Personnel Association (ACPA), the National Association of Student Personnel Administrators (NASPA), and has been used by hundreds of colleges and universities across North America. In 2001 he was awarded the Diversity Award by the president of Duke University, which is given to a single employee that has shown a consistent commitment to diversity and inclusion on campus. Additionally, his work with Lavender Graduation ceremonies was cited by *Instinct* magazine as among the best of LGBTQIA+ offerings on college campuses.

Outside his work in higher education, he dreams of being a superstar DJ; regularly puts out a consistently ranked house music podcast "Club Kerry NYC"; follows extreme storms while pretending to be a meteorologist on social media; and dotes on his constant companion tuxedo cat, named Miss Oreo.

About the Contributors

Pierre R. Berastaín serves as the Assistant Director of Innovation & Engagement for the National Latin@ Network, a project of Casa de Esperanza. Prior to Casa de Esperanza: National Latin@ Network, Pierre worked for Renewal House, a domestic violence shelter in Boston, Massachusetts, as the Restorative Justice Advocate, and served as the Director of Media Relations for the Hispanic Black Gay Coalition. He is the co-founder of the Massachusetts Restorative Justice Collaborative and served as the co-chair of the Massachusetts Gay/Lesbian/Bisexual/Transgender (GLBT) Domestic Violence Coalition. Pierre was a 2012–2013 Fellow at the Gay Lesbian Alliance Against Defamation's National People of Color Media Institute. As a contributor to the *Huffington Post*, he writes on domestic violence, restorative justice, and general issues of social justice. He currently sits on the executive board for MERGE (Men Embracing their Role for Gender Equality). Originally from Peru, Pierre immigrated to the United States with his family in 1998 and remained an undocumented immigrant for fourteen years. He holds a Bachelor's in Social Anthropology and a minor in Ethnic Studies/Human Rights from Harvard University as well as a Master of Divinity from Harvard Divinity School.

Lindsey Bickers Bock is a natural community builder that works with broad school and worksite-based initiatives to move the needle on prevention. She currently leads the Strategic Coaching team at Prevention Partners, which guides individual organizations and community partners in reshaping policies, benefits, environments, and systems to accelerate change and positively influence health behaviors. Prior to joining Prevention Partners, Lindsey worked for several years at Duke University and the University of North Carolina at Chapel Hill, coordinating outreach and prevention efforts on campus. She is a recipient of the Outstanding Staff Award from the Duke University Center for Lesbian, Gay, Bisexual and Transgender Life and the Southern College Health Association's New Professional Award. Lindsey is also a cook who loves to experiment, a runner who loves exploring new places on foot, and a group fitness instructor. Lindsey earned a Master of Public Health, with a concentration in Health Behavior & Health Education from the Gillings School of Global Public Health at the University of North Carolina at Chapel Hill. She has a Bachelor of Arts with concentrations in Women's Studies and Brain & Cognitive Science from the University of Rochester.

Matt Bruno is the co-chair of the Consortium of Higher Education LGBT Resource Professionals (2015–2018) and also works at American University as the Coordinator of LGBTQ Programming in the Center for Diversity & Inclusion. He has taught courses in Women, Gender, and Sexuality Studies at American University (AU) and through the Integrative Studies Program at George Mason University (GMU). Bruno has worked on, facilitated, and created curriculum for Safe Zone and similar programs since 2001, where he started as an undergraduate facilitator. In the M.A. program (Higher Education Administration at George Mason University), he wrote his thesis on the Impact of the Safe Zone Program at GMU. In addition to his work in higher education, Bruno has facilitated LGBTQ Inclusion trainings for government and non-profit agencies in the DC metropolitan area.

Ezekiel Reis Burgin received his M.S.W. from Simmons. In his clinical work he focuses on creating social justice both as a means to mental health and an end in itself. His publications include the chapter "Liberation Health and

LGBT Communities" in *Social Justice in Clinical Practice: A Liberation Health Framework for Social Work* and an essay on *Manning Up: Transsexual Men on Finding Brotherhood, Family & Themselves.* To help friends and family practice the use of gender-neutral pronouns, his cats have graciously agreed to exist outside the gender binary.

Erica M. Cornelius, Ph.D., has worked in higher education most of her adult life in teaching, student affairs, and staff diversity training. She is also a philosopher who conducts practical research within Western esotericism. In these diverse activities, she is interested in helping each human being uncover and live in accordance with their own deepest values, as only they can define.

D. A. Dirks is the co-chair of the Consortium of Higher Education LGBT Resource Professionals (2015–2018). He works at the University of Wisconsin System Administration as a Senior Academic Planner. From 2012 to 2014, D. A. was contract faculty in the departments of General Education and Humanities at Mount Royal University. He taught courses that examined diverse genders and sexualities. D. A. was the Coordinator of Student Organizations for Social Justice & LGBT Resource Center at Northwestern University, 2006–2012, and the Coordinator of LBGT Student Services at Western Michigan University, 2005–2006. D. A. has a B.A. and an M.A. from the University of Calgary, and an M.A. and a Ph.D. (Dissertation Title: "Transgender People on University Campuses: A Policy Discourse Analysis") from Western Michigan University. When not advocating for social justice, D. A. runs with friends and rescues cats, but not simultaneously.

Abigail Francis is MIT's first-ever full-time Director of LBGTQ Services under the Division of Student Life. She holds a B.S. in Psychology and Pre-Medical studies from Bates College and a master's in Social Work and Urban Leadership from Simmons College. In overseeing MIT's Rainbow Lounge she offers one-on-one support for students, advising 12 LBGTQ student groups, collaborates with community partners, and provides consistency and resources to help build and empower the LBGTQ and Ally community at MIT. Abigail heads up the organization called LBGTQ@MIT, a community resource offering quality programming, services, collaboration, and education to all of MIT. Currently LBGTQ@MIT offers diversity trainings, student leadership development, campus climate assessment, the provision of inclusive Institute policies and procedures, and various forms of LBGTQ community building. LBGTQ@MIT works closely with the Black Students' Union, the Latino Cultural Center, the Office of Minority Education, MIT Medical, and Women and Gender Studies. As the first Director of LBGTQ Services, Abigail has had a powerful impact on the level of LBGTQ visibility, inclusion, support, and comfort within the MIT community as a whole. Her work has been recognized with the Infinite Mile award, highlighting "exceptional qualities and professionalism in contribution to MIT's mission," and twice with the MIT Excellence Award for Diversity and Inclusion, as well as the MIT Office of Multicultural Programs award for Best Multicultural Advocate.

Eli R. Green, Ph.D., C.S.E., is an interdisciplinary sexualities scholar, assistant professor of Public Health at William Paterson University and adjunct assistant professor in the Center for Human Sexuality Studies graduate program at Widener University. Dr. Green is a nationally recognized trainer who helps non-profits, direct service, medical providers, and educational professionals expand their LGBQ and transgender-related cultural competency. Dr. Green's book, co-authored with Luca Maurer, *The Teaching Transgender Toolkit: A Facilitator's Guide to Increasing Knowledge, Reducing Prejudice & Building Skills*, is the first of it's kind and offers best practices and lessons for teaching transgender content. As a consultant, he has developed and leads LGBQ & transgender specific train-the-trainer courses, and provides ongoing technical assistance and coaching for current educators and trainers. His award-winning research focuses largely on reducing prejudice toward transgender people and communities through education and training. Dr. Green holds a Ph.D. in Human Sexuality Studies from Widener University, in addition to Master's Degrees in Human Sexuality Education (Widener University) and Applied Women's Studies (Claremont Graduate University). He is a Certified Sexuality Educator (CSE) through the American Association of Sexuality Educators, Counselors & Therapists (AASECT).

Holly M. Kent is assistant professor of History at the University of Illinois Springfield, where she teaches classes in U.S. women's history, nineteenth-century U.S. history, fashion history, and the history of slavery and abolition. Her scholarship on nineteenth-century fashion culture and feminist pedagogy is forthcoming in the *Women's History Review* and *The Seneca Falls Dialogues Journal*, and she has written an introduction for a new edition of the antebellum abolitionist novel *Madge Vertner* for Hastings College Press.

Samuel Lurie, M.S.W., MED., has been providing training on transgender issues to health care providers, advocates and activists since 1998, directly training over 30,000 providers in thirty states and three countries. Samuel has consulted and trained in higher education/student affairs around the United States, helping to build not only awareness around gender diversity but also skills and strategies to implement gender-inclusive policies and practice. Samuel served on the board of Outright Vermont, the statewide queer youth organization and in 2013 was the proud recipient of their Lifetime Queer Youth Advocate Award. He has a master's in Education in Health Education from the University of Vermont and an M.S.W. from Smith College School for Social Work. In addition to his training and consulting work (www.tgtrain.org), he is a clinician in community mental health and has a private practice working with queer, trans and gender-questioning clients and their families in Burlington, Vermont.

Ryan McConville attended the University of Illinois Springfield where he earned a B.A. in Political Science and a minor in Philosophy. His interests focused on the relationship between citizens and their government, and the obstacles preventing the implementation of meaningful reforms necessary for legal equality of all citizens. He is currently studying law at the University of Missouri-Kansas City School of Law with a concentration in Litigation/Advocacy. While his immediate future will be learning the nuances of the U.S. legal system, both as a student and attorney, his long-term goal is to directly influence the creation and implementation of public policy.

Michele Miller is assistant professor of psychology at the University of Illinois Springfield. She has been working in higher education consistently since the summer of 2008, instructing both undergraduates and graduates in a variety of courses in Developmental Psychology (Child Development, The Role of Play in Child Development, Adolescence, Life-span Developmental Psychology) and Methods (Statistical Research Methods for the Social Sciences, Research Methods in Psychology) at the University of Wisconsin-Madison and the University of Illinois Springfield. Dr. Miller's past and current research employs multi-method assessment approaches and advanced quantitative statistical techniques to investigate the broad areas of temperament, emotion, and psychopathology risk. Additionally, she has explored these concepts in ways that control for genetic differences. Currently, her research focuses on the associations between early temperament, school readiness, and later cognitive development. In addition to her teaching and research obligations, Dr. Miller is devoted to community mental health and has a private practice working with queer, trans, and gender-questioning clients and their families in Burlington, Vermont.

Robyn Ochs, Ed.M., is a national speaker who has been an advocate for LGBTQ+ people since 1982. From 1983 to 2009, she worked as an administrator at Harvard University, during which time she co-founded Harvard's LGBT Faculty and Staff group, the Trans Task Force, and the LBQ Women's Lunches, served on the Board of Directors of the Harvard Gender & Sexuality Caucus, and advised Harvard College's LGBTQ student organization. She is an activist and educator, writing and speaking on identity and sexuality, with a focus on the middle sexualities. Robyn is editor of the *Bi Women Quarterly*, and co-editor of two anthologies: *Getting Bi: Voices of Bisexuals Around the World* (2nd ed. 2009); and *RECOGNIZE: The Voices of Bisexual Men* (2014). She has served on the board of MassEquality (Massachusetts' statewide LGBTQ advocacy organization) since 2004 and has also served as a Commissioner on the Massachusetts Commission on LGBTQ Youth (www.robynochs.com).

Jessica Pettitt, M.Ed., is a Certified Speaking Professional focusing on Diversity, Social Justice, and LGBT Advocacy. After working in Student Affairs for 10 years, she now travels from organization to organization with a writing curriculum, consulting on policy, facilitating tough conversations, and keynoting at events pulling from her professional and personal experience as a teacher, stand-up comedian, and crisis manager to serve others. Jess has served on dozens of boards, collaborated and continues to support the Consortium of LGBT Higher Education Professionals, Campus Pride, Social Justice Training Institute, Association of Fraternal Leadership Values, Delta

Gamma Fraternity, and the National Speakers Association. American College Personnel Association recently honored Jess for her dedication and contributions to Trans Inclusion in Higher Education through the Diamond Honoree award. In an attempt for things to be as accessible as possible, Jess offers live and online education, as well as a number of affordable products and free downloads on her site GoodEnoughNow.com.

Jeffrey Pierce graduated from the University of Southern California with a B.A. in Theater. Having worked as an actor throughout the United States and Canada, Jeffrey moved to Miami, Florida, to fulfill a two-year commitment with Teach for America where he taught Creative Writing to high school students. Jeffrey is currently pursuing his JD at the University of Miami with a concentration in both litigation and entertainment law. He has been happily married to his husband since 2010.

Pamela M. Salela, M.A., M.S. (UIUC), is associate professor, Library Instructional Services Program in Brookens Library, University of Illinois at Springfield (UIS). Before coming to UIS in 2005, she was at Miami University (Ohio) as well as St. Cloud State University (Minnesota). In addition to being the liaison to Women & Gender Studies and Public Administration she oversees the Central Illinois Nonprofit Resource Center. Salela is also associate faculty in the Women & Gender Studies Department where she teaches. She has developed courses on women and poverty as well as the politics of reproduction. She has been a member of UIS' SafeZone for several years, regularly teaching the workshop on Multiple Identities.

Brady Sullivan is an instructor and doctoral student at the University of Missouri–St. Louis. He is a Licensed Professional Counselor (LPC), Associate Licensed Marriage and Family Therapist (ALMFT), and a Certified Alcohol and Other Drug Abuse Counselor (CADC). His research interests include spirituality within the LGBTQIA community, and the effects of culture and society on gay male body image. He received the Outstanding Performance on the Comprehensive Examination Award for his final master's presentation. He also received the Prairie Star Address award for his contributions to the religion and spirituality session as part of the Safe Zone Program at the University of Illinois–Springfield. He is currently working on his degree in Counselor Education.

Nancy Jean Tubbs has directed the University of California, Riverside's LGBT Resource Center since 2000. She holds a master's degree in Educational Administration from Texas A&M University, and has published articles on allies' development and transgender-inclusive campus policies. Nancy Jean founded the UCR Allies Program and currently facilitates the Trans Allies Seminars for members. She is active in the Consortium of Higher Education LGBT Resource Professionals. Nancy Jean is a radical bureaucrat who enjoys improving policies, spending budgets, writing reports, questioning gender, dialoguing sexuality, challenging systems of oppression, and wearing comfortable shoes.

Michael Stephens started his career with topics of sexual and gender identity in his master's program at the University of Illinois-Springfield. He worked as a graduate assistant for the UIS LGBTQA Resource Office, facilitating workshops described in this book as well as helping to create the Safe Dating and Relationships workshop. He currently is working as an in-home family therapist in Pennsylvania and a Ph.D. candidate in Duquesne University's Counselor Education and Supervision Program. As well as experience working for a gender and sexuality resource office, his experience has been in working with individuals and families struggling with identity issues (such as sexual and gender identity issues), couples and families working through a variety of presenting problems, and is trained in systemic therapy, play therapy, and developmental therapy techniques for children, adolescents, and families. Michael has experience and interest in qualitative multicultural research topics such as racial, gender, and sexual identity development and autism spectrum disorders.

Evangeline Weiss is a social change instigator with a twinkle in her eye. Evangeline has over 18 years of community-building and organizational development experience facilitating values-based capacity building to sustain leaders and organizations on a path towards greater wholeness, intentionality, and purpose. As a White anti-racist and queer mommy, Evangeline believes that intersectional approaches to social justice are key to forging spaces which are inclusive and authentic. After earning a master's degree from UW-Madison in educational policy studies, Evangeline has worked with clients such as Coaching Corps, Southern Poverty Law Center, Leadership for Educational Equity, Ipas, International Planned Parenthood Federation, Highlander Education and Research Center, Goddard College, and Emerge Maine. Evangeline is a poet, community builder justice worker, living with her beloved soul mate and son, and their most adorable dog, Sherlock. She is extremely grateful to call Greensboro, North Carolina, home.

Debra Wells-Ply has worked in higher education for seven years as the manager of the Office of Undergraduate Education at the University of Illinois Springfield (UIS). A longtime advocate for LGBTQIA+ issues, Wells-Ply serves as a committee member on the UIS Safe Zone Coordinating Committee and co-facilitates the campus Safe Zone Fundamentals and Religion workshops.